The City and Suburbs of

# PHILADELPHIA
## 1794

N O R T H E R N

R I V E R

# CITY TAVERN
# BAKING & DESSERT
## COOKBOOK

# City Tavern
# Baking & Dessert
## Cookbook

200 Years of
Authentic American Recipes

❧

by Walter Staib
with Jennifer Lindner

Running Press
PHILADELPHIA • LONDON

9   8   7   6   5   4   3   2   1
Digit on the right indicates the number of this printing

Library of Congress Control Number: 2002115206

ISBN 0-7624-1554-1


Cover and insert photography by Zave Smith
Picture research by Susan Oyama
Cover and interior design by Bill Jones
Edited by Justin Schwartz
Typography: Adobe Garamond, Caslon Antique and Old Claude

This book may be ordered by mail from the publisher.
Please include $2.50 for postage and handling.
***But try your bookstore first!***

Running Press Book Publishers
125 South Twenty-second Street
Philadelphia, Pennsylvania 19103-4399

Visit us on the web!
www.runningpress.com

I dedicate this book to

my mother, Hertha Staib,

my uncle and aunt, Walter and Ruth Eberle,

and my uncle, Karl Hintze,

from whom I learned my true and lifelong passion

for the culinary arts

# Contents

# Acknowledgments

First I would like to thank the U.S. Department of the Interior, National Park Service, for their unwavering trust and confidence in me as the operator of the unique and historic City Tavern in Philadelphia, Pennsylvania.

As always, I would like to thank my wife Gloria for her unwavering support and assistance in realizing my dreams.

When I decided to write this book, I had only one coauthor in mind, Jennifer Lindner. I met Jennifer when she was editor of *Art Culinaire* and was impressed by her dedication to her two biggest passions: pâtisserie and history. She was a perfect match for me in writing this book. A very thorough and talented writer, Jennifer has made an enormous contribution to this book and through her writing has helped me realize my goal of further exploring the cultural influences that converged to create this unique brand of eighteenth-century cuisine and relating them to everyday life in Philadelphia, then and now.

I also owe a great deal of gratitude to my corporate pastry chef, Christian Gatti, also a highly accomplished pastry chef and historian, who makes every single bread and dessert served at City Tavern every day. His assistance with writing and testing the recipes in this book was invaluable, and I am fortunate to have such a talented culinary professional on my team.

Also, many thanks go to my assistant and director of communications, Paul Bauer, who maintained control of this project from inception to publication, compiling the manuscript from the many sources of information we used, arranging the photography, handling the edits, and more. As always, he was the cohesive force that held this project together and ensured its timely and accurate completion.

A very heartfelt thanks goes to our nation's foremost historian, David McCullough, for his gracious and insightful foreword.

Special thanks to the Winterthur Museum for all of the wonderful historic illustrations; to Dr. Lorna Sass; and to Barbara Kuck, chief archivist at Johnson & Wales University.

Last but certainly not least, I want to thank the entire staff of City Tavern for their daily commitment to the accurate re-creation of history that makes City Tavern one of a kind. My most heartfelt thanks to all of you for realizing my vision!

# City Tavern Timeline

**1772 to 1773:** Fifty-three prominent citizens commission the building of City Tavern, which is to be "a large and commodious tavern" that will be worthy of Philadelphia's standing as the largest, most prosperous city in the colonies.

**December 1773:** City Tavern opens for business. The building has five levels and includes kitchens, a bar room, two coffee rooms, and three dining rooms; the second largest ballroom in the New World; five lodging rooms and servants' quarters. Daniel Smith, its first proprietor, leases the Tavern for £300 per year, an amount roughly equivalent to five years of wages for the common man. He resides there from 1774 to 1778.

**May 1774:** Paul Revere arrives at the Tavern to announce Parliament's closing the port of Boston. The next day, two-to-three hundred prominent Philadelphians meet at City Tavern to select a committee of correspondence to draft a letter of sympathy for Revere to take back to Boston.

**September to October 1774:** City Tavern is the unofficial meeting place of the delegates before and after sessions of the first Continental Congress, convened at nearby Carpenters' Hall. George Washington, Thomas Jefferson, John Adams, Richard Henry Lee, and Peyton Randolph are among the participants.

**1776 to 1777:** Continental and British troops use City Tavern to house prisoners of war. Military courts-martial are also held there.

**July 4, 1777:** America's first Fourth of July celebration is held at City Tavern.

**August 3 to 5, 1777:** General Washington and his aides-de-camp share table and quarters at City Tavern, making the Tavern the official headquarters of the Continental Army for three days.

**1778:** On December 10, politician John Jay is elected president of the Continental Congress, while staying as a guest at the Tavern.

**1783:** The Pennsylvania Society of the Cincinnati is formed at City Tavern in the second floor northwest dining room.

**1784:** Original subscribers sell City Tavern to Samuel Powel, a prominent Philadelphian and former mayor of the city.

**January 1789:** City Tavern's two front rooms become headquarters of the Merchants' Coffee House and Place of Exchange.

**April 1789:** City Tavern hosts a banquet for George Washington as he passes through Philadelphia on his way to New York for his inauguration.

**March 1834:** City Tavern's roof catches fire; the building is heavily damaged.

**1854:** The surviving structure is razed.

**1948:** Congress authorizes Independence National Historical Park to preserve certain important buildings and sites of significant national importance, encompassing more than forty buildings on forty-two acres, including the site of the original City Tavern.

**1975:** Historically accurate replication of the original Tavern is completed according to period images, written accounts, and insurance surveys.

**1976:** The newly rebuilt Tavern opens in time for the bicentennial. The restaurant is managed by a large food service company.

**December 31, 1992:** The restaurant concession at the Tavern closes.

**1994:** Walter Staib wins congressional approval as operator of the Tavern, which re-opens for business on July 4, featuring eighteenth-century style gourmet cuisine.

# Forewords

Of all those worthy patriots who gathered for the first Continental Congress in Philadelphia in late summer of 1774—and of those who later fixed their signatures to the immortal Declaration of Independence—none wrote so fully or candidly about the setting of the historic drama, or the human side of life for the protagonists, than did John Adams of Massachusetts. And quite fitting it is that Adams, describing his arrival in Philadelphia for the first time, on August 29, 1774, singled out City Tavern for lavish praise. Indeed, to judge by John Adams's diary, the then-new hostelry on Second Street was the only thing about Philadelphia that made an impression that first day.

Adams and the others traveling with him had been on the road since early morning, and "dirty and dusty and fatigued" as they were, they could not resist the Tavern, where, Adams wrote, they received a "fresh welcome," "a supper . . . as elegant as ever was laid on a table." What time they sat down to eat he did not record, but it was eleven before they pushed back their chairs and called it a night, all of them, one gathers, departing amply fortified to face whatever might lay in store. For his part, Adams decided that here was the finest tavern in all America.

It was an endorsement few would have disputed, and it came from a man who dearly loved to eat, who all his life loved and appreciated good food, good drink, good talk around a convivial table.

Philadelphia in the late eighteenth century was the largest, most prosperous city in America, the busiest port, and a cornucopia without equal. Nowhere could one find such bountiful evidence of American abundance; such quantities of fresh fruit and vegetables, fresh fish, meats, sausages, wild game, and cheeses on sale; or such a variety of "elegant" cooking. Delegates from the far-flung colonies, visitors from abroad—visitors of all kinds—marveled at the produce on display at the city's enormous central market. Twice weekly, on market days, German-speaking country people rolled into the city in huge wagons laden with produce, live chickens, ducks, and pigs. One signer of the Declaration of Independence, Stephen Hopkins of Rhode Island, counted seventy farm wagons on Market Street.

In such an atmosphere, not surprisingly, minimalist cuisine was not the fashion. Dinner at City Tavern, or at any of the fine homes of Philadelphia, could include twenty or more different dishes, not counting dessert. As John Adams reported to his wife, Abigail, even "plain Quakers" served ducks, hams, chicken, and beef at a single sitting, while such desserts as served at the home of Mayor Samuel Powel on Third Street were dazzling—custards, flummery, jellies, trifles, whipped syllabubs, floating islands, fruits, nuts, everything imaginable.

But for the delegates to the Congress, City Tavern remained the great gathering place. It was there that Adams and George Washington first met. It was there that so many came and went, not yet figures in history, but flesh-and-blood human beings, let us never forget—Sam Adams, Richard Henry Lee, Patrick Henry, Jefferson, Franklin, Dr. Benjamin Rush. And here they made history, shaped much about the world we live in, with what they said among themselves, bargaining, politicking, speaking their minds, talking small things and large over the rattle of dishes and the steady hubbub of surrounding tables. Nothing of what was said was recorded. No artist is known to have sketched such scenes. Further, the original City Tavern is gone. The present City Tavern, on the same site, is an exact reproduction. Still, the feeling of entering another time is strong and appealing, and it makes City Tavern a must experience for anyone with even a little interest in history—and most especially when the food comes on.

The great pull of the place is the same as long before, with the marvelous array of things to eat. Under the direction of chef/restaurateur Walter Staib, the offerings are never static, never routine, any more than in days of old, when the likes of Adams and Washington climbed the marble stairs to the front door. That this sumptuous cookbook, devoted solely to desserts and breads, contains no less than 180 tantalizing receipts certainly makes the point.

The founding era of America, now more than two centuries past, was a vastly different time from our own. The people, too, were different, and more so than generally understood. Yet it is possible to make contact with them as fellow human beings. We can enter their world, we can come to know them through the letters they wrote, their diaries, the books they read, their music, their architecture, the ways they worshipped, the poetry they loved and learned by heart, and yes, God be praised, by the food they ate.

Besides, with such a guide at hand as this wonderful volume, along with its companion work, the *City Tavern Cookbook*, we are able now to enjoy such singular delights as they knew right in our own homes.

It is all well and good to read that in the eighteenth century the pleasures of the table ranked high among the pleasures of life, but quite another thing to savor the real fare itself. To dine as John Adams and his contemporaries once did at City Tavern is to be reminded of how full-flavored life at best must have been for them, and that they themselves, at their best, were anything but dull company.

—*David McCullough*

As a Philadelphia chef who has long been intrigued by the city's history, I am pleased to contribute to this book, which admirably explores the baking and confectionery popularized here, and specifically at City Tavern, during the eighteenth century. The recipes in these pages accurately reveal the breadth of cultural influences that helped to shape Philadelphia's sweetmeat tables. I commend the time and effort Chef Staib, Christian Gatti, Paul Bauer, and Jennifer Lindner spent in researching historic documents and cookery books to make this material come alive for us.

I have long admired Walter Staib, not only as a chef and restaurateur but also for his ability, through food, to engage patrons with the awesome beacon that was eighteenth-century Philadelphia.

As we progress into the twenty-first century, the cultural and culinary diversity of the city continue to be integral to the development of its distinguished and innovative restaurants. This continuum of converging traditions is exciting, giving way to an ever-evolving array of inspired dishes and styles of dining. At the same time, the city maintains the richness of its eclectic heritage, as Philadelphians carry on the foodways that express their own unique cultures and ethnicities. It is this celebrated diversity that allows chefs and restaurateurs to freely borrow from different traditions and introduce us to new and creative ways of eating.

The colorful, culturally vibrant city we enjoy today is, in many ways, little changed from that which City Tavern knew in the late eighteenth century.

Philadelphia was founded on the acceptance of diverse peoples. As they met and forged lives within the city limits and on rural farms, they not only influenced one another but maintained the integrity of their traditions as well. Food was one way early Philadelphians identified with their many different heritages while simultaneously assimilating into a New World defined by new rules, expectations, and opportunities.

Baked goods and confectionery played a special role in Philadelphia's culinary history. Due to the high cost of ingredients such as sugar, chocolate, nuts, citrus, and spices, sweet dishes were greatly prized. Indeed, only wealthy Philadelphians could afford to prepare or purchase these items with regularity. Research, however, shows that shops around the city commonly sold expensive, imported ingredients from Europe, the Caribbean, and neighboring colonies, and that confectioners selling prepared goods maintained a steady patronage.

Eighteenth-century Philadelphia was a bustling, cosmopolitan center in which its inhabitants and their foodways represented the traditional finery and finesse of Europe as well as the newness and innovation of the Americas. The ideals and aspirations of our Founding Fathers exemplified the merging of these two, often disparate worlds. One need only look to men like George Washington, Thomas Jefferson, and Benjamin Franklin—three City Tavern patrons—who maintained respect for European tradition and culture while enthusiastically adopting and shaping American mores. Indeed, these three did so as much through political activity as through dining and farming.

The sweet dishes of Philadelphia underscored the Founding Fathers' ideals. The city enthusiastically welcomed French ice cream and pastry, German breads and cookies, and English puddings and jellies alongside New World confections featuring such native ingredients as apples, cranberries, molasses, maple syrup, and corn. There is no doubt that Americans' admiration for Europe waxed and waned. Yet, Philadelphians so highly regarded European baking, pastry, and confectionery that these items became symbols of culture and status and often graced some of the finest tables in the city, including those at City Tavern.

It is appropriate that Walter Staib decided to devote his second book not only exclusively to baking and confectionery but also to exploring more fully the culinary heritage of the city. The elegance and perfection of the eighteenth-century sweet table beautifully represents the high character of the city itself in this period—a time when the very streets we travel today were filled with men and women whose ideals and grand visions helped to shape the country we now share. Thank you, Walter Staib and City Tavern, for reminding us of our elegant, inspiring past.

—*Robert Bennett*

# Preface

When I penned the *City Tavern Cookbook*, I conducted a great deal of research on the cuisine and culinary customs of the eighteenth century. Surprisingly, there was a great deal of information—recipes, anecdotes about dining experiences in prominent homes, menus from the original City Tavern, and so on. Perhaps the single most prominent theme in my research was the eighteenth-century sweet table, an abundant display of cakes, pies, pastries, fruits, preserves, ice cream and sorbet, and sweetmeats. To detail the elaborate displays of confectionery talent were sweet table drawings and diagrams so precise that they could be considered culinary architectural plans.

Unfortunately, we did not have enough space in the *City Tavern Cookbook* to do the eighteenth-century sweet table justice, so I decided to shelve all of the information we collected until I was ready to write this sequel cookbook. Another important aspect of eighteenth-century cuisine in Philadelphia left unexplored in the *City Tavern Cookbook* was the influence of the many varied cultural traditions and foodways that blended to create a unique and varied culinary culture.

Realizing that what I uncovered while writing the *City Tavern Cookbook* was only the tip of the iceberg, I searched for a unique talent to assist in this endeavor. I met Jennifer Lindner when she was editor of *Art Culinaire* and recognized immediately her passions for patisserie and history, so I asked her to join me in this endeavor to delve further into the cultural origins of eighteenth-century cuisine in Philadelphia and to help research more historical recipes. Being an accomplished pastry chef and historian, she offered a unique perspective, and her contribution to this book is invaluable.

So how did a German become a custodian of eighteenth-century American culinary history? I began my culinary career in Pforzheim, Germany, a small town located at the entrance to the Black Forest, and had my first culinary apprenticeship in Nagold, in the heart of the Black Forest. My uncle Karl Hintze was a Master Confissier and Master Pâtissier in Pforzheim both at the Café Frei and at the Café Wagner, and my mother, Hertha Staib, was a great baker and chef; the entire family had a passion for baking, cooking, and gardening. We made our own preserves, canned fruits and vegetables, baked our own breads and pastries—all of the techniques that mirrored what the early Americans did back in 1773.

At a very young age, I spent a great deal of time in my uncle and aunt's restaurant, Gasthaus zum Buckenberg, complete with its own huge bakeshop. I started out doing odd jobs and was soon learning about food and developing cooking skills. My aunt was also a very accomplished baker and always enlisted my help in making the pastries and sweets (essentially a sweet table) that were enjoyed with coffee every Sunday in the Black Forest—a tradition that continues to this day.

It came to my attention that City Tavern closed its doors on December 31, 1992. After inquiring with the National Park Service, which supervises the Tavern, I received a prospectus to apply for its operation. Although it seemed complex and too full of governmental jargon and red tape, I took it with me on a trip to Asia. It was on the return flight from Tokyo that the project really captured my imagination. I couldn't believe the lifestyle and level of sophistication those early Philadelphians had. It quickly became clear to me that City Tavern had been, without a doubt, the greatest restaurant in eighteenth-century North America.

The more I learned about City Tavern and its special place in social, political, and gastronomic history, the more I started to believe in its potential. Realizing that, with the right management and cuisine, the Tavern could once again rival any restaurant in America, I began to feel like a culinary crusader, impassioned about keeping America's gastronomic heritage alive. I submitted a proposal.

Before we opened our doors on July fourth of that same year, we had completely renovated the kitchen, removed the freezers and the commercial laundry facility, and installed a pastry and bakeshop. Independence National Historical Park chief curator Karie Diethorn worked closely with us to re-create the most authentic City Tavern experience possible, with slight adjustments to make room for the modern-day context. The walls were painted in the Tavern's original colors, the rooms were decorated in reproduction furniture and fabrics, and we dressed our service staff in handmade eighteenth-century attire. We chose reproduction table settings, including candlesticks, plates with a china pattern based on one from 1793, and lead-free pewterware in the mid-eighteenth-century style for our tabletops. Even our glassware, which was imported from Italy or hand blown by artisans in West Virginia, was selected to reflect the styles used in the late eighteenth century. And for an authentic ambience, we decided to commission colonial-period "characters" for special events, such as Thanksgiving, and to provide live harpsichord music on weekends.

As critical as the setting was, the most important thing for me as a chef was to work diligently on the food and dining experience. I was fortunate enough to have had a head start—a few years earlier, as a consultant to a restaurant of the same period in Richmond, Virginia, I had researched colonial culinary and dining traditions with acclaimed New York food historian Dr. Lorna Sass. It became my mission to re-create the culinary heritage of City Tavern, a one-of-a-kind restaurant.

The experience turned out to be a delightful awakening as I discovered how close to "home" eighteenth-century food was for me. Having grown up in the Old World, where everything was done the old-fashioned way, I found the original City Tavern recipes comfortably familiar. Many of them could have come right from my own grandmother's kitchen.

In keeping with the Old World tradition, my food philosophy for the Tavern continues to be "from the farm to the table, as fresh as possible." Accordingly, breads and pastries are baked each morning, and we use no walk-in freezers—our products are delivered daily and prepared in the same manner as they were in the early colonial era.

City Tavern is indeed more than a restaurant. It is a piece of history, a living culinary museum that offers diners an experience unavailable anywhere else—insight into our country's vast and underappreciated culinary heritage. I wrote this book to extend that experience to a larger audience and to solidify City Tavern's place in American gastronomic history.

This collection of recipes reflects the sophistication of City Tavern's chefs and the high esteem in which the Tavern was held by America's first gourmands, the Founding Fathers. These are the same recipes we faithfully re-create every day. Although I strive to preserve the authentic nature of the colonial-era recipes we use, I have had to adapt some of them to modern tastes and equipment.

I hope you enjoy this sweet lesson in our country's extraordinary culinary history. Bon appétit!

—*Walter Staib, chef/proprietor*

# A Taste of History

## Important Events Held at the Tavern

City Tavern's role as the backdrop for the unfolding of American history is indisputable and well documented. When Paul Revere rode six days from Boston with news that the British had closed the port in retaliation for the famous tea party, he went directly to City Tavern to deliver the news. As the delegates of the first Continental Congress began to arrive in the Fall of 1774, they stopped first at City Tavern. In fact, when John Adams arrived in town, dusty and fatigued from the long ride, he went straight to the Tavern, "the most genteel one in America." George Washington did the same, not proceeding to his lodgings until first supping at City Tavern.

The delegates of the Continental Congress frequented the Tavern the entire time they were assembled, where they often conducted informal discussions outside of the more formal confines of Carpenters' Hall.

When the battles of Concord and Lexington were announced by a rider at City Tavern on April 24, 1775, it became the center of military activity during the war. As battles raged, the funerals of war heroes such as Colonel John Haslet of Delaware and General Hugh Mercer took place at the City Tavern, with full military honors.

In 1777, the nation's first Fourth of July celebration was held at the Tavern, "with festivity and ceremony becoming the occasion," according to John Adams. When Washington moved his headquarters to Philadelphia in August of the same year, his letters indicate that he used the Tavern as his informal headquarters—although he would not allow his troops entrance, for fear of their corruption.

When the British retook Philadelphia that fall, innkeeper Daniel Smith welcomed his countrymen with open arms—and an open till. The Tavern was commandeered as a center for officer recreation, including a weekly series of balls where Philadelphia's Tory belles were entertained. The fun was not always so wholesome—record of a horse theft in front of the tavern was made in October 1777.

Soon after the Continental Army reoccupied Philadelphia in 1778, Smith returned to England. Gifford Dalley and then George Evans succeeded him as innkeepers. City Tavern once again hosted special events for the upper crust of America and abroad. During Dalley's tenure, the Coffee Room developed into an exchange room and seat of business. When the second Continental Congress convened, a series of dazzling balls and national affairs of state took place, often continuing until the wee hours of the morning. With the establishment of the new political order, Philadelphia was suddenly inundated by politicians needing entertainment, room, and board—exactly the kind of trade most restaurants pray for.

The most lavish party held at the Tavern was most likely the election and installation of the state's chief executive, the president of the Supreme Executive Council in 1778. A party of 270, including ambassadors and ministers of France and Spain, attended. The bill was £2995—only £500 of that for food. The rest was for a stupefying amount of alcohol, including 522 bottles of Madeira, 116 large bowls of punch, nine bottles of toddy, six bowls of sangria, 24 bottles of port, and two tubs of grog for artillery soldiers. Understandably, the party turned boisterous—the bill also covered 96 broken plates and glasses, as well as five decanters.

In 1785, the Tavern was sold to Samuel Powel, one of the original proprietors, the former mayor of the city and a man of great wealth and social standing. When thirty-nine delegates, representing twelve of the thirteen states, approved a constitution for the United States of America, on September 17, 1787, they then adjourned, according to the record, "to the City Tavern, dined together and took a cordial leave of each other."

From 1785 to 1824, City Tavern served primarily as a hotel, merchants' exchange, and coffee house. The merchants' exchange, a forerunner of the Philadelphia-Baltimore-Washington stock exchange of today, was a bustling center of industry, a lively place where sea captains, insurance salesmen, and farmers haggled and exchanged gossip. The Tavern's fortunes gradually declined in the early 1800s, and in 1834 its roof caught fire, damaging the Tavern irreparably. In 1854, when City Tavern was demolished, *The Pennsylvania Gazette* wrote, ". . . nobody is going to miss this Tavern except those persons living in the past."

# City Tavern Rises Again in the Twentieth Century

Fortunately, that period of the Tavern's obscurity ended when the U.S. Department of the Interior was authorized by the Truman Administration to create Independence National Historical Park, a surviving group of pivotal historic sites that formerly included City Tavern. Although that decision was made in 1948, it took more than twenty-five years of research to recreate the Tavern, brick by brick, according to historic documentation of the original structure. City Tavern finally opened in 1976, just in time for the country's bicentennial celebration.

While there are other restaurants on the Atlantic seaboard that attempt to recapture America's past, only City Tavern has faithfully revisited the high culinary standards of the day. City Tavern is clearly an American original, a restaurant famous both for its Revolutionary cuisine and its formidable place in our nation's history. This unique twofold attraction appeals to tourists and locals alike and guarantees City Tavern a distinguished place in culinary history, both for its vibrant past and its utterly delicious present.

# Touring the Tavern

In 1975, after painstaking research, the National Park Service rebuilt City Tavern. Today, the Tavern appears essentially as it did 200 years ago, even down to the front awning, which shades the Tavern from the direct summer sun. Every year, 12,000 to 20,000 guests are drawn to City Tavern because of its reputation for fine, authentic colonial dining, as well as for its historic élan. At the Tavern, they enjoy a taste of the past in the same atmosphere of gentility and good cheer enjoyed by our nation's founders. Here's a quick "guided" tour through the seven dining and public rooms of this accurately reconstructed inn.

The original City Tavern was comprised of five levels. The cellar housed the kitchens; the first and second floors contained the public areas; the third floor was devoted to lodging rooms; and the attic probably served as servants' quarters. The first and second floors, which we will tour in detail here, were the heart of the Tavern's operation.

**First Floor**

As you walk up a set of marble stairs into the Tavern from Second Street, you first enter a long hallway. On your right is the Subscription Room, so-called because the magazines and newspapers, ships' manifests, and letters of decree to which the Tavern subscribed were located there.

Behind the Subscription Room is the Bar Room, with its high-backed wooden booths and central fireplace. Although it doesn't have a "bar" as we know them today, per se, it does have a narrow, closet-sized room that can accommodate the bartender and, of course, the liquor. It has a window and a Dutch door that doubles as a shelf, with barred gate that slides down on top of it. In the 1700s, this was commonly used to separate the innkeeper and his liquor from the patrons. Since tempers and political arguments were often stoked by alcohol consumption, whenever the innkeeper felt threatened, he would lower and lock "the bar" to protect himself, thereby explaining the derivation of the modern-day term. Back then, the bar would have functioned as the Tavern's nerve center, where patrons would arrange to rent a room, order a meal, or hear the latest news.

Across the hallway from the Subscription Room is a Coffee Room. From the very beginning of the Tavern's history this Coffee Room was the place where merchants would discuss ship movements and other business over a cup of coffee or stronger drink—one reason why maps remain on the Coffee Room wall today.

In the room next door is a second Coffee Room, representative of the Tavern's public dining spaces.

Back in the main hallway, to our left is the back door, which leads out to the porch and garden area, and doubled as the entrance for the gentry class en route to balls and private parties commonly held upstairs.

## Second Floor

The stairs in the main hallway lead to the second floor. At the top of the stairs, straight through the hallway, is the Long Room—the scene of countless elegant balls, brilliant musical performances, large meetings, and card games. In fact, it was in the Long Room that Congress held the first Fourth of July celebration in 1777.

Adjoining the Long Room are two private dining rooms. Originally, these rooms would have accommodated clubs or groups desiring privacy. On the left at the top of the stairs, is the Cincinnati Room (originally called the Northwest Dining Room), named in 1975 in honor of the Pennsylvania chapter for the Society of the Cincinnati, which helped refurbish this room. This organization is composed of direct descendants of the Revolutionary officers who founded the original Pennsylvania chapter at City Tavern in 1783.

Across the hallway is the Charter Room, named in honor of the fifty-three original Tavern subscribers and once reserved for their private use. This room also serves to honors the members of the national Home Fashions League, who contributed toward furnishing the present City Tavern.

## Lower Level

The adaptation of City Tavern's cellar provides insight into the historical aspect of food storage, preparation, and service. From 1773 to 1848, the cellar served the vital purpose of being both a work and storage area. Fresh foodstuffs were delivered to the Second Street entrance. At the rear of the building, casks, barrels, and boxes were loaded into the cellar through the cobblestone alley. Because there was access to water pumps on the public street, this area also served for dishwashing.

The back cellar room was used for the long-term storage of bulk foodstuffs such as flour. The larder room located on the southeast corner was possibly used as a storeroom for prepared foods like pickled meat and preserved fruits. From the kitchen on the northeast corner, food was prepared and distributed.

In 1994, the cellar area was opened to the public for dining.

# Introduction

CITY TAVERN, PHILADELPHIA. DANIEL SMITH begs leave to inform the PUBLIC, that the Gentlemen Proprietors of the CITY TAVERN have been pleased to approve of him, as a proper person to keep said tavern: in consequence of which he has completely furnished it, and, at a very great expence [*sic*], has laid in every article of the first quality, perfectly in the stile [*sic*] of a London tavern. . . .

He has also fitted up a genteel Coffee Room, well attended, and properly supplied with English and American papers and magazines.

He hopes his attention and willingness to oblige, together with the goodness of his wines and larder, will give the public entire satisfaction, and prove him not unworthy of the encouragement he has already experienced.

The City Tavern in Philadelphia was erected at a great expence, by a voluntary subscription of the principal gentlemen of the city, for the convenience of the public, and is by much the largest and most elegant house occupied in that way in America.

—*Pennsylvania Gazette*, February 16, 1774

When City Tavern first opened in Philadelphia in December 1773, it was considered one of the most elegant establishments of its kind in colonial America. The city was growing rapidly in this period, becoming ever more cosmopolitan, wealthy, and politically significant, and its inhabitants and visitors required taverns to suit their social and mercantile needs. In 1756, there were already more than 120 taverns in Philadelphia (more than in New York or Boston). By the mid-1770s, surely even more taverns were needed to serve a city bursting with over twenty-one thousand residents (as many as in New York and four thousand more than in Boston) (Rice 31). With the opening of City Tavern, genteel Philadelphians, for the first time, had a place to gather for business, social events, political meetings, and, of course, food and drink, otherwise known in the period as "entertainment." When proprietor Edward Moyston opened the first two front rooms of the City Tavern as a "Merchants' Coffee-House &

Place of Exchange" in 1789, it became even more business-oriented. Writing in the early 1790s, French visitor Moreau de St. Mery declared it "an extremely useful establishment" (Roberts et al. 354). The rest of the building, however, remained virtually unchanged, continuing to serve patrons who desired food, drink, and lodging.

Although City Tavern altered and expanded during the nearly twenty years that it remained Philadelphia's most fashionable public house, the information offered in the above advertisement defined the unchanging essence of this establishment. Of course, the sale of food and drink was one among many services City Tavern offered Philadelphians. As one of the most important services, however, the quality of these "entertainments" was implied in the advertisement. Daniel Smith took pride in characterizing his establishment as being "perfectly in the stile [*sic*] of a London tavern"; he emphasized the "goodness of his wines and larder"; and, of course, he described it as "the largest and most elegant house . . . in America." How does this language relate to the dishes, particularly the desserts, served at City Tavern and in numerous Philadelphia dining rooms during the eighteenth century? It reveals that the sweet preparations were as cosmopolitan, abundant, and "elegant" as the city itself. Set amid the businesses, stores, confectioners' shops, and elite homes that populated the streets just blocks away from the waterfront, City Tavern catered to the fashionable tastes of its patrons, who could obtain the finest imported and prepared foods in shops and private dining rooms throughout Philadelphia. Like imported furniture, silver, ceramics, and so forth, foodstuffs from all over the world arrived daily at the city's ports, ready to be celebrated on fashionable tables. In the same way, just as European craftspeople brought their skills to the colonies and inspired American artisans, so did transplanted European confectioners and cooks not only serve welcoming Americans who patronized their shops and taverns but also influence those who cooked in Philadelphia kitchens.

At City Tavern, the sweet dishes served to merchants, Masonic societies, diplomats, and congressmen were much like those prepared in elite households. Seasonal and preserved fruits and vegetables, locally butchered meats and dairy products, fresh breads, nuts, and a wealth of imported spices and exotic ingredients were just some of the products Philadelphians enjoyed. Although tensions ran high between the British and the Americans during the 1770s and 1780s (most of City Tavern's heyday), the cakes, breads, puddings, sweetmeats, and so forth served there and in private homes were based on traditional English cookery. Most colonists could trace their roots back to England, after all, and best enjoyed the dishes with which they were most familiar. The popularity of English cookbooks in Philadelphia and other large cities during the eighteenth century is further testament to Americans' predilection for English cooking.

Although City Tavern served some of the most elegant dishes of the period, it nonetheless employed the frugality that was so admired and necessary during the period. Taverns in many large cities vied for patrons by emphasizing the quality of their "entertainments" in local advertisements (Rice 86). Yet, in the 1770s and 1780s, as the colonies prepared for and went to war with England, even the wealthiest of diners at least occasionally enjoyed simply prepared dishes at home as well as in public houses. On November 17, 1779, for example, a notice appeared in the *Pennsylvania Gazette* describing a governmental procession that was followed by a meal at City Tavern. It stated that only "a cold collation was provided, consistent with that frugality and oeconomy [*sic*] which the situation of our public affairs not only renders necessary but honourable." It is unclear from the notice what time of day this meal took place, but "cold collations" (light meals) were usually served for supper or the evening meal.

In the eighteenth century, frugality and preparedness were essential to managing a successful kitchen. Although food in Philadelphia was plentiful, households and public houses could not afford to waste it. If the dishes found on menus at City Tavern resembled those served in private Philadelphia homes, so were their methods of storing food similar. Root cel-

lars were vital to the eighteenth-century kitchen. There, packed between layers of sand to keep them cool and, to some extent, out of the reach of vermin, vegetables and some fruits remained fresh during the fall and winter months. Drying, preserving, and pickling were additional methods of storing these items over long periods of time. Poured into ceramic jars and most often covered with paper, jams, preserves, conserves, jellies, and pickles were integral to well-stocked pantries. Households and public houses similarly maintained supplies of meats, which were salted, dried, or pickled, and stored in cellars, larders, or icehouses (Philadelphia having the good fortune of having an abundance of ice). Even butter and eggs could be kept fresh. Butter was generously salted and packed in casks between additional layers of salt or in brine, which were then stored in a cool place. Eggs were preserved with a coating of lime or wax and also kept in a cool storage space. With their skillful knowledge of food preservation and preparation, Philadelphia cooks were able to take full advantage of the city's abundant supply of local and imported ingredients.

If Philadelphia's primarily English character caused it to resemble other eighteenth-century colonial American cities, its general acceptance of other cultural groups made it unique among them. To be sure, mid- to late-eighteenth-century Philadelphia experienced a veritable acculturation, whereby such groups as the Dutch, Swedes, Irish, Jews, French, and Germans influenced the daily life of this cosmopolitan center. Within this climate of cultural diversity, Philadelphians were exposed not only to a variety of social mores but also to traditions, many of which included foodways. That many kinds of sweet dishes—from gingerbread to crème brûlée to linzertorte to ice cream—were available in eighteenth-century Philadelphia seems obvious today. Yet, only when one understands the degree to which diverse peoples shaped the city is it possible to truly appreciate how their foods became popularized and were incorporated into the culture that was cosmopolitan Philadelphia.

During their travels to the city, many European visitors kept journals in which they described the cultural diversity they witnessed. Writing in the 1790s, Moreau de St. Mery declared of Philadelphia's Caucasian men, "They are made up of English, Scotch, Irish and all the nationalities of Europe." The city, in fact, reflected Americans around the country, who, St. Mery explained, "have extremely diversified European ancestors" (Roberts et al. 276-277). Writing in his journal nearly fifty years before St. Mery, Dr. Alexander Hamilton similarly described Philadelphia's eclectic cultural landscape. In 1739, Hamilton left his native Scotland to practice medicine in Annapolis, Maryland. Then, on May 30, 1744, due to health reasons and his interest in the colonies, he began a journey that took him to Maine and then back to Maryland. On Friday, June 8, Dr. Hamilton wrote of dining at a Philadelphia tavern, where he experienced not only the cultural but also the religious diversity of its patrons:

> I dined att [sic] a taveren [sic] with a very mixed company of different nations and religions. There were Scots, English, Dutch, Germans, and Irish; there were Roman Catholicks [sic],

Church men, Presbyterians, Quakers, Newlightmen, Methodists, Seventh day men, Moravians, Anabaptists, and one Jew. The whole company consisted of 25 planted round an oblong table in a great hall well stoked with flys [sic] (Bridenbaugh 20).

As they wrote about the city's cultural diversity, many visitors to Philadelphia particularly emphasized the large size of the German community. In addition to the English, Welsh, Irish, and Scots, the Germans were some of the earliest settlers in Pennsylvania, and their numbers continued to increase throughout the eighteenth century. The German community was large outside of the city, but it maintained a strong presence in Philadelphia as well. In June of 1744, Dr. Hamilton wrote in his journal, "The Germans and High Dutch are of late become very numerous here" (Bridenbaugh 29). While visiting Philadelphia in 1765, Scottish traveler Lord Adam Gordon similarly explained in his journal, "The Germans in this province are not under 60,000" (Peckham 261). Some fifty years later, Moreau de St. Méry expressed similar thoughts. "The population includes many foreigners, especially Germans," he wrote. "Above Third

Street in Northern Liberties, as I have said before, there are only Germans. Their peaceful character, their love of work, the similarity of their language to English, which easily lets them understand and be understood—all these things bring them in great numbers to the American continent" (Roberts 264). As Germans farmed the land and opened businesses in the city, they maintained many of their traditions, including their foodways, which undoubtedly profoundly influenced the food culture of Philadelphia.

Next to the Germans, it was arguably the stylishness, attitudes, and traditions of the French that most colored Philadelphians' way of life. This particularly occurred when France entered the Revolution in 1778. As late as the 1790s, however, Moreau de St. Méry believed, "The misfortunes existing in the colonies have also brought many French to Philadelphia. Twenty-five thousand are estimated to have sought refuge in the United States" (Roberts 265). As large numbers of French travelers, émigrés, and diplomats passed through and settled in the city, Philadelphians became ever more inspired by their social mores and sense of fashion. The degree to which people were influenced by the French and other cultures was apparent not only in the way they dressed and behaved but also in their ability to communicate with foreigners. While most Philadelphians probably learned German and French out of necessity and convenience, proficiency in the latter was also a sign of gentility. German and French émigrés had little choice; they needed to learn English. It is thus most appropriate that, in the 1780s, a language school opened across the street from City Tavern—the most cosmopolitan and elegant establishment of its kind in the city. The instructor, Mr. Becker, clearly saw a need for such courses and listed the following advertisement in the *Pennsylvania Gazette*:

February 7, 1781 . . . HENRY BECKER, Living Second street, opposite the City Tavern, proposes to wait upon those LADIES and GENTLEMEN that intend to learn the FRENCH, GERMAN AND ENGLISH LANGUAGES, At their respective Houses, any hour of the day, on the most reasonable terms.

N. B. An EVENING SCHOOL will, be opened by said Becker, at his Lodgings, for those that it will not suit to attend in the Day.

Philadelphians expressed their admiration of French culture in many ways. They not only learned the language and adopted various polite French mannerisms but also came to appreciate and desire French foods. Thomas Jefferson was undoubtedly one of the greatest proponents of French cuisine, and, after his term in Paris as Minister Plenipotentiary to the Court of Louis XVI from 1784 to 1788, Americans became more familiar with it than ever before. Before and after the Revolution, they were exposed to many French foods, from wine to cheese to ice cream. One can only imagine the influence that French confectioners, bakers, and chocolatiers had in Philadelphia, as they opened shops to discriminating patrons eager to partake of fashionable delicacies.

French culture was seductive—so much so that even English cookbook author Eliza Smith, writing from London in the early eighteenth century, included French recipes in her otherwise English cookbook, which she wrote "in such a Manner as is most agreeable to *English* Palates." Sensitive to the animosity that had long existed between England and France and, yet, aware of the British taste for French style, she explained, "I have so far temporized, as, since we have, to our Disgrace, so fondly admired the *French* tongue, *French* Modes, and also *French* Messes, to present you now and then with such Receipts of the *French* Cookery as I think may not be disagreeable to *English* Palates" (Smith, *Preface*).

By the late 1770s, French culture was colorfully influencing daily life in Philadelphia. Local diarists referred to it frequently. On May 3, 1783, young Philadelphia socialite Nancy Shippen described her preparation earlier in the day for a party that took place that evening—one that importantly called for French fashion:

10 o'clock at night—Spent a most delightfull [*sic*] Eveng at Mrs. Powells. I heard in the Morning there was to be a very large Company.—I spent great part of the day in making preparation—I wish'd to look well. Sett [*sic*] off about six oclock [*sic*]—my glass told me I look'd well—was dressed in pink with a gause [*sic*] peticoat [*sic*]—an Elegant french [*sic*] Hat on, with five white plumes nodding different ways—[and] a bouquet of natural flowers" (Armes 141-142).

Another prominent Philadelphian, Elizabeth Drinker, also frequently remarked in her diary upon the French people and events she encountered in the city. Referring to Philadelphia's feting of the recently born dauphin, on June 15, 1782, she wrote, "Great doings this evening at the French Ambassadors, (who lives at John Dickinsons [*sic*] House up Chesnut [*sic*] Street) on account of the Birth of the Dauphine [*sic*] of France—feasting fire-Works &c, for which they have been preparing for some weeks" (Drinker 401).

Ironically, while Philadelphians prided themselves on incorporating such things as French mores and foodways into their daily lives, many French visitors chastised them, and Americans in general, for their inferiorities. Among the dining practices they encountered, the French generally found Americans' large consumption of tea ridiculous. Monsieur Roux was one of the many who wrote scathingly of the "immoderate use of tea and coffee at all repasts" (Sherrill 82). The French also believed Americans ate too frequently. Monsieur Chastellux, commenting on dining with a Mr. Brick in Boston, remarked that "supper was served exactly four hours after we had risen from the table. It can be easily imagined that we took practically nothing. Nevertheless, the Americans did very well at it. In general they eat less than we during a single meal, but they eat as often as they wish—a custom which I consider very bad" (97). And the French found foolish Americans' desire to eat copious amounts of meat and small amounts of, what they considered to be, poor quality bread. "They [Americans] eat seven or eight times as much meat as bread," wrote St. Méry, and while the French often complimented the meals they ate in the colonies, they thought little of the bread offered to them (99). Monsieur de Bourg commented, "Their only grain is Indian corn, which accounts for their eating only that kind of bread—the meanest and worst in the world" (100).

Although this was hardly the case, such a criticism was a common one. Monsieur Revel remarked that some Americans looked unhealthy. "It is possible that their food is partly to blame," he suggested, "for they not only eat no bread, but there are some of them who never even heard of it. They make a sort of biscuit on the hot cinders with corn meal, which they cultivate in great quantities" (Sherrill 100-101). Some of the worst attacks came from a Monsieur Robin, who not only attributed Americans' physical ailments to the paucity of quality bread, but claimed that American bread could not even satisfy French troops:

> [T]he women, generally very pretty, are often deprived of these precious ornaments (teeth) at eighteen or twenty years of age. . . . I presume this to be the effect of hot bread. . . . [Americans], who have such fine wheat, nevertheless do not know the precious art of making it more digestible by kneading and fermentation. Whenever it is required they make a cake which they put to half-cook on an iron plate; the French who went to war in America could not become accustomed to it, and taught them to improve on it a little. It is to be found passable in the inns, but still very inferior to that of our Army (101).

Despite such criticism, however, the French did offer some compliments. Most referred to Americans' cleanliness, the abundance of food in America, and how well Americans provided for themselves. Monsieur Brissot found that American "kitchens are kept clean, and do not give out the disgusting smell to be found in the best kitchens of France. The dining rooms, which are generally on the ground floor, are also clean and well aired; cleanliness and fresh air is to be found everywhere" (Sherrill 106). Furthermore, with poverty ever increasing in Europe, French visitors were startled at the veritable lack of want in America. Monsieur Beaujour was adamant on this point:

> It must be remarked that the poorest individual, the ordinary day-laborer, is better fed and clad here than in any other country. Every day of their lives they eat more in the United States than in France, and that too of expensive things, and those which elsewhere are considered luxuries. They calculate (based on the receipts of the Custom House) that each man consumes annually ten pounds of sugar, two and a half of coffee, one of tea and about fifteen of molasses (80).

The many cultures that lived and thrived together in Philadelphia profoundly influenced one another in multiple ways. This diversity gave rise to many shared traditions, one of the most important of which was cookery. Through food, each culture maintained its unique identity while at the same time it inspired others. The continuous arrival of European immigrants, as well as the constant importation of goods from Europe and the Caribbean, exposed Philadelphians to new and exotic foods, which they then incorporated into their own traditional recipes.

Food in general was important to eighteenth-century Philadelphians, but they arguably revered the preparation of sweet dishes and baked goods in a unique way. As they were in Europe, not only did sweetmeats, cakes, breads, preserves, and the like demand a lot of time and skill to prepare, but the ingredients were very costly as well. Sugar was, for many people, a luxury throughout the eighteenth century; hence the popularity of less expensive maple syrup and molasses in the period. The processes of purchasing, grinding, cooking, and removing the impurities from sugar were also time-consuming. Indeed, if families could afford to do so, they often purchased baked goods and confections from nearby shops.

Although period cookbook authors often encouraged readers to purchase various ingredients or finished dishes in order to save time and money, it is clear that Philadelphians, like their European neighbors, admired the skill required to prepare baked goods and sweet dishes at home. Nearly all households had domestic help; sometimes a woman relied on the abilities of her cook, while at other times she prepared baked goods and other such dishes herself, desirous of displaying her own skills. In many diaries of this period, Philadelphia girls and women recounted such activities as preparing pastry, sweetmeats, and preserving fruit, thus revealing that these were among the most celebrated and important of cooking skills. Eighteenth-century advertisements further emphasize this. On June 4, 1767, Mary McCallister appealed "To the LADIES or [of] PENNSYLVANIA, and the adjacent Provinces" in an advertisement she listed in the *Pennsylvania Gazette*. She detailed her plans to open a boarding school in Philadelphia, where she would teach such classes as:

> Literature . . . the English and French Languages, with their proper Accent and Emphasis; Needle Work in Silks, Worsted and Linens. . . . [T]he Arts of Painting on Glass, Japanning with Prints, Wax and Shell Work . . . Writing, Arithmetic, Music, or Dancing. . . . [And] I likewise intend, on a certain Day in every Week, to instruct the Ladies in Pastry, with some other beneficial and amusing Articles, too tedious to mention.

It is clear that learning how to make proper pastry and "other beneficial . . . Articles" was as important to a girl's development and to her becoming an accomplished woman as were other artistic endeavors, such as learning a language, needlework, painting, or playing an instrument.

Other advertisements reveal that even though women who managed their households were skilled in the kitchen, they sought domestics who were also knowledgeable about cookery. Women considered trained help highly desirable, as they required little supervision. The woman who listed an advertisement with the *Pennsylvania Gazette* on September 17, 1767, was surely aware of her appealing qualifications. "WANTS a PLACE, in a genteel Family," she wrote, "who is capable of . . . Pastry, in the genteelist Manner; [and] can preserve and pickle." She also added, "She has lived in some of the best Families in London, and in this Country, in that Station"—experiences that would certainly have pleased a Philadelphia family interested in emulating fashionable styles of dining. Yet another advertisement might have appealed to a household or shop owner. On August 5, 1772, the *Pennsylvania Gazette* listed the services of "A LIKELY NEGROE FELLOW, about 23 Years old, has had the Smallpox, can cook, and do all Kinds of Housework, is thoroughly acquainted with the Chocolate Manufactory, in all its Branches." Certainly this man would have been suited to work in one of the city's many chocolate shops, but it is possible he could have been hired to cook for

a family as well. These advertisements are significant, as they reveal the sorts of culinary skills Philadelphians most valued.

When City Tavern opened to the public, Philadelphia was already a cosmopolitan city and becoming ever more so. Despite its economic difficulties during the Revolution, Philadelphia saw significant growth in many industries and occupations, especially in the last decades of the century. Food-related businesses experienced this as much as any other. Among the many that existed by 1790, the city had 114 bakers, 26 biscuit bakers, 11 sugar refiners, 9 chocolate makers, 7 sugar bakers, 5 pastry cooks, and 3 cake bakers (Schweitzer 125). City residents were virtually surrounded by culinary artisans, eager to provide their goods and services. In this environment of elegant dining, locally grown and imported foodstuffs, and fashionable taste, City Tavern provided Philadelphians with new dining and socializing experiences. The colonies saw much change in the late eighteenth century, but Philadelphia's City Tavern set standards that public houses up and down the East Coast continued to emulate well into the nineteenth century.

# Cakes

Cakes were among the most popular of eighteenth-century confections. Not only did Philadelphians prepare them in home kitchens, but they were also able to purchase many varieties in local bakeries. Period cookbooks and advertisements in the *Pennsylvania Gazette* reveal that city residents enjoyed the simplest of sponge and pound cakes, as well as more elaborate and costly spice cakes, fruit- and cream-filled trifles, and rich cheesecakes.

Like today's finest baking instructors, those of the eighteenth century emphasized that understanding basic baking methods was essential to preparing successful cakes. Some, like Elizabeth Raffald, author of *The Experienced English Housekeeper,* opened her chapter on cakes with clear instructions that applied to the recipes that followed. Today's bakers would benefit as much from these suggestions that are more than two hundred years old as they would from any other:

## Observations upon Cakes

When you make any kind of cakes be sure that you get your things ready before you begin. Then beat your eggs well, and don't leave them till you have finished the cakes; or else they will go back again and your cakes will not be light. If your cakes have butter in, take care you beat it to a fine cream before you put in your sugar, for if you beat it twice the time it will not answer so well. . . . Bake all kinds of cake in a good oven according to the size of the cake, and follow the directions of your receipt, for though care hath been taken to weigh and measure every article belonging to every kind of cake, yet the management and the oven must be left to the maker's care (134).

British butler Samuel Adams described the ceremonies in such American houses as Christopher Gore's: "When the ladies have retired from the dining-room and the drawing-room bell rings for coffee, the footman enters with the tray . . . of coffee . . . bread and butter, cakes, toast, &c., the under butler or some other servant following to take away the empty cups and saucers on a waiter or other tray" (Belden 382–383).

# Sour Cream Coffee Cake

By the mid- to late 1600s, coffee was being enjoyed in the French court and in London. Ever interested in imitating European fashion, colonists, too, were enjoying this beverage that the Dutch had introduced into their homes and taverns by 1670 (Mariani 89–90). Whether taken in the morning, afternoon, or evening, coffee was commonly enjoyed with a variety of cakes. This one, with its streusel topping, reflects the German foodways that were so prevalent in colonial America.

Makes one 9-inch cake; serves 10 to 12

**Crumb Topping**
½ cup granulated sugar
½ cup chopped walnuts
2 tablespoons all-purpose flour
2 tablespoons unsalted butter, melted
1 teaspoon ground cinnamon

**Cake**
2 cups sifted all-purpose flour
1½ teaspoons baking powder
½ teaspoon baking soda
½ teaspoon salt
1 cup granulated sugar
¼ pound (1 stick) unsalted butter
2 large eggs
1 teaspoon vanilla extract
8 ounces (1 cup) sour cream

*In* The Complete Confectioner, *the recipe for "Coffee" is as follows:*
*"FOR four bottles of brandy, take one pound of coffee in powder, the very best Turkey [Turkish]; a little salt, two cloves, a little cinnamon; then mix altogether for twelve hours before you distil it; two pounds of sugar, two bottles and half a pint of water clarified with whites of eggs, filtered through the paper"* (Nutt, 82).

1. Preheat the oven to 350°F. Lightly grease one 9 x 2½-inch round cake pan with butter, and coat lightly with flour.
2. Prepare the Crumb Topping: In a small bowl, combine the ½ cup sugar, walnuts, 2 tablespoons flour, 2 tablespoons melted butter, and cinnamon. Set aside.
3. Prepare the Cake: In a large bowl, sift together the 2 cups flour, baking powder, baking soda, and salt.
4. In the bowl of an electric mixer, beat the 1 cup sugar and ¼ pound butter on medium speed until light and fluffy, scraping down the sides of the bowl often. Add the eggs and vanilla extract slowly and beat well, scraping down the sides of the bowl often.
5. With the electric mixer on low speed, slowly add the dry ingredients, alternating with the sour cream, and mix until just combined.
6. Pour the batter into the prepared pan. Sprinkle the Crumb Topping on top of the batter. Bake for 45 to 50 minutes, or until golden brown and a toothpick inserted near the center comes out clean.
7. Cool the cake in the pan on a wire rack for 10 minutes. Remove from the pan. Cut into slices and serve.

# Pound Cake

Nearly every recipe book available in colonial America included a recipe for pound cake. Because they were ever interested in incorporating exotic spices into their baked goods, it is hardly surprising that most eighteenth-century recipe writers suggested adding caraway seeds as well. Named for each pound of its ingredients—flour, butter, sugar, and eggs—it was a rich, dense cake that remained moist for a number of days and complemented the coffee, tea, or spirited beverages that often accompanied it. This recipe, like most contemporary interpretations of the traditional favorite, alters the original ratio of ingredients to produce a somewhat lighter, easier-to-prepare cake.

**Makes two 8-inch loaves**

> 4 cups granulated sugar
> ¼ pound (1 stick) unsalted butter, at room temperature
> 6 large eggs
> ½ tablespoon vanilla extract
> 4 ounces (½ cup) sour cream
> 2½ cups plus 2 tablespoons sifted all-purpose flour
> ½ teaspoon baking powder
> ½ teaspoon baking soda
> ¼ teaspoon salt

**1.** Preheat the oven to 325°F. Grease two 8½ x 4½ x 2½-inch loaf pans with butter.

**2.** In the bowl of an electric mixer, beat the sugar and butter together on medium to high speed until light and fluffy, scraping down the sides of the bowl often.

**3.** Add the eggs and vanilla extract slowly and beat well. Add the sour cream and beat well.

**4.** In a separate bowl, sift together the flour, baking powder, baking soda, and salt. With the electric mixer on low speed, slowly add the dry ingredients, and mix until just combined.

**5.** Divide the batter between the two prepared pans. Bake about 1 hour, or until golden brown and the cakes pull away from the sides of the pans.

**6.** Cool the cakes in the pans on wire racks for 10 minutes. Remove the cakes from the pans, and completely cool before serving. To store for later use, wrap the cakes well in plastic wrap and freeze for up to 4 weeks.

In _The Complete Confectioner_, author Frederick Nutt included a recipe for "Coffee":

> FOR four bottles of brandy, take one pound of coffee in powder, the very best Turkey (Turkish); altogether for twelve hours before you distil it; two pounds of sugar, two bottles and half a pint of water clarified with whites of eggs, filtered through the paper (82).

# Gingerbread

Although gingerbread is commonly associated with early American comfort food, its popularity dates back many centuries. Chinese recipes for this spicy sweet emerged in the tenth century, and by the Middle Ages Europeans had developed versions of their own. Through more than three millennia of trade, ginger, an Asian spice, made its way to such far-reaching places as the Middle East and Africa; after the Spanish introduced it to the West Indies, Jamaican ginger was one of a variety of exotic spices available in European shops.

Ever popular in England, gingerbread naturally maintained its fashion in colonial America. Recipes commonly appear in eighteenth- and early-nineteenth-century American receipt books. Quite a few, like M. E. Rundell's *A New System of Domestic Cookery,* list more than one variety; among the four this author included in her book were "A good plain sort" and "A good sort without butter" (236).

**Makes one 10-inch cake; serves 10**

2½ cups dark brown sugar
3 large eggs
1⅓ cups bread flour
1 tablespoon baking powder
½ teaspoon baking soda
2 tablespoons ground cinnamon
1 teaspoon ground ginger
1 teaspoon ground cardamom
½ teaspoon ground cloves
½ teaspoon salt
6 ounces (1½ sticks) unsalted butter, melted
¾ cup whole milk, at room temperature
Chantilly Cream (see page 120), for serving (optional)

1. Preheat the oven to 350°F. Grease one 10-inch round pan with butter, and coat lightly with flour.
2. In the bowl of an electric mixer on high speed, beat together the brown sugar and eggs until light and foamy, about 8 minutes.
3. In another bowl, sift together the bread flour, baking powder, baking soda, cinnamon, ginger, cardamom, cloves, and salt. Add the dry ingredients to the sugar and egg mixture in two increments, mixing on low speed between additions until just combined.
4. In a separate bowl, combine the butter and the milk and add to the batter slowly, scraping down the sides of the bowl.
5. Pour the batter into the prepared pan. Bake for 45 minutes, or until golden brown and a toothpick inserted near the center comes out clean.
6. Cool the cake in the pan on a wire rack for 10 minutes. Remove from the pan, and completely cool before serving. Serve with Chantilly Cream, if desired.

# Martha Washington's Chocolate Mousse Cake

The sweet chocolate beverages and confections that came to be enjoyed in colonial America had their roots in ancient Aztec culinary traditions. Columbus might have introduced cocoa beans to Spain, but it was Hernando Cortés who, having drunk chocolate with Montezuma, showed his countrymen how to utilize the beans (Mariani 79). The bitter, spicy beverage enjoyed by the Aztecs did not appeal to the Spanish, however; not until they added sugar to it did Europeans develop a passion for this exotic drink. The enthusiasm that led a Frenchman to open the first "cocoa house" in London in 1657 spread to the colonies, where drinking chocolate became increasingly fashionable throughout the eighteenth century. Like many of the fashionable Europeans with whom Thomas Jefferson mingled, Jefferson's particular fondness for chocolate was based on his belief that it was healthier than coffee or tea. George Washington, too, was keen on the confection, and it is likely that Martha Washington kept a recipe for a cake like this one in her cookery books.

**Makes two 9-inch cakes; serves 10 to 12**

### Chocolate Cake
2 cups granulated sugar
½ pound (2 sticks) unsalted butter
4 large eggs
5 cups sifted cake flour
¼ cup sifted unsweetened Dutch cocoa powder
2 teaspoons baking soda
½ teaspoon salt
1 cup whole milk

### Chocolate Mousse
4 ounces semisweet chocolate
4 large eggs, separated
½ cup heavy cream

### Chocolate Ganache
1 pint (2 cups) heavy whipping cream
24 ounces semisweet chocolate
Candied flowers or chopped nuts, for garnish (optional)

**Chef's Note**

*This recipe calls for eggs that are only partially cooked, which may present a health concern for the young, the elderly, or those whose immune systems are compromised.*

1. Prepare the Chocolate Cake: Preheat the oven to 350°F. Lightly grease two 9-inch round cake pans with butter, and line the bottoms with parchment paper circles.
2. In the bowl of an electric mixer fitted with the paddle attachment on medium-high speed, beat the sugar and butter until light and fluffy, scraping down the sides of the bowl often. Add the 4 eggs slowly, scraping down the sides of the bowl often.
3. In a separate bowl, sift together the cake flour, cocoa powder, baking soda, and salt. With the mixer on low speed, add the dry ingredients to the butter-sugar mixture, alternating with the milk, scraping down the sides of the bowl as necessary. Mix until just combined.
4. Divide the batter between the two prepared pans. Bake for 30 to 35 minutes, or until firm to the touch or until a toothpick inserted in the middle comes out clean.

5. Cool the cakes in the pans on wire racks for 10 minutes. Remove the cakes from the pans, and completely cool before assembling.

6. Prepare the Chocolate Mousse: Place water in the bottom pan of a double boiler so that the top of the water is ½ inch below the upper pan. Place the chocolate in the upper pan. Then place the boiler over low heat. Stir the chocolate constantly until it is melted. The water in the bottom of the double boiler should not come to a boil while the chocolate is melting.

7. Remove the melted chocolate from the heat, and let cool for a minute. Add the egg yolks and beat well with a whisk. Set aside to cool.

8. In a chilled bowl of an electric mixer with chilled beaters, beat the ½ cup heavy cream on medium speed until soft peaks form. Cover with plastic wrap and refrigerate until chilled.

9. In a separate, clean and dry bowl of an electric mixer, whip the egg whites on medium speed until soft peaks form. Reserve.

10. With a rubber spatula, gently fold the chilled whipped cream into the chocolate mixture until the cream is just combined into the mixture. Do not over fold. Gently fold the reserved whites into the chocolate until just combined. Cover the mixture with plastic wrap, and refrigerate for at least 1 hour before using.

11. Prepare the Chocolate Ganache: In a heavy 1-quart saucepan, bring the 2 cups heavy cream just to a boil, stirring frequently. Remove the saucepan from the heat.

12. In a large bowl, place the chocolate. Pour the hot cream over the chocolate and let sit for 1 minute. Whisk to thoroughly combine ingredients. (The chips should have melted from the heat of the cream.) Allow to cool. When the mixture is room temperature, cover with plastic wrap and refrigerate. Remove 1 hour before ready to use.

13. When the cake has cooled completely, using a serrated knife carefully cut each cake in half horizontally into 2 layers, for a total of 4 layers.

14. To assemble, place the first cake layer on a large serving plate. Alternate the cake layers and mousse filling, spreading the mousse evenly onto each cake layer.

15. Frost the outside of the cake with the Chocolate Ganache. Refrigerate the cake until ready to serve. Garnish with candied flowers or chopped nuts, if desired.

Like Thomas Jefferson, George Washington had a fondness for chocolate. Records at Mount Vernon reveal that he first ordered chocolate from England in 1757 and that he received twenty pounds one year later. Correspondences between the general and his guests reflect that he served chocolate as a special beverage to them during his presidency (Curatorial Registrar to James C. Rees, "Washington's Chocolate Purchases," Mount Vernon memo 1988).

# Yule Log

The Yule log, as it was called in England, was based on the French bûche de Noël, a decorative, rolled sponge cake filled with buttercream. Although this cake doesn't appear in American cookbooks until later in the nineteenth century, the French who emigrated to colonial America certainly brought such confectionery traditions with them and influenced American cooks and cookbook authors. The sponge cake upon which the Yule log is based appears in Martha Washington's recipe book, as well as those written by such noted eighteenth- and nineteenth-century authors as Eliza Leslie, Lydia Maria Child, and Susannah Carter.

Be sure to have a clean kitchen towel ready that is as long as your jelly-roll pan. You will need it for rolling up the sponge cake layer after it's baked.

**Makes one jelly roll; serves 8 to 10**

### Chocolate Filling
9 ounces semisweet chocolate
1 cup whole milk
4 large egg yolks
1 pound (2 sticks) unsalted butter
1 cup sifted confectioners' sugar

### Chocolate Sponge Cake
4 large eggs
½ cup granulated sugar
¾ cup sifted all-purpose flour
¼ cup sifted unsweetened Dutch cocoa powder

Candies and chocolates, for garnish (optional)

1. Prepare the Chocolate Filling: Place water in the bottom of a double boiler so that the top of the water is ½ inch below the upper pan. Place the chocolate in the upper pan. Then place the double boiler over low heat. Stir the chocolate constantly until it is melted. The water in the bottom of the double boiler should not come to a boil while the chocolate is melting. Transfer to a bowl and set aside.

2. Wash and dry the upper pan of the double boiler. Add the milk and yolks, stir to combine, and heat just until warm.

3. Add the melted chocolate to the milk and yolk mixture, stirring until combined. Transfer to a bowl. Cover with plastic wrap and refrigerate for 30 minutes.

4. In the bowl of an electric mixer fitted with the paddle attachment on medium to high speed, beat the butter and confectioners' sugar until light and fluffy, scraping down the sides of the bowl often.

5. Add the cooled chocolate-milk mixture to the electric mixer bowl and mix until combined. Refrigerate.

6. Prepare the Chocolate Sponge Cake: Preheat the oven to 400°F. Grease a 15 x 10 x 1-inch jelly-roll pan with butter, and line the bottom with parchment paper.

7. In the bowl of an electric mixer fitted with the whip attachment on high speed, beat the eggs and sugar for 5 minutes, or until pale yellow and thick. With a rubber spatula, gently fold in the flour and cocoa.

8. Pour the batter into the prepared pan. Bake for 12 to 15 minutes, or until golden and the cake springs back when lightly touched and pulls away from the sides of the pan.

9. While the cake is still warm, immediately turn it out onto a towel sprinkled with confectioners' sugar.

10. Carefully peel back the parchment paper. With the towel under the cake, gently roll up the long side of the cake into a jelly-roll shape so that the towel is both rolled up inside and covers the outside of the cake. Let the cake cool completely.

11. To assemble the cake, unroll the cake. Spread with a third of the Chocolate Filling, reserving the rest for coating the outside. Roll the cake back up into a log shape, with the seam side down. To make the roll look like a log, cut a ½-inch diagonal piece from each end of the roll. Form "branches" by placing these wedge-shaped pieces of the cake on either side of the log's "trunk," and secure with toothpicks.

12. Spread the remaining Chocolate Filling evenly on the outside of the log and around each of the branches to secure them in place. To give the log a realistic look, carefully score the frosting with the tines of a fork, so that it resembles the irregular texture of bark. Dust the "bark" with cocoa powder and then some confectioners' sugar to create "snow." If desired, decorate with candies and chocolates. Refrigerate until ready to serve. To serve, cut the roll into slices and serve on dessert plates.

# Lebkuchen

Gingerbread was available in many forms in eighteenth-century Philadelphia. Confectioners and home cooks baked firm ginger cookies as well as soft cakes, and period cookbooks are filled with many variations of gingerbread. *Lebkuchen* is neither a cookie nor a cake in consistency but, rather, somewhere in between. It is characterized not only by its intense ginger flavor but also by the honey, citron, and almonds that are mixed into it and the glaze that cloaks each piece in a sheer, sugary shroud. Like many of the firm colonial American gingerbreads that were pressed into molds before baking, *lebkuchen* is often baked in decorative molds to create a similar surface ornamentation (Herbst 255).

German immigrants from Nuremberg brought memories and recipes of this cake with them to the colonies, where they continued to prepare it as a testament to their cultural identity.

Makes one 9 x 13-inch cake; serves 12 to 16

1 cup honey
¾ cup light brown sugar
3 large egg yolks
1 tablespoon orange juice
2 cups all-purpose flour
½ cup plus 1 tablespoon bread flour
3 tablespoons unsweetened Dutch cocoa powder
½ teaspoon baking soda
1 teaspoon ground cinnamon
1 teaspoon ground allspice
½ teaspoon ground cardamom
⅓ cup sliced almonds, toasted (see Chef's Note, page 38) and cooled
2 tablespoons roughly chopped Candied Orange Peel (see page 234)
2 tablespoons roughly chopped Candied Lemon Peel (see page 234)
2 teaspoons roughly chopped Candied Ginger (see page 235)

1. Preheat the oven to 350°F. Grease a 9 x 13-inch baking pan with butter, and coat lightly with flour.
2. In a medium-size bowl, whisk together the honey, brown sugar, yolks, and orange juice.
3. In another large bowl, sift together the all-purpose flour, bread flour, cocoa, baking soda, cinnamon, allspice, and cardamom three times.
4. Stir the dry ingredients into the wet ingredients. Stir in the almonds and candied fruit.
5. Transfer the batter to the baking pan, and spread it out evenly. Cover the batter with plastic wrap, and chill it into the refrigerator overnight.
6. Bake for 15 minutes, or until a toothpick inserted near the center comes out clean. Cool for at least 30 minutes before cutting into portions and serving.

# Vanilla Cheesecake

Eighteenth- and nineteenth-century recipe books commonly included cheesecake—a practice that dates to the fifteenth century (Mariani 68). Today we are most familiar with cheesecakes made from either cream cheese or ricotta cheese. In the eighteenth century, however, all of these cakes called for a cheese the consistency of ricotta or cottage cheese, which was beaten smooth and often pushed through a fine sieve to create an even silkier texture. Although cheese was available for purchase, period recipes detail the cheese-making process, suggesting that many women did, in fact, prepare their own.

Unlike cheesecakes today, eighteenth-century varieties nearly always called for the additional textures and flavors of crushed macaroons, almonds, Naples biscuits (similar to ladyfingers), and nutmeg. This recipe relies exclusively on the scent and flavor of vanilla, which was not only very expensive in the period, but also seemingly somewhat of a novelty, even in cosmopolitan Philadelphia.

**Makes one 9-inch cheesecake; serves 12 to 14**

1 vanilla bean
1½ cups Graham Cracker Crust (see page 74)
Two 8-ounce packages cream cheese, softened
1 cup granulated sugar
3 large eggs
16 ounces (2 cups) sour cream
1 tablespoon vanilla extract
¼ teaspoon salt

1. With a paring knife, cut the vanilla bean in half lengthwise, and scrape out the tiny black seeds with the back of the knife. Set aside.
2. Preheat the oven to 350°F. Grease a 9 x 3-inch springform pan with butter. Wrap the bottom of the pan with aluminum foil to prevent water from seeping in around the side of the springform pan during the water bath.
3. Press the Graham Cracker Crust mixture onto the bottom and about 2 inches up the side of the pan. Set aside.
4. In the bowl of an electric mixer fitted with the paddle attachment on medium to high speed, beat the cream cheese and sugar until combined, scraping the sides of the bowl down often.
5. With the mixer on low speed, add the eggs. Mix until just incorporated.
6. Add in the sour cream, vanilla seeds, and salt, and mix on medium speed until incorporated.
7. Pour the batter into the prepared pan. Place the pan into a larger high-sided roasting pan, and carefully pour boiling water into the roasting pan around the springform pan to a depth of 1½ inches. (This step reduces cracking on the top of the cheesecake.)
8. Bake for 40 to 45 minutes, or until the middle of the cheesecake is nearly set when shaken and slightly puffy. Remove from the oven and let cool completely on a wire rack before serving. Wrap and store the cake in a refrigerator for up to 5 days.

# Hazelnut Cheesecake

Until the mid-twentieth century, hazelnuts were mostly imported to American shores from Italy, Spain, France, and Turkey. Like other nuts, they were highly prized and added to a variety of baked goods.

**Makes one 9-inch cheesecake; serves 12 to 14**

> 1½ cups Graham Cracker Crust (see page 74)
> Two 8-ounce packages cream cheese, softened
> 1 cup granulated sugar
> 3 large eggs
> 16 ounces (2 cups) sour cream
> ¼ teaspoon salt
> ½ cup hazelnuts, toasted, skinned, and finely chopped (see Chef's Note, page 51)
> ¼ cup hazelnut-flavored liqueur (Frangelico)

1. Preheat the oven to 300°F. Grease a 9 x 3-inch springform pan with butter. Wrap the bottom of the pan with aluminum foil to prevent water from seeping in around the side of the springform during the water bath.

2. Press the Graham Cracker Crust mixture onto the bottom and about 2 inches up the side of the pan. Set aside.

3. In the bowl of an electric mixer fitted with the paddle attachment on medium to high speed, beat the cream cheese and sugar until combined, scraping down the sides of the bowl often.

4. With the mixer on low, slowly add the eggs and beat well. Add the sour cream and salt and beat well. Add the hazelnuts and the liqueur and beat well.

5. Pour the batter into the prepared pan. Place the pan into a larger high-sided roasting pan, and carefully pour boiling water into the roasting pan around the springform pan to a depth of 1½ inches. (This step reduces cracking on top of the cheesecake.)

6. Bake for 40 to 45 minutes, until the middle of the cheesecake is nearly set when shaken and slightly puffy. Remove from the oven and let cool on a wire rack. Refrigerate overnight. Carefully remove the side of the pan before serving.

In her recipe book of 1772, originally entitled The Frugal Housewife, or Complete Woman Cook, Susannah Carter included two recipes for cheesecake. The first began with the method for making cheese and reveals just how laborious a task it was to prepare this otherwise simple cake: "First warm a pint of cream, and then add to it five quarts of milk that is warm from the cow; and when you have put a sufficient quantity of rennet to it, stir it about till it comes to a curd; then put the curd into a cloth, or linen bag, and let the whey be very well drained from it; but take care not to squeeze it hard; when it is sufficiently dry, throw it into a mortar, and beat it till it is as fine as butter" (107).

# Ricotta Cheesecake

This recipe was inspired by the many cheesecakes that appeared in period cookbooks. More than merely creamy confections, these cakes were often elaborately flavored compositions that took advantage of many imported ingredients, such as the spices, fruits, and wine included in this version.

**Makes one 10-inch cake; serves 10 to 12**

2 pounds *Pâte Sucrée* (see page 73)

**Ricotta Filling**
4½ cups (40 ounces) ricotta cheese
¾ cup granulated sugar
½ cup honey
½ cup cake flour
4 large egg yolks
3 large whole eggs
1 cup whole milk
1 tablespoon vanilla extract
1 teaspoon almond extract
1 lemon, zest grated
1 orange, zest grated
1 teaspoon ground nutmeg
1 teaspoon ground cinnamon
½ teaspoon ground cardamom
¼ cup finely chopped dried pineapple, soaked overnight in ¼ cup Madeira wine
¼ cup raisins, soaked overnight in ¼ cup Madeira wine

1.  Grease one 10-inch round cake pan or cake ring, and coat lightly with flour. Refrigerate for 45 minutes.
2.  Lightly flour your work surface and rolling pin. Roll the short dough to a ¼-inch-thick, rough, 14-inch-diameter circle. Fit it into the prepared cake pan/ring, making certain the edges are flush with the sides and top of the mold. Patch wherever necessary with dough scraps. Prick the base and sides of the dough with a fork. Refrigerate overnight.
3.  Prepare the Ricotta Filling: The night before you want to bake the cake, line a medium-size bowl with cheesecloth. Fill the cloth with the ricotta, set a plate atop the cheese, and let sit in the refrigerator overnight. The following day, wrap the ricotta cheese in the cheesecloth and wring out as much liquid as possible. Transfer the cheese to a fine mesh sieve and, using a plastic spatula, force the cheese through into a large stainless steel bowl.
4.  Preheat the oven to 400°F. Weight the chilled shell with foil and beans, and bake until the shell just begins to brown, 7 to 10 minutes.
5.  Whisk the sugar and honey into the ricotta cheese. Sift the cake flour over the cheese mixture and whisk it in. Add the egg yolks and whole eggs in three additions, whisking thoroughly after each. Whisk in the milk. Whisk in the vanilla and almond extracts, lemon and orange zests, nutmeg, cinnamon, and cardamom, and stir in the soaked pineapple and soaked raisins.
6.  Reduce the oven temperature to 300°F. Pour the mixture into the prebaked shell, and bake until the cake is golden and a toothpick inserted in the center comes out clean.
7.  Cool the cake completely on a wire rack, then unmold. Serve at room temperature or chilled.

# Apple–Walnut Cakes

These cakes utilize two of the most popular ingredients in Early America: apples and walnuts. Many wealthy Philadelphians kept country houses complete with a variety of gardens and orchards. It was common for travelers from abroad to remark on them. "The country . . . [around] the great and noble city of Philadelphia is extremely pleasant, well inhabited, fruitful, and full of orchards," Lord Adam Gordon wrote in his journal of 1765 (Peckham 259). Walnuts were abundant as well. George Washington was particularly fond of eating a variety of nuts after dinner. Recalling the meals he enjoyed, Eleanor Parke Custis Lewis in 1823 wrote, "After dinner he drank three glasses of Madeira. I ate a small plate of Indian [Native American] walnuts" ("Description of Meals," Mount Vernon memo).

These cakes, reminiscent of quick bread, are easy to prepare, aromatic, and flavorful due to the generous amounts of cinnamon and nutmeg.

**Makes eight 3 x 1½-inch (½-cup) ramekins; serves 8**

> 2 medium McIntosh or Granny Smith apples, peeled, cored, and chopped (about 2 cups)
> ½ cup B&B liqueur
> 1 cup packed light brown sugar
> ¾ cup vegetable oil
> 2 large eggs
> 1 cup sifted all-purpose flour
> 1 tablespoon ground cinnamon
> 1 teaspoon baking soda
> 1 teaspoon ground nutmeg
> ¾ cup walnuts, toasted (see Chef's Note), ground and chopped

1. In a medium bowl, combine the chopped apples and liqueur, adding more liqueur if necessary to make sure the apples are covered so they don't turn brown. Allow to marinate for 8 hours or overnight in the refrigerator.

2. When ready to bake the cake, preheat the oven to 350°F. Grease eight 3 x 1½-inch (½-cup) ramekins with butter, and coat lightly with flour.

3. In the bowl of an electric mixer fitted with the paddle attachment on medium speed, beat the brown sugar, oil, and eggs until just combined.

4. In a separate bowl, sift together the flour, cinnamon, baking soda, and nutmeg.

5. With the electric mixer on low, add the dry ingredients to the sugar-and-oil mixture and mix until combined. With a rubber spatula, gently fold in the marinated apples and walnuts.

6. Divide the batter among the prepared ramekins and place them on a baking pan. Bake for 20 to 25 minutes, or until slightly puffed and golden brown and a toothpick inserted near the center comes out clean.

*Chef's Note*

*Toasting Nuts—Preheat oven to 350°F. Spread out the nuts in a single layer on a sheet pan. Bake for about 20 minutes, or until golden brown. Let cool. Sliced, slivered, or chopped nuts require less time to toast— watch carefully.*

# Orange–Ricotta Coffee Cake

Imported from Spain, citrus fruit remained expensive throughout the eighteenth century and was enjoyed mostly in wealthy, fashionable households. Just as numerous exotic spices arrived on trade ships, so were many varieties of oranges available in Philadelphia's markets and shops. Both the Seville, or "bitter" orange, and the "sweet" orange were imported and used in a multitude of sweet and savory dishes. In her cookery book *The Art of Cookery Made Plain and Easy,* Hannah Glasse listed recipes for orange pudding, tarts, fool, butter, cream, jelly, wine, marmalade, preserves, wafers, cakes, loaves, and biscuits. Although the wealthy could afford to purchase oranges, they were frugal in their use of the entire fruit. The rind was valued as highly as the juice; it was often candied and enjoyed as a delicate sweetmeat or used in cakes and breads.

**Makes one 9-inch cake; serves 8 to 10**

¼ cup warm water (105° to 115°F)
1 package (2¼ teaspoons) active dry yeast
½ cup granulated sugar
½ cup warm whole milk (105° to 115°F)
½ cup ricotta cheese
1 tablespoon grated orange zest
½ cup strained fresh orange juice
1 large egg
½ teaspoon salt
3½ to 4 cups sifted all-purpose flour

**Icing**
1 cup sifted confectioners' sugar
2 tablespoons strained fresh orange juice

**Chef's Note**

*The word* boule *(pronounced bool), is French for ball. In baking, it usually refers to a round loaf of bread.*

1. In the bowl of an electric mixer on low speed, add the warm water and yeast and mix briefly, until combined and the yeast is dissolved.
2. Using the dough hook attachment and with the mixer on low speed, slowly add the granulated sugar, warm milk, ricotta cheese, orange zest and ½ cup juice, egg, and salt to the mixer bowl. Mix until just combined.
3. With the mixer on low speed, gradually add 2 cups of the flour, until the mixture starts to form a dough. Gradually add the remaining 1½ to 2 cups flour, adding only enough flour to make the dough stiff. Turn the dough out onto a lightly floured surface and knead with your hands for 5 minutes.
4. Place the dough in a large, greased bowl and cover loosely with a damp towel. Place the bowl in a warm area, such as on top of the oven, but away from drafts for 1 to 1½ hours to allow the dough to rise; it should double in size. Punch it down.
5. Preheat the oven to 350°F. Grease one 9 x 2½-inch round cake or springform pan with butter, and coat lightly with flour.
6. Shape the dough into a *boule* (ball) and gently place in the pan. Bake 50 to 60 minutes, or until golden brown and a toothpick inserted in the center comes out clean.
7. Cool the cake in the pan on a wire rack for 10 minutes. Remove the cake from the pan.
8. Prepare the Icing: In a small bowl, combine the confectioners' sugar and 2 tablespoons orange juice and stir until smooth. Drizzle the icing over the top of the cooled cake in a decorative pattern.

# Almond Cake

Recipe books of the eighteenth and nineteenth centuries commonly referred to frangipane as "almond cake" or "French almond cake." It was baked in a variety of pans, including large and small tins and decorative molds, and it was served tender and moist, as well as fairly firm and crisp.

Naturally, almond cake is based on almond paste. This slightly sweet and crumbly paste is a traditional component of many European pastries. In the eighteenth century, almond paste was most commonly used as the main ingredient in "marchpane"—an early term for marzipan—and marchpane cakes (candy-coated marzipan).

America, like England, imported almonds from Spain, and these almonds are often referred to as Jordan almonds in recipe books of the eighteenth and nineteenth centuries. Bitter almonds, considered poisonous and now illegal in the United States, were also frequently used in almond cake, although peach kernels (the meaty center of the pit) were considered an acceptable substitute.

Almond cakes were served either plain or, like Eliza Leslie's version, iced with a lemon-flavored meringue (*Seventy-Five Receipts, for Pastry, Cakes, and Sweetmeats* 53). This variation is finished a bit more luxuriously with a coffee buttercream and a garnish of chocolate sauce, although it is equally delicious simply served with fruit.

Makes one 15 x 10-inch cake; serves 8 to 10

### Almond Paste
1 cup granulated sugar
1 cup water
10 ounces (3 cups) dry, blanched almonds
2¼ cups confectioners' sugar

### Cake
1⅓ cups Almond Paste, or use purchased
13 ounces (3 sticks plus 2 tablespoons) unsalted butter, softened
1¾ cups granulated sugar
¼ cup sifted cake flour
9 large eggs

### Coffee Buttercream (makes about 3 cups)
5½ cups plus 2 tablespoons sifted confectioners' sugar
8 large egg whites
1¼ pounds (5 sticks) unsalted butter, cubed and softened
½ cup very strong cold coffee

1 cup Chocolate Sauce (see page 239)

1. Prepare the Almond Paste: In a small saucepan, combine the 1 cup granulated sugar and water and bring to a boil over medium-high heat. Cook, stirring often, until the sugar dissolves. Remove from the heat and let cool. Set aside.
2. In a food processor bowl, add the almonds and grind to a fine, powder-like consistency. Stop the processor and scrape down the sides of the bowl.
3. Add the 2¼ cups confectioners' sugar to the food processor, and process with on/off pulses for 30 seconds. Scrape down the sides of the bowl.
4. With the processor running, gradually add the cooled sugar syrup through the feed tube and mix until the mixture forms a paste. (The amount of syrup needed will vary depending on how dry the almonds are.)

5. Remove the almond paste from the bowl. If not using immediately, wrap the almond paste tightly in plastic wrap and chill in the refrigerator until ready to use. Almond paste will keep in the refrigerator for up to 4 weeks if well sealed.

6. Prepare the Cake: Preheat the oven to 400°F. Grease two 15 x 10 x 1-inch jelly-roll pans with butter, and line the bottoms with parchment paper.

7. In the bowl of an electric mixer fitted with the paddle attachment on medium speed, begin creaming the allmond paste. Add the butter in chunks gradually, until combined.

8. Add the 1¾ cups granulated sugar and beat well. With the mixer on medium-low speed, add the flour, a little at a time, until just combined. Slowly add the eggs and continue to beat well, scraping down the sides of the bowl often.

9. Evenly divide and spread the mixture into the two prepared pans. Bake for 12 to 15 minutes, or until golden and the cakes pull away from the sides of the pans.

10. Turn the cakes out of the pans onto cooling racks. Let cool for 10 minutes; then peel off the parchment paper and let the cakes cool completely. Trim ½ inch off the edges of the cake on all sides.

11. Prepare the Coffee Buttercream: In a 1-quart saucepan, bring 1 inch of water to a boil. In a large bowl, combine the 5½ cups plus 2 tablespoons confectioners' sugar and the egg whites. Place the bowl over the saucepan of boiling water, and whisk the mixture until hot (about 160°F on a candy thermometer).

12. Remove the bowl from the heat, and transfer the egg whites to a clean, dry bowl of an electric mixer fitted with the whip attachment. Beat on high speed until the whites become stiff (meringue) and the bowl is cool to the touch.

13. When the meringue is completely cool, add the 1¼ pounds softened butter a little at a time. Beat until the mixture becomes slightly thick and fluffy.

14. Add the prepared coffee a little at a time to desired taste.

15. To assemble the cake, place the first layer of the cake on a large serving plate. Spread evenly with 1 to 1½ cups of the coffee buttercream. Top with the second cake layer. Frost the top and then the sides of the cake with the remaining buttercream. If desired, use any extra buttercream to pipe a decorative border.

16. To serve, cut the cake into 3-inch squares and transfer to dessert plates. Garnish each square with about 1 tablespoon of the prepared Chocolate Sauce.

Almond cake was one of the simplest of confections, consisting usually of four or five ingredients: almonds, flour, eggs, sugar, and rose water or lemon essence. We are reminded, however, once again that eighteenth-century baking was a time-consuming and labor-intensive task. Imported almond paste was available but very expensive, so cooks often chose to process almonds themselves (Belden 186). Martha Washington, as did many other recipe writers, explained this procedure clearly; one of her almond cakes called for "a quarter of a pound of almonds, blanched in well water, & beaten in rose water" (Hess 321). The other ingredients required refining as well. Sugar was mostly available in hard lumps or cones, so these recipes often called for "loaf-sugar, powdered and sifted" (Seventy-Five Receipts, for Pastry, Cakes, and Sweetmeats 52) and "fine flower, well dryed against ye fire" (Hess 321). In addition, it would have taken quite a few hours to heat an oven and usually another hour or so to bake the cake.

# Raspberry Trifle

The British trifle required little translation in the American colonies. Recipe books reveal that this simple but often highly decorative dessert required a few select ingredients: pieces of cake or biscuit; custard; sack (wine); syllabub (a mixture of wine or cider, fresh milk, and cream); and decoration, such as jelly, flowers, small candies, or additional biscuits.

Unlike the traditional version, in which the soaked biscuits or cake were simply covered with one layer of custard and jelly, this trifle is built in colorful, multiple layers, with the final layer consisting of custard rather than of strongly flavored syllabub.

**Makes one 3-quart (12-cup) trifle; serves 12**

### Yellow Cake
4 large eggs
½ cup granulated sugar
½ teaspoon vanilla extract
¼ teaspoon almond extract
⅔ cup sifted all-purpose flour
3 tablespoons butter, melted and cooled

### Whipped Cream Filling
2½ cups heavy whipping cream
½ cup sifted confectioners' sugar

1 cup brandy
1 cup Raspberry Preserves (see page 244)
4 cups Pastry Cream (see page 119)
4 pints (8 cups) fresh raspberries

1.  Prepare the Yellow Cake: Preheat the oven to 350°F. Grease one 9-inch cake pan with butter. Line the bottom of the pan with parchment paper, and grease the top of the paper with butter.

2.  In a medium-size metal bowl set over a saucepan of simmering water, whisk the eggs and sugar until warm—do not allow the eggs to curdle. Remove the bowl from the heat, and whisk in the vanilla and almond extracts.

3.  Transfer the warmed egg mixture to the bowl of an electric mixer fitted with the whip attachment. Beat on high speed until the mixture is pale yellow and has thickened and tripled in volume.

4.  Remove the bowl from the mixer and sift ⅓ cup of the flour over top of the eggs, gently folding with a rubber spatula. Repeat sifting and folding with the remaining ⅓ cup of flour. Fold in the melted butter, being sure to scrape down the sides of the bowl.

5.  Pour the mixture into the prepared cake pan and bake for 20 to 25 minutes, or until golden and a toothpick inserted in the center comes out clean. Cool the cakes on a wire rack for 10 minutes before removing from the pan.

6.  Using a serrated knife, cut the cake layer horizontally into four layers.

7.  Prepare the Whipped Cream Filling: In the chilled bowl of an electric mixer fitted with the whip attachment, beat the heavy cream on medium speed until soft peaks form. Add the confectioners' sugar and beat a few seconds more. Cover with plastic wrap and chill in the refrigerator until ready to use.

8. Assemble the trifle: Place one cake layer into the bottom of a 10-inch glass trifle bowl. Using a pastry brush, brush the cake with the brandy. With a spoon, spread ⅓ cup of the Preserves over the cake layer. Spread one-third of the prepared Pastry Cream over the preserves, and cover with 1 pint of the raspberries.

9. Repeat the layering process two more times, and top with a cake layer.

10. Using a 12-inch decorator bag fitted with a star tip, transfer the reserved chilled Whipped Cream Filling into the bag, leaving enough room to close and twist the top of the bag. Pipe the filling around the edges of the bowl. Fill the center with the remaining raspberries. Chill in the refrigerator for 2 hours before serving.

In <u>The Art of Cookery Made Plain and Easy</u>, Hannah Glasse's recipe for trifle called for three types of biscuit and cake: "Naples biscuits [ladyfingers] broke in pieces, mackeroons [*sic*] broke in halves, and ratafia cakes [crisp almond cookies]." Her version was particularly decorative among those of the period, for she suggested, "You may garnish it with ratafia cakes, currant jelly, and flowers, and stew [*sic*] different coloured nonpareils over it." It was clear, however, that she was attempting to make the decorating task as simple as possible for the busy cooks creating this dessert, as she added at the end, "Note, these are bought at the confectioners" (180).

# Fruitcake

Eighteenth-century cookbooks are filled with recipes for rich butter cakes flavored with dried and candied fruit, spices, and wine or liquor. Fruitcake, however, referred to a specific type of cake—one dense with fruit and nuts and flavored liberally with spices and brandy. According to British tradition, this cake was commonly served at weddings and so became known as "Bride Cake," recipes for which most often appear in English cookery books of the period (Raffald 134). Surely the practice of serving fruitcake at weddings continued in colonial America. The celebratory connotations of this cake seem to have led further to its frequent appearance on holiday tables, much as rich plum puddings and fruit-filled yeast breads had for centuries in Europe.

Makes one 10-inch cake; serves 10 to 12

½ cup shredded carrots
½ cup slivered almonds
¼ cup sweetened flaked coconut
¼ cup finely chopped Candied Citrus Peel (orange, lemon, etc., see page 234)
2 tablespoons cup dried currants
2 tablespoons golden raisins
2 tablespoons finely chopped dried pineapple
2 tablespoons finely chopped Candied Ginger (see page 235)
1 cup dark rum
2¼ cups sifted bread flour
1 tablespoon baking powder
2 teaspoons baking soda
1 teaspoon each ground nutmeg, ginger, allspice, and cloves
Pinch of ground cardamom
Pinch of ground mace
1 teaspoon salt
2 cups brown sugar
2 cups olive oil
9 large eggs
¼ cup honey
1 tablespoon vanilla extract
1 teaspoon almond extract
2 teaspoons rose water
2 cups Apricot Preserves (see page 243)
1 tablespoon peeled and finely chopped fresh ginger
Confectioners' sugar, for dusting
Maple Whipped Cream (see page 121), for serving

1. In a medium-size container, combine the carrots, almonds, coconut, Candied Citrus Peel, currants, raisins, dried pineapple, and Candied Ginger. Add the rum and soak overnight.
2. Preheat the oven to 375°F. Grease two 10-inch round cake pans with butter, and coat lightly with flour.
3. In a mixing bowl, sift together the flour, baking powder, baking soda, nutmeg, ginger, allspice, cloves, cardamom, mace, and salt.

4. In a large bowl, whisk together the brown sugar and olive oil until light in color. Add the eggs one at a time, whisking after each addition. Whisk in the honey, vanilla and almond extracts, and rose water.

5. Whisk the dry ingredients into the wet ingredients in three additions. Using a spatula, fold in the Apricot Preserves and fresh ginger, followed by the presoaked dried and candied fruits.

6. Divide the batter between the 2 prepared cake pans. Bake for 30 minutes, or until set and a toothpick inserted near the center of each comes out clean. Allow the cakes to cool in the pan, and then unmold and dust with confectioners' sugar. Serve with Maple Whipped Cream.

In an advertisement that appeared in the <u>Pennsylvania Gazette</u> on June 12, 1766, Samuel Frauncis detailed many of the confections he was selling at his Water Street shop. In addition to the many sweetmeats he mentioned, he made a particular point of declaring, "Said Frauncis undertakes also, by giving him timely Notice, to make Wedding Cakes, of all Sorts, and to fix Deserts [*sic*] for Wedding Suppers." Although it is unclear just exactly what "sorts" of cakes these were, one can assume at least some of them were traditional English fruitcakes.

# Rice Torte

Just as white rice thrived in the warm and humid South, wild rice grows best in the cool air of its native northern states. Both varieties are cultivated in water. Yet, while white rice develops in water-filled rice paddies, wild rice is not rice at all but, rather, a marshy grass. As with so many other foods, wild rice was a foodstuff that Native Americans grew for centuries and that colonial Americans adopted and enjoyed in sweet and savory dishes.

This torte clearly refers to eighteenth-century rice puddings that were often brightly flavored with spices, liqueurs, and preserved fruits. The addition of ground macaroons not only recalls the perfume and flavor of almonds that were so desired in the eighteenth century but also gives body and texture to the filling.

**Makes one 9-inch cake; serves 8 to 10**

> 3 cups finely ground Macaroons (see page 137), or substitute store-bought Italian-style amaretti cookies
> ¼ pound (1 stick) unsalted butter, melted
> 1 teaspoon ground cinnamon
>
> **Rice Filling**
> 2 cups water
> ½ cup Madeira wine
> ¾ cup long-grain wild rice
> 2½ cups whole milk
> Pinch of salt
> ½ cup granulated sugar
> 3 large eggs
> ¼ pound (1 stick) unsalted butter, melted
>
> 2 tablespoons chopped Candied Lemon Peel (see page 234)
> 2 tablespoons dark rum
> 1 teaspoon vanilla extract
> 1 teaspoon ground cardamom
> 4 large egg whites
> 1 tablespoon confectioners' sugar

1. Preheat the oven to 350°F. Brush a 9-inch round cake pan with melted butter.
2. Once you have ground the Macaroons in a food processor, with the processor still running, add the melted butter; pulse a few times to combine. Add the cinnamon and pulse briefly to combine. Spread the crumb mixture evenly on the base and up the sides of the pan. Set aside.
3. Prepare an ice bath in a large stainless steel bowl and set aside.
4. Prepare the Rice Filling: In a 2-quart saucepan, bring the water and Madeira to a boil; then add the rice. Simmer, covered, for 15 to 20 minutes. Let stand, covered, for 5 minutes and drain, if necessary.
5. In a separate medium-size saucepan, bring the milk and salt to a boil. Stir in the drained rice and cook, covered, until the grains are soft, about 10 minutes more. Strain the rice, discarding the milk.

6. In a large bowl, whisk together the granulated sugar, whole eggs, butter, Candied Lemon Peel, rum, vanilla extract, and cardamom.

7. Gradually stir the hot rice into the egg mixture. Return the mixture to the saucepan and cook, stirring constantly over low heat, until the mixture thickens, about 3 minutes.

8. Transfer the rice pudding to a medium-size stainless steel bowl. Place the bowl into the ice bath and stir to cool.

9. Meanwhile, in an immaculately clean bowl of an electric mixer fitted with the whip attachment on medium speed, whip the egg whites to soft peaks. Adjust the speed to low, and add the confectioners' sugar. Adjust the speed to high and whip the meringue further, until stiff peaks form.

10. Fold the meringue into the rice pudding, making certain no streaks of meringue remain, but do not overmix. Pour the mixture into the prepared cake pan.

11. Bake, covered with foil, for 20 to 30 minutes, or until a knife inserted near the center comes out clean. Sprinkle additional cinnamon on top as a garnish.

In her cookbook <u>American Cookery</u>, author Amelia Simmons devoted no less than six entries to "Rice Pudding," each of them a variation of the one before, and all of them incorporating such ingredients as cinnamon, nutmeg, wine, and rose water (30–31).

# Eggnog Puff Pastry Torte

The rich flavor and creamy texture today associated with eggnog characterized many of the custards prepared in eighteenth-century kitchens. They commonly appear in period cookbooks as sweetened mixtures of cream, eggs, spices, and sack (imported white wine) that are baked in ceramic cups or in pastry. The substitution of rum, brandy, and bourbon for sack in this recipe refers to the availability of these spirits in eighteenth-century Philadelphia.

The addition of gelatin in this eggnog custard transforms it into a Bavarian—a filling that remains firm when the torte is sliced. In the eighteenth century, obtaining gelatin was not as easy as it is for today's cooks, who purchase it in granulated or sheet form; early Americans obtained gelatin by laboriously boiling calves' feet. Once sufficiently cooked, the resulting liquid was strained and skimmed, and the fat was separated from the desired jelly.

Makes one 10-inch torte; serves 10 to 12

3 pounds Puff Pastry (see page 188), or use store-bought

**Eggnog Bavarian**
1 tablespoon plus 1 teaspoon unflavored gelatin
1 tablespoon dark rum
1 cup whole milk
4 tablespoons granulated sugar
1 tablespoon vanilla extract
2 cinnamon sticks
Freshly grated nutmeg, to taste
3 large egg yolks
¼ cup eggnog
1 tablespoon brandy
1 tablespoon bourbon
1¼ cups heavy whipping cream, whipped to medium peaks

4 Poached Pears (see page 239)

1. Preheat the oven to 375°F.
2. Roll out the Puff Pastry to ½-inch thickness. Grease an 11 x 17-inch baking pan or jelly-roll pan with butter and line with parchment paper. Place the sheet of pastry on the baking pan; place another sheet of parchment paper atop the pastry, and weight it down by placing two more baking pans directly on top of the parchment paper. Bake for 10 minutes, or until the pastry just begins to brown.
3. Remove the puff pastry from the oven and allow it to cool. Using a 10-inch-diameter bowl and a paring knife, cut an 10-inch puff pastry round. Return the round to the oven and bake until golden, 3 to 5 minutes more.
4. Prepare the Eggnog Bavarian: Prepare an ice bath in a large stainless steel bowl. Bring a small pot of water to a simmer. In a small bowl, sprinkle the unflavored gelatin over the rum, and whisk to combine. Let the gelatin soften for 10 minutes.
5. In a medium-size pot, bring the milk, 2 tablespoons of the sugar, vanilla extract, cinnamon sticks, and nutmeg to a boil.

6. Meanwhile, in a medium-size bowl, whisk together the egg yolks and the remaining 2 tablespoons of sugar. Temper the hot milk mixture into the yolk mixture by adding ¼ cup of the hot liquid at a time to the yolks, whisking all the while. Return the custard to the pot and cook, stirring constantly, over low heat until the mixture reaches a temperature of 185°F on a candy thermometer and is thickened. Strain this mixture back into the medium-size bowl.

7. Dissolve the softened gelatin by setting the bowl over the pot of simmering water and stirring constantly until it liquefies. Whisk the gelatin into the custard. Whisk in the eggnog, brandy, and bourbon. Set the bowl of custard in the ice bath and whisk until the mixture is cool.

8. In a large bowl, add ½ cup of the cooled eggnog custard and the whipped cream, and stir to combine. Fold the remaining eggnog custard into the whipped cream mixture with a hand-held whisk. Set the Bavarian in the refrigerator for later assembly.

9. Line a 10-inch round cake pan with plastic wrap. Trim the edges of the prebaked puff pastry round, if necessary, so that it fits precisely inside the pan.

10. Fill the tart with the Bavarian. Freeze 1 hour.

11. To unmold the cake, turn it upside down, hold the plastic down, and pull up on the pan. Carefully turn the Bavarian right side up.

12. Slice each Poached Pear in half. Remove the core and stem. Slice each pear into ¼-inch slices. Arrange the pears nicely atop the Bavarian.

In her cookbook <u>The Art of Cookery Made Plain and Easy</u>, Hannah Glasse included a recipe entitled "To make baked Custards," which is certainly an early relation of this Eggnog Bavarian: "One pint of cream boiled with mace and cinnamon; when cold, take four eggs, two whites left out, a little rose and orange flower water and sack, nutmeg and sugar to your palate; mix them well together, and bake them in china cups" (173).

# Dacquoise

This dessert, an elegant, flavorful combination of crisp nut meringue and creamy coffee buttercream, pays tribute to the influence of French culture and cuisine in eighteenth-century Philadelphia, as well as to the foodstuffs available there. Items such as hazelnuts and coffee were imported and sold in shops around the city, while raspberries grew wild in the country and raspberry preserves were common to many a household pantry.

Makes one 9-inch torte; serves 8 to 10

**Hazelnut Meringue**
2½ cups hazelnuts, toasted (see Chef's Note) and skins removed
    by rubbing in a kitchen towel
2 tablespoons confectioners' sugar, plus extra for dusting
1½ cups granulated sugar
12 large egg whites

**Coffee Cream**
6 large egg whites
2 cups granulated sugar
2 pounds (8 sticks) unsalted butter, at room temperature
¼ cup brewed espresso, at room temperature

1 cup Raspberry Preserves (see page 244)
3 pints fresh raspberries
Cocoa powder, for garnish
Fresh mint sprigs, for garnish

1. Preheat the oven to 375°F. Grease three 9-inch round cake pans with butter, and line them with parchment paper.
2. Prepare the Hazelnut Meringue: Bring a medium-size pot of water to a boil. In a food processor, pulse the toasted hazelnuts with the confectioners' sugar until finely ground—do not make a paste.
3. Place the granulated sugar and egg whites in a medium-size stainless steel bowl. Set the bowl over the pot of simmering water. Whisking slowly, cook the whites until the sugar dissolves and the mixture reaches a temperature of 165°F on a candy thermometer.
4. Immediately transfer the whites to an immaculately clean bowl of an electric mixer fitted with the whip attachment. Whip the meringue until it is cool and stiff peaks form. Gently fold in the ground hazelnuts using a plastic spatula.
5. Divide the batter evenly among the 3 parchment-lined cake pans. Bake 15 minutes, or until light golden and firm. Turn the oven off. Let the layers cool on wire racks; then unmold.
6. Prepare the Coffee Cream: Place the egg whites and granulated sugar in a medium-size stainless steel bowl. Set the bowl over the pot of simmering water. Whisking slowly, cook the whites until the sugar dissolves and the mixture reaches a temperature of 165°F on a candy thermometer.

7. Immediately transfer the whites to an immaculately clean bowl of an electric mixer fitted with the whip attachment. Whip the meringue until it is cool and stiff peaks form.

8. Once the meringue has been whipped to stiff peaks, begin incorporating the butter. With the mixer running on medium speed, add the room-temperature butter by the stick; wait until each stick of butter has been fully incorporated before adding the next. Beat until the mixture doubles in volume.

9. Once all the butter has been added, with the mixer running on its slowest speed, slowly drizzle in the espresso. Whip the mixture until all ingredients are well combined.

10. Final assembly: Because the meringue is fragile, carefully spread a thin layer of preserves evenly atop each of the three meringues with an angled spatula.

11. Place approximately 1½ cups of Coffee Cream atop each preserve-covered meringue and, using an angled spatula, spread it evenly across the surface.
Arrange 1 pint of raspberries nicely atop two of the cream-covered meringues. Apply light pressure to each berry, securing it in the cream. Stack one raspberry-covered meringue atop the other, and stack the layer without berries on top.

12. Using a pastry bag fitted with a number #16 fluted tip, fill the bag with Coffee Cream and pipe a shell border around the perimeter of the final cream-covered meringue round. Fill the center of the round with the remaining pint of raspberries. Garnish with cocoa powder, confectioners' sugar, and a sprig of mint.

*Toasting and Skinning Hazelnuts—Preheat the oven to 350°F. Arrange whole hazelnuts in a baking pan and bake for 15 minutes, or until they are golden brown and aromatic. Remove from the oven and let cool. When the nuts are still warm, place them in a kitchen towel and roll back and forth to remove the skins.*

George and Martha Washington's records reveal that they ordered hazelnuts a number of times. They purchased some in December 1766 and two additional bushels in January 1767. They bought another bushel in 1769 and 1771, as well as ten pounds in June 1798 ("Foods used in the Christmas Table Setting," Mount Vernon memo 1989).

# Strawberry Short Cake

Simple combinations of fruit and cake were enjoyed in the eighteenth century as much as they are today. This marriage of light cake, cream, and fresh and preserved strawberries is particularly suited to summer months, when ripe berries are available. In the eighteenth century, cooks took advantage of the season's harvest to prepare the strawberry preserves that were consumed throughout the fall and winter.

Recipes for sponge cake appear in many period cookbooks under that title as well as under "*biscuit de Savoye*" or "*biscuit de Savoie*" ("Savoy sponge"), as they do in Thomas Jefferson's collection of recipes (Kimball 36). Ladyfingers are essentially small sponge cakes that appear in eighteenth-century recipe books as "sponge biscuits" and "Naples biscuits."

Makes one 15 x 10-inch cake; serves 12

### Sponge Cake
½ cup plus ½ tablespoon cake flour
½ cup cornstarch
6 large eggs
1 cup plus 2 tablespoons granulated sugar
2½ tablespoons unsalted butter, melted and cooled

### Whipped Cream
2 quarts heavy whipping cream
¾ cup confectioners' sugar
3 tablespoons orange liqueur (such as Cointreau or Triple Sec)
1 teaspoon vanilla extract

3 pints fresh strawberries
2 cups Vanilla Simple Syrup (see Chef's Note, page 54)
2 cups Strawberry Preserves (see page 244)
Confectioners' sugar, for dusting

1. Prepare the Sponge Cake: Preheat the oven to 375°F. Line three 15 x 10 x 1-inch jelly-roll pans with parchment paper, and grease the paper with butter.
2. Place a medium-size pot of water on the stove and bring it to a boil. Meanwhile, over a large bowl, sift together the flour and cornstarch three times.
3. In a stainless steel bowl, combine the eggs and sugar and set the bowl on top of the boiling pot of water. Whisk together the eggs and sugar until the sugar dissolves and the eggs are lukewarm. Transfer the egg mixture to the bowl of an electric mixer fitted with the whip attachment. Whip the eggs on high speed until thick and cool and ribbons form.
4. In a separate small bowl, whisk together one quarter of the whipped eggs and the melted, cooled butter. Set aside.
5. Fold the sifted dry ingredients into the whipped egg-sugar mixture in three additions. Fold in the whipped egg-butter mixture.
6. Divide the batter evenly among the trays, and spread it across the surface. Bake for 8 minutes, or until golden and the cake pulls away from the sides of the pan. Allow the cakes to cool and invert each onto the back of sheet pans. Turn the oven off.

7. Prepare the Whipped Cream: Place the whipping cream and confectioners' sugar in the clean bowl of an electric mixer fitted with the whip attachment. Whip on medium speed until medium peaks form. Add the liqueur and vanilla extract, and whip to stiff peaks.

8. Assemble the Cake: Take 1½ pints of the strawberries, remove the stems, and slice the strawberries in half. Cut the stems off the remaining strawberries.

9. Soak each sheet cake with Vanilla Simple Syrup. Spread a thin layer of Strawberry Preserves atop each cake.

10. Cover one preserve-coated sheet cake with 1 heaping cup of Whipped Cream. Cover the surface of the whipped cream with halved strawberries. Spread a very thin layer of whipped cream atop the strawberries.

11. Stack a second preserved-coated sheet cake atop the first. Repeat the process in step #10 above. Stack the final layer atop the second layer. Spread a thin layer of whipped cream atop the final layer using an angled spatula. Arrange the whole, hulled strawberries nicely atop the final layer. Dust with confectioners' sugar.

Sponge cake is celebrated for its light, delicate texture—a quality achieved by combining its few ingredients in a manner unique to this cake. Eggs and sugar are whipped to their maximum volume, and only then are the flour, flavorings, and butter (if it is included) gently folded in stages into them. Although pastry chefs have, for centuries, been intimately familiar with the details of preparing this seemingly simple cake, many home cooks are not. Eighteenth- and early-nineteenth-century cookbook authors, however, were usually very clear in their instructions, priding themselves on their ability to convey the intricacies of cooking to their audiences. Included in her book Seventy-Five Receipts, for Pastry, Cakes, and Sweetmeats, Eliza Leslie's method for preparing "Spunge Cake" [sic] is one such example of the detailed explanations authors offered. Today's home cooks would benefit as much from her 185-year-old recipe as from any other:

Beat the eggs as light as possible. Eggs for spunge or almond-cakes require more beating than for any other purpose. Beat the sugar, by degrees, into the eggs. Beat very hard, and continue to beat some time after the sugar is all in.

No sort of sugar but loaf, will make light spunge-cake. Stir in, gradually, the spice and essence of lemon. Then, by degrees put in the flour, a little at a time, stirring round the mixture very slowly with a knife. If the flour is stirred in too hard, the cake will be tough. It must be done lightly and gently, so that the top of the mixture will be covered with bubbles. As soon as the flour is all in, begin to bake it, as setting will injure it (51).

# Peach Torte

Peaches grew abundantly in eighteenth-century America. Many varieties were indigenous to the soil and had been cultivated for centuries by Native Americans. As European peaches were introduced with the colonists, new varieties were planted and became widely available. George Washington and Thomas Jefferson are among the well-known gardeners who grew peach trees on their estates, enthusiastically sharing in the country's fondness for the fruit (Leighton 237).

This cake not only refers to the many eighteenth-century cakes that were flavored with spices and rose water, but also complements the fresh flavor and creamy texture of the peach mousse.

**Makes one 10-inch torte; serves 12**

### Cake
1 cup plus 3 tablespoons pastry flour
1½ teaspoons baking powder
1 teaspoon baking soda
1 teaspoon salt
1 teaspoon ground allspice
1 teaspoon ground cinnamon
1 teaspoon ground ginger
3 tablespoons whole milk
3 tablespoons sour cream
5 ounces (1¼ sticks) unsalted butter, at room temperature
½ cup plus 2 tablespoons granulated sugar
3 large eggs
1 tablespoon honey
2 tablespoons rose water

### Peach Mousse
2 tablespoons unflavored gelatin
¼ cup orange juice
½ cup granulated sugar
¼ cup water
1 tablespoon honey
4 large egg yolks
1 cup peach purée, or substitute frozen peaches, thawed and puréed
1½ pints heavy whipping cream, whipped to soft peaks

2 cups Simple Syrup (see Chef's Note)
3 peaches, pitted and cut into ½-inch wedges
2 cups apricot Glaze (see page 116)

*To prepare Simple Syrup—In a medium-size saucepan, combine 1 cup water and 1 cup granulated sugar. Bring just to a boil, stirring occasionally, until the sugar is dissolved. Remove from the heat and cool to room temperature. Makes 2 cups.*

*To prepare Vanilla Simple Syrup—Add 1 tablespoon vanilla extract to the Simple Syrup after you remove it from the heat and before you cool it to room temperature.*

1. Prepare the Cake: Preheat the oven to 375°F. Grease one 10-inch round cake pan with butter, and coat lightly with flour.
2. In a medium-size bowl, sift together the flour, baking powder, baking soda, salt, allspice, cinnamon, and ginger. In another bowl, whisk together the milk and sour cream.

3. In the bowl of an electric mixer fitted with the paddle attachment, cream the butter and sugar on medium speed until light and fluffy. Scrape down the sides of the bowl as needed.

4. With the mixer still running, add the eggs and honey. Mix on medium speed for 5 minutes. Add the rose water and mix briefly.

5. With the mixer running on low speed, add one third of the flour mixture and mix until just combined. Add half of the milk mixture and mix until just combined. Repeat the process until all of the wet and dry ingredients have been incorporated.

6. Transfer the batter to the prepared cake pan and bake for 30 minutes, or until golden and a toothpick inserted near the center comes out clean. Let cool in the pan for 10 minutes; then turn over and unmold. Finish cooling on a wire rack. Turn off the oven.

7. Prepare the Peach Mousse: Prepare an ice bath in a large stainless steel bowl. Bring a small pot of water to a simmer. In a small bowl, sprinkle the unflavored gelatin over the orange juice and whisk to combine. Let the gelatin "soften" for 10 minutes.

8. In a medium-size pot, bring the sugar, water, and honey to a boil. Cook the mixture until it reaches a temperature of 255°F on a candy thermometer.

9. In the bowl of an electric mixer fitted with the paddle whip attachment, whip the yolks on high until they are pale and ribbons form. Temper the hot sugar syrup into the yolk mixture by adding it in a thin steady stream. Whip the mixture until it is cool.

10. Dissolve the softened gelatin by setting the bowl over the pot of simmering water, stirring constantly until it liquefies. In another large bowl, whisk the gelatin into the peach purée. Whisk in the cool egg mixture. Set the bowl of peach base in the ice bath and whisk until the mixture is cool.

11. In a large mixing bowl, transfer ½ cup of the cool peach mixture into the whipped cream, and stir to combine. Fold in the remaining peach mixture with a hand-held whisk. Set in the refrigerator for later assembly.

12. Final assembly: Line a 10-inch round cake pan with plastic wrap. Slice the Cake in half. Place one half of the cake in the bottom of the lined cake pan, and brush it with Simple Syrup. Fill the pan halfway with the Mousse.

13. Place the second half of cake atop the mousse and brush it with simple syrup. Fill the pan with the remaining mousse. Freeze the cake for 1 hour.

14. Unmold the cake. Arrange the peaches nicely atop the mousse. Brush with the apricot Glaze.

# Mango Mousse Torte

Mangoes were certainly enjoyed in eighteenth-century America but in a manner much different than today. Asian pickled mangoes were first imported to England in the seventeenth century, where they were met with an enthusiastic reception. Desirous of reproducing this flavorful import, colonial Americans followed the English lead and developed recipes themselves. The only problem was, of course, that fresh mangoes were not available in England or in America and, as a result, other fruits and vegetables were used in lieu of the exotic item (Hooker 88). So closely associated were pickled mangoes and these new vinegary preparations, however, that the fruit was used as a verb as well as a term for other pickled foods. For example, recipe titles such as "To Mango Muskmellons or Cucumbers" became common, as did "To pickle or make Mangoes of Melons" (Hooker 88; Simmons 62). Even Elizabeth Raffald's recipe "To pickle Mango" was erroneous, as it, in truth, instructed how to pickle cucumbers (178). All of this misnaming further forces one to question the authenticity of the "home made Pickles, amongst which are Mangoes" that shop owner Samuel Frauncis advertised June 12, 1766 in the *Pennsylvania Gazette*.

Regardless of whether or not the fruit was pickled or simply used as a general reference, mangoes certainly enjoyed celebrity in America and abroad. This torte pays tribute to this phenomenon, complementing the fresh flavor of mango mousse with delicate chocolate sponge cake.

Makes one 10-inch torte; serves 10 to 12

### Mango Mousse
1 tablespoon plus 2 teaspoons unflavored gelatin
¼ cup orange juice
1 cup mango purée
4 large egg yolks
¼ cup granulated sugar
1 teaspoon honey
2 tablespoons water
1½ pints heavy whipping cream, whipped to stiff peaks

1 layer Chocolate Cake (see page 30)
2 cups Simple Syrup (see Chef's Note, page 54), combined with 3 tablespoons dark rum
6 mangoes, peeled and sliced ¼ inch thick

1.  Prepare the Mango Mousse: Bring a small pot of water to a simmer. In a small bowl, sprinkle the gelatin over the orange juice and whisk to combine. Let the gelatin "soften" for 10 minutes. Bring the mango purée to room temperature.
2.  In the bowl of an electric mixture fitted with the whip attachment, whip the egg yolks until light in color and tripled in volume.
3.  In a second small pot, stir together the sugar, honey, and water. Wash down the sides of the pot with a pastry brush and cool water, making certain no sugar crystals remain. Bring the mixture to a boil over medium-high heat. Cook the sugar syrup until it reaches a temperature of 245°F on a candy thermometer.

4. Decrease the mixer's speed to low and slowly pour the hot sugar syrup into the yolk mixture in a thin, steady stream. Try to avoid hitting the sides of the bowl or whip when adding the syrup. Once all the syrup has been added, increase the speed to high and whip until the mixture cools.
5. Transfer the cool yolk mixture to a medium-size bowl. Whisk in the mango purée.
6. Dissolve the "softened" gelatin by stirring it over the pot of simmering water until the gelatin liquefies. Add the gelatin to the mango-egg mixture.
7. In a large mixing bowl, add one third of the mango mixture to the whipped cream and gently whisk it together. Add the mango-cream mixture back to the mango mixture, and fold it together using a wire whisk.
8. Final assembly: Line a 10-inch springform pan with plastic wrap.
9. Slice the Chocolate Cake in half. Place one half in the base of the pan. (You can freeze the other half for another use.) Brush the layer in the pan with the rum and Simple Syrup mixture.
10. Fill the pan with Mango Mousse, and chill for 1 hour in the refrigerator.
11. Arrange the mango slices nicely atop the torte. Unmold and cut into slices to serve.

# Vanilla Cream Torte

This torte celebrates the vanilla bean. Although native to South America, vanilla remained desirable in Europe, particularly in England and France, for nearly two hundred years before it became popular in the colonies. It is hardly surprising that Thomas Jefferson was responsible for initiating this culinary trend after returning from Paris in 1789. He became enamored with vanilla at the same time that he was joyously introduced to French ice cream that was perfumed with it. Back in America, he ordered vanilla beans from France and became renowned for his rich ice cream (Mariani 338). To be sure, Jefferson would have been quite happy with this torte, whose every component is flavored with vanilla.

Makes one 10-inch cake; serves 12 to 16

**Vanilla Cream**
1 vanilla bean
2 cups whole milk
6 tablespoons granulated sugar
5 large egg yolks
2 tablespoons plus 1 teaspoon cornstarch
6 ounces (1½ sticks) unsalted butter

**Buttercream**
1¼ cups granulated sugar
¼ cup water
1 tablespoon light corn syrup
6 large egg whites
1½ pounds (6 sticks) unsalted butter, at room temperature
1 tablespoon vanilla extract

2 layers Sponge Cake (see page 52)
2 cups Vanilla Simple Syrup (see Chef's Note, page 54)

1. Prepare the Cream: Using a paring knife, slice the vanilla bean in half lengthwise. Scrape the beans from the pod with the back of the knife. Place the beans, pod, milk, and 3 tablespoons of the sugar in a medium-size pot, and bring the mixture to a boil.

2. Meanwhile, in a medium-size bowl, whisk together the egg yolks, the remaining 3 tablespoons sugar, and the cornstarch.

3. Remove the vanilla bean pod from the milk using a slotted spoon. Temper the milk mixture into the yolk mixture, adding the hot liquid slowly, ¼ cup at a time, to the yolks, whisking all the while. Once all the milk has been added, return the custard back to the pot and cook, stirring constantly, until the mixture thickens and boils. Boil the mixture for 1 minute, stirring vigorously.

4. Strain the mixture into a clean, medium-size plastic or glass bowl, and set the bowl in an ice bath. Cover the cream directly with plastic wrap. Occasionally stir and then again cover the cream with the plastic wrap.

5. In the bowl of an electric mixer fitted with the paddle attachment, cream the butter on medium-high speed until light in texture.

6. Once the cream is at room temperature, fold the whipped butter into the cream. Set it aside for final assembly.

7. Prepare the Buttercream: Stir together 1 cup of the sugar, the water, and the corn syrup in a small saucepan. Wash down the sides of the pot with a pastry brush and cool water, making certain no sugar crystals remain. Bring the mixture to a boil over medium heat, and cook until it reaches a temperature of 245°F on a candy thermometer.

8. Place the egg whites in the clean bowl of an electric mixer fitted with the whip attachment. Whip the whites on medium speed until foamy. Slowly add the remaining ¼ cup of sugar, 2 tablespoons at a time. Once all the sugar has been added, continue to whip the whites to medium peaks.

9. Decrease the mixer's speed to low, and slowly add the hot sugar syrup to the whites in a thin steady stream. Try not to hit the whip or the sides of the bowl when adding the syrup.

10. Increase the mixer's speed to high, and whip the meringue until it is stiff and cool.

11. Once the meringue has been whipped to stiff peaks, begin incorporating the butter. With the mixer running on medium speed, add the room-temperature butter by the stick; wait until each stick of butter has been fully incorporated before adding the next. Once all the butter has been incorporated, add the vanilla extract. Whip the mixture until all ingredients are well combined. Set aside for later assembly.

12. Final assembly: Using a serrated knife, slice the tops off each Sponge Cake, making them level. Slice each cake in half, for a total of four layers.

13. With a pastry brush, brush each cake slice with Vanilla Simple Syrup. Divide the Vanilla Cream evenly among three of the layers, and spread it evenly across each surface.

14. Stack each layer atop the other, ending with the unfinished layer. Chill the cake for 1 hour before icing.

15. Set the cake atop a rotating cake table. Using a cake spatula, spread an even layer of Buttercream evenly across the top of the cake. Ice the sides of the cake. Hold the cake spatula parallel lightly against the sides of the cake and spin the table. The buttercream will naturally rise evenly up the sides of the cake and will become smooth. Square off the sides of the cake with the edge of a butter knife.

16. Score the cake into 12 portions. Pipe a rosette atop each portion.

As he did with a number of foodstuffs, Thomas Jefferson is credited with introducing vanilla to America. During his tenure as secretary of state in 1791, he wrote to American chargé at Paris William Short: "Petit informs me that he has been all over the town in quest of vanilla, & it is unknown here. I must pray you to send me a packet of 50 pods (batons) which may come very well in the middle of a packet of newspapers. It costs about 24 s a baton when sold by the single baton" (Kimball 13–14).

# Plum Cake

Wild plums grew plentifully in the New World, and, as was the case with many fruits, new varieties developed as settlers cultivated plum stones brought to American shores from Europe. George Washington and Thomas Jefferson grew American and European plums at Mount Vernon and Monticello, respectively, and most likely enjoyed them fresh, dried, and preserved (Leighton 240–241).

With the exception of plum preserves, all eighteenth-century plum recipes call for raisins or currants (or both) rather than plums. This suggests that the word "plum" was used not only for a particular sort of fresh fruit but also as a general term for small dried fruit. Eighteenth-century cookbook writers, like their audiences, knew that raisins and currants were dried grapes, but perhaps the similarities between these dried fruits led to this general use.

**Makes one 10-inch cake; serves 10 to 12**

**Sweet Dough**
2 cups all-purpose flour
4 tablespoons (½ stick) unsalted butter, at room temperature
2 tablespoons honey
¼ teaspoon salt
¼ cup whole milk, at room temperature
1 large egg
2 large egg yolks
½ tablespoon active dry yeast

**Topping**
7 large plums
1 cup (8 ounces) sour cream
3 tablespoons honey
1 lemon, zest grated
1½ cups slivered almonds
¼ cup light brown sugar
Pinch of ground cardamom
1 teaspoon ground cinnamon
2 tablespoons unsalted butter, melted

Chantilly Cream (see page 120), or whipped cream, for serving (optional)

1. Prepare the Sweet Dough: In the bowl of an electric mixer fitted with the dough hook attachment, place the flour, butter, honey, and salt.
2. In a small mixing bowl, whisk together the milk, egg, yolks, and yeast, and add these wet ingredients to the electric mixer bowl. Mix on low speed for 4 minutes. Increase the speed to medium, and mix for another 4 minutes, or until the dough pulls away from and slaps against the sides of the bowl.
3. Cover the dough with plastic wrap and allow it to rise in a warm place until doubled in volume, about 1 hour.
4. Preheat the oven to 375° F. Grease a 10-inch round cake pan with butter, and coat lightly with flour.

5. Prepare the Topping: Slice the plums in half and remove the stones. Slice each half into thirds. Set the plums aside.
6. In a medium-size mixing bowl, whisk together the sour cream, honey, and lemon zest.
7. Once the dough has doubled in volume, punch it down and set it inside the prepared cake pan. Spread the sour cream mixture atop the dough. Sprinkle the almonds atop the sour cream, and arrange the sliced plums nicely atop.
8. In a small bowl, stir together the brown sugar, cardamom, and cinnamon. Brush the sliced plums with the melted butter, and dust the top of the cake with the sugar mixture. Allow the dough to relax for 30 minutes.
9. Bake in the preheated oven for 40 minutes, or until the plums have caramelized and a toothpick inserted comes out clean. Let the cake cool in the pan for 20 minutes, then turn out onto a serving plate. The cake can be served either warm or at room temperature. Serve with Chantilly Cream or whipped cream, if desired.

Like many authors, Amelia Simmons included a recipe for "Plumb Cake" in her cookbook <u>American Cookery</u>, which called for currants rather than plums. Although the dried fruit was incorporated into the sweetened yeast dough instead of mixed with a topping, the ingredients in her recipe reveal the similarity between this cake and City Tavern's version: "Mix one pound currants, nutmeg, mace and cinnamon one qr. of an ounce each, 12 eggs, one quart milk, and a sufficient quantity of raisins, 6 pound of flour, 3 pound of sugar, 2 pound of butter, and 1 pint yeast" (40).

# Apple Cake

This cake is based on the many eighteenth-century spice cakes that often included cooked or preserved fruit. "Cider cake"—a spice cake prepared with currants, brandy, and cider—occasionally appeared in period cookbooks as well, incorporating apples in yet another form (*Directions for Cookery* 347–348). The combination of fresh apples and applesauce in this version lends an intense fruit flavor to the cake, and the buttery, crunchy streusel topping complements its moist texture.

**Makes one 10-inch cake; serves 10 to 12**

2 Granny Smith apples

**Streusel**
1¾ cups plus 1 tablespoon light brown sugar
¾ cup bread flour
½ pound (2 sticks) unsalted butter, cold
2½ cups chopped walnuts
1 cup old-fashioned oats

**Cake**
½ cup cake flour
¾ cup all-purpose flour
1 tablespoon baking powder
1 tablespoon ground cinnamon
1 teaspoon ground nutmeg
2 cups Applesauce (see page 241)
2 large eggs
¼ cup plus 3 tablespoons light brown sugar
2 tablespoons apple cider
6 tablespoons olive oil
1 tablespoon Grandma's dark molasses
1 tablespoon plus 1 teaspoon honey

Confectioners' sugar, for dusting
Ground cinnamon, for dusting
Molasses Whipped Cream (see page 121), for serving

1. Preheat the oven to 375°F. Grease a 10-inch round cake pan with butter, and coat lightly with flour.
2. Peel, core, and cut the apples into 1-inch cubes.
3. Prepare the Streusel: In a medium-size bowl, stir together the brown sugar and bread flour. Cut the cold butter into ¼-inch cubes, and add it to the bowl. Place the bowl in the refrigerator for 1 hour to chill thoroughly.
4. Transfer the streusel ingredients to the bowl of an electric mixer fitted with the paddle attachment. Pulse the mixer on and off until the mixture begins to resemble a coarse meal. Add the nuts and oats, and pulse a few times, only until all ingredients are incorporated. The topping should remain crumbly and should not be creamed together. Set the topping in the refrigerator for later use.

5. Prepare the Cake: In a large bowl, sift together the cake flour, all-purpose flour, baking powder, cinnamon, and nutmeg; set aside.

6. In a medium-size bowl, whisk together the Applesauce, eggs, brown sugar, cider, oil, molasses, and honey. Add the dry ingredients to the wet ingredients, and stir, using a plastic spatula, until the ingredients come together. Pour the cake batter into the prepared cake pan.

7. Final assembly: Top the cake batter with the cubed apples. Top the apples with the streusel.

8. Bake the cake in the preheated oven for 35 minutes, or until a toothpick inserted comes out clean. Allow the cake to cool before unmolding from the pan. To unmold, turn the pan upside down and tap on the bottom to release.

9. Turn the cake right side up, and sift confectioners' sugar and cinnamon over the top. Serve with Molasses Whipped Cream.

# Cobblers & Crisps

The most practical eighteenth-century desserts were those that relied on seasonal, fresh ingredients or on preserved foodstuffs requiring little preparation. Cobblers and crisps, inspired by English and German food traditions, were thus not only practical but also easy to make and subject to much delicious variation. Nearly any kind of fruit—fresh, cooked, or preserved—was, and still is, suitable for these desserts. Baked in pans or individual dishes, the sweetened fruit becomes comfortingly soft and juicy, while the cloak of butter, flour, sugar, spices, and/or oats and nuts transforms into a crisp, complementary topping.

# Streusel

This German-inspired topping is the perfect complement to baked, fruit-based desserts and coffeecakes.

*Makes 4 cups*

>2 cups all-purpose flour
>1 cup packed light brown sugar
>¾ cup granulated sugar
>1 tablespoon ground cinnamon
>6 ounces (1½ sticks) cold unsalted butter, cut into cubes
>2 cups chopped walnuts

1. In the bowl of an electric mixer on medium speed, mix the flour, brown sugar, granulated sugar, and cinnamon until combined.
2. Add the butter and mix well, until the texture becomes crumbly. With a wooden spoon, stir in the walnuts.
3. Use immediately, or transfer to a covered container and store in the refrigerator for up to 2 weeks.

# Oat Topping

The addition of oats to the basic Streusel topping creates a crunchy, flavorful variation that marries well with fruit-based breads and pastries.

*Makes 2 cups*

>½ cup all-purpose flour
>½ cup old-fashioned oats
>½ cup packed light brown sugar
>4 tablespoons (½ stick) cold unsalted butter, cut into cubes
>½ cup chopped walnuts

1. In a medium bowl, combine the flour, oats, and brown sugar. Stir to combine.
2. Transfer the mixture to the bowl of a food processor, add the butter, and process until the texture becomes crumbly. You may also do this by hand, cutting the butter into the dry ingredients with two knives. With a wooden spoon, stir in the walnuts.
3. Use immediately, or transfer to a covered container and store in the refrigerator for up to 2 weeks.

# Blueberry Cobbler

This cobbler was as simple to prepare in the eighteenth century as it is today. Sweetened fresh berries are topped with a basic streusel made with sugar, flour, butter, and spices and baked until the fruit is soft and juicy and the topping is golden.

**Makes eight 3 x 1½-inch (½-cup) ramekins or one 1½-quart baking dish; serves 8**

> 4 pints (8 cups) fresh blueberries
> 1 cup granulated sugar
> ¼ cup cornstarch
> 2 tablespoons freshly squeezed lemon juice
> 4 cups Streusel (see page 65 )

1. Preheat the oven to 350°F. Grease eight 3 x 1½-inch ramekins or one 1½-quart shallow baking dish with butter.
2. In a large bowl, gently toss together the blueberries, sugar, cornstarch, and lemon juice.
3. Evenly divide the mixture among the prepared ramekins (or place in the baking dish).
4. Top each ramekin with ½ cup of the Streusel (or spread all of the topping over the baking dish).
5. Place the ramekins (or baking dish) on a baking pan. Bake for 25 to 30 minutes, or until the tops are golden brown and the filling starts to bubble. Serve warm.

# Pear and Sour Cherry Cobbler

In the eighteenth century, cherries were frequently preserved, made into wine, dried, and used in baked goods. The puddings (baked or boiled in pastry) and cherry pies that were also common inspired this cobbler, which marries the soft and tart fruit with a crisp, German streusel.

Makes eight 3 x 1½-inch (½-cup) ramekins or one 1½-quart baking dish; serves 8

> 1½ cups dried tart red cherries
> ½ cup brandy
> 8 pears, peeled, cored, and sliced
> 1 cup granulated sugar
> 3 tablespoons cornstarch
> 4 cups Streusel (see page 65)

1.  In a small bowl, combine the dried cherries and brandy and soak for 2 hours, or until softened.
2.  Preheat the oven to 350°F. Grease eight 3 x 1½-inch ramekins or one 1½-quart shallow baking dish with butter.
3.  In a large bowl, combine the pears, sugar, and cornstarch. Add the softened cherries, and gently toss together.
4.  Evenly divide the mixture among the prepared ramekins (or place in the baking dish).
5.  Top each ramekin with ½ cup of the Streusel (or spread all of the topping over the baking dish).
6.  Place the ramekins (or baking dish) on a baking pan. Bake for 25 to 30 minutes, or until the tops are golden brown and the filling starts to bubble. Serve warm.

Dried and candied fruit were available in various shops in eighteenth-century Philadelphia, but cookbooks of the period offered recipes for women who wished to engage in the time-consuming task of drying fruit themselves. In The Art of Cookery Made Plain and Easy, Hannah Glasse included a recipe for "How to dry Cherries":

Take eight pounds of cherries, one pound of the best confectioners' sugar, stone the cherries over a great deep bason [*sic*] or glass, and lay them one by one in rows, and strew a little sugar: thus do till your bason is full to the top, and let them stand till next day; then pour them out into a great posnet, set them on the fire, let them boil very fast a quarter of an hour, or more; then pour them again into your bason, and let them stand two or three days; then take them out, lay them one by one on hair-sieves, and set them in the sun, or an oven, till they are dry, turning them every day upon dry sieves; if in the oven, it must be as little warm as you can just feel it, when you hold your hand in it (255).

# Apple-Cranberry Cobbler

Colonial Americans found native cranberries similar in flavor to the lingonberries with which they had been familiar in Europe, although they quickly learned that the cranberry required quite a bit of sweetening. In the eighteenth century, cranberries were most often preserved or stewed to sweeten them for use in pies.

This cobbler relies upon the apples and the oat topping to add sweetness to the cranberries and to create a light dessert that is pleasantly tart.

*Makes eight 3 x 1½-inch (½-cup) ramekins or one 1½-quart baking dish; serves 8*

> 6 Granny Smith apples, peeled, cored, and cut into 8 slices each
> 2 cups whole fresh cranberries
> ½ cup granulated sugar
> 2 tablespoons cornstarch
> 1 teaspoon ground cinnamon
> 2 cups Oat Topping (see page 65)

1. Preheat the oven to 375°F. Grease eight 3 x 1½-inch ramekins or one 1½-quart shallow baking dish with butter.
2. In a large bowl, combine the apples, cranberries, sugar, cornstarch, and cinnamon.
3. Evenly divide the mixture among the prepared ramekins (or place in the baking dish).
4. Top each ramekin with ¼ cup of the Oat Topping (or spread all of the topping over the baking dish).
5. Place the ramekins (or baking dish) on a baking pan. Bake for 25 to 30 minutes, or until the tops are golden brown and the filling starts to bubble. Serve warm.

This cobbler is an updated version of the sort that appeared in late-eighteenth-century cookbooks like Amelia Simmons's <u>American Cookery</u>. Her recipe for cranberry tart called for "Cranberries. Stewed, strained, and sweetened, put in paste No. 9 [a sweet, butter pastry], add spices till grateful, and baked gently" (29).

# Apple–Fig Crumble

The Spanish introduced figs to the Americas in the early 1500s, and they have thrived on these shores for nearly five hundred years. Throughout the eighteenth century, Philadelphians purchased imported figs and grew them locally as the climate permitted. George Washington, in fact, is known to have had a fondness for the fruit. Records show that in 1772 he sent an order to the West Indies for "A Pot of good dryed Figs" and desired them only if they were reasonably priced. By 1797, he was growing the fruit at Mount Vernon as well, possibly for enjoying them both fresh and dried ("Foods used in the Christmas Table Setting," Mount Vernon memo 1989).

This richly flavored crumble relies not only on the concentrated sweetness of dried figs, but also on the intense flavor achieved by precooking the fruit with Madeira, sugar, cinnamon, and vanilla—ingredients that were popular in the eighteenth century as well.

**Makes eight 3 x 1½-inch (½-cup) ramekins or one 1½-quart baking dish; serves 8**

1 bottle (750 ml) Madeira wine
1½ cups granulated sugar
15 dried figs, stemmed and cubed
3 sticks cinnamon
1 vanilla bean, split lengthwise
8 Granny Smith apples, peeled, cored, and sliced
4 cups Streusel (see page 65)
1½ cups *Crème Anglaise* (see page 122)

1. Preheat the oven to 350°F. Grease eight 3 x 1½-inch ramekins or one 1½-quart shallow baking dish with butter.

2. In a medium saucepan, bring the Madeira, sugar, figs, cinnamon sticks, and vanilla bean to a boil. Reduce the heat to medium and cook for 20 to 30 minutes, or until thickened and reduced by half.

3. Place the apples in a medium, ovenproof bowl. Remove the saucepan from the heat and pour the mixture over the apples. Stir the mixture until well combined. Discard the vanilla bean and cinnamon stick.

4. Evenly divide the mixture among the prepared ramekins (or place in the baking dish).

5. Top each ramekin with ½ cup of the Streusel (or spread all of the topping over the baking dish).

6. Place the ramekins (or baking dish) on a baking pan. Bake for 25 to 30 minutes, or until the tops are golden brown and the filling starts to bubble.

7. Serve warm with *Crème Anglaise* or, if desired, a high-quality purchased vanilla ice cream.

# Rhubarb-Strawberry Crisp

In the eighteenth century, desserts and savory dishes reflected the use of seasonal ingredients. Fruit, like other foods, was certainly preserved, and nearly every period cookbook included recipes for a wide variety of sweetmeats, including fruit jellies. When prepared in season, however, baked goods like this crisp were based on fresh fruit, which Philadelphians obtained from local markets or, in the case of wealthier families, from country houses outside of the city.

Here, the tart flavor of rhubarb is combined with ripe strawberries and streusel to create a simple dish of varied textures and complementary flavors.

**Makes eight 3 x 1½-inch (½-cup) ramekins or one 1½-quart baking dish; serves 8**

> 1½ pounds fresh rhubarb, leaves removed and diced
> 1 pint (2 cups) fresh strawberries, stems removed and halved
> ¼ cup granulated sugar
> ¼ cup packed light brown sugar
> 2 tablespoons water
> 1 teaspoon freshly squeezed lemon juice
> 4 cups Streusel (see page 65)

1. Preheat the oven to 350°F. Grease eight 3 x 1½-inch ramekins or one 1½-quart shallow baking dish with butter.
2. In a large bowl, combine the rhubarb and strawberries. In a separate bowl, combine the sugar, brown sugar, water, and lemon juice; mix well. Pour the sugar mixture over the fruit. Gently toss together.
3. Evenly divide the mixture among the prepared ramekins (or place in the baking dish).
4. Top each ramekin with ½ cup of the Streusel (or spread all of the topping over the baking dish).
5. Place the ramekins (or baking dish) on a baking pan. Bake for 25 to 30 minutes, or until the tops are golden brown and the filling starts to bubble. Serve warm.

Elizabeth Drinker and her family were wealthy Philadelphia Quakers. They kept a garden at their home on Front Street, just a few blocks from City Tavern, as well as at their country estate, Clearfield Farm, 6 miles from the city (Drinker xi, xii). Elizabeth Drinker kept her diary from 1758 to 1807, and during the spring and summer months her entries were filled with references to the produce available at Clearfield. Writing from the city on May 28, 1794, she explained that although there was a great quantity of fruit and vegetables available at the farm, the inclement weather deterred her from traveling to the country: "[O]ur Gardener . . . brought from the plantation this morning about 11 2 peck green peas, and 3 pints of Strawberries—there is a bundence of both, either wasted or perishing there, but it does not suit to leave home while the weather continues dull" (561). The garden at Clearfield continued to produce strawberries late into the summer of the same year, for on August 22, Elizabeth, writing from the farm, mentioned that one of her domestics was "hear [sic] to day [sic] weeding the Strawberries" (585).

# Peach and Raspberry Crisp

Eighteenth-century Philadelphians enjoyed preserved peaches and raspberries year-round, but they would have prepared a crisp such as this one to take advantage of the summer's bounty of fresh fruit. The walnuts in the oat topping are the perfect complement to the soft texture of the cooked peaches and raspberries.

**Makes eight 3 x 1½-inch (½-cup) ramekins or one 2-quart baking dish; serves 8**

> ½ cup granulated sugar
> ⅓ cup sour cream
> 1 large egg
> 2 tablespoons all-purpose flour
> 1 teaspoon vanilla extract
> 5 ripe peaches, sliced, skin on
> 1 pint (2 cups) fresh raspberries
> 2 cups Oat Topping (see page 65)

1. Preheat the oven to 375°F. Grease eight 3 x 1½-inch ramekins or one 2-quart baking dish with butter.
2. In a large bowl, combine the sugar, sour cream, egg, flour, and vanilla extract. Gently fold in the peaches and raspberries.
3. Evenly divide the fruit mixture among the prepared ramekins (or place in the baking dish).
4. Top each ramekin with ¼ cup of the Oat Topping (or spread all of the topping over the baking dish).
5. Place the ramekins (or baking dish) on a baking pan. Bake for 15 to 20 minutes, or until the tops are golden and the filling starts to bubble.

In eighteenth-century Philadelphia, crisps of this sort were prepared from fresh and preserved fruit. During the summer, Elizabeth Drinker most likely took advantage of the ripe peaches she obtained from her garden and local markets, but it is possible that she used preserved fruit during warm months as well. In April 1779, she wrote that "all our Fruit in the Yard and Garden spoild [sic] with the Frost" (Drinker 343). Perhaps it was due to this devastating event that in May of the same year she thought it important to mention in her journal that a relative "brought over some dry'd [sic] peaches this afternoon" (347). Once re-hydrated in water or brandy, these peaches would have added a deliciously concentrated flavor to any fresh-fruit-based dessert.

# Pies & Tarts

Pies and tarts, these seemingly ordinary, uncomplicated dishes, were among the most important baked items of the eighteenth century. In Philadelphia, as in other early American cities and towns, they were made in confectioneries, in taverns, and in home kitchens. Some were elegant and expensive, prepared with puff pastry and imported spices and citrus, while others were modest and frugal, consisting of a short dough and custard. The two terms were often used interchangeably and referred to a wide variety of dishes. They were sweet or savory; they were filled with fresh fruit, dried fruit, preserves, custards, or puddings; they had top crusts, bottom crusts, or both; they were prepared in deep dishes or shallow tins; and they were baked in ovens as well as in bake kettles (lidded pans that stood in hot coals in the fireplace, covered with additional embers).

As they are today, pies and tarts of the eighteenth century were considered pastries, for they were based on "pastes," or doughs—a term derived from the French word for pastry, *pâte*. Despite the many varieties available in the period, all pies and tarts were assembled and baked in pans. They differ, therefore, from the pastries discussed in the Pastries chapter (see page 186), the components of which were, and still are, most often prepared separately before being assembled.

Eighteenth-century cookbook authors included numerous recipes for pies and tarts in their books, testament to the significance of these dishes during the period. Elizabeth Raffald included five "paste," or pie and tart dough, recipes in *The Experienced English Housekeeper*; Susannah Carter and Hannah Glasse included six such recipes in *The Frugal Housewife* and *The Art of Cookery Made Plain and Easy*, respectively; and Amelia Simmons published nine recipes in her *American Cookery*, six of which were for puff pastry alone. As great as these figures are, they pale in comparison to the quantities of pie and tart recipes that accompanied them, which often numbered in the dozens. To be sure, these authors were committed to sharing as much information as possible with their readers, who undoubtedly understood the importance of preparing proper pastry.

Most authors of the period wrote in great detail about the preparation of pastes as well as individual pies and tarts. Elizabeth Raffald, however, was fairly succinct in her introductory suggestions, which served as an informative overview of the subject:

Raised pies should have a quick oven and [be] well closed up or your pie will fall in the sides. It should have no water put in till the minute it goes into the oven, it makes the crust sad and is a great hazard of the pie running [*sic*]. Light paste requires a moderate oven but not too slow, it will make them sad, and a quick oven will catch and burn it and not give it time to rise. Tarts that are iced require a slow oven or the icing will be brown and the paste not near baked. These sort of tarts ought to be made of sugar paste and rolled very thin (Raffald 71).

# Pâte Brisée (Basic Pie Dough)

This French term, which literally translates as "short pastry," refers to a flaky dough that is suitable for sweet and savory fillings.

**Makes 12 ounces; enough for one 9-inch pie crust**

> 1⅓ cups sifted all-purpose flour
> ¼ teaspoon salt
> 4 tablespoons (½ stick) cold unsalted butter, cubed
> ¼ cup cold vegetable shortening
> 4 to 5 tablespoons ice-cold water

1. In a medium bowl, stir together the flour and salt. Using a pastry cutter or two knives, cut in the butter and shortening until the mixture resembles coarse crumbles.
2. Sprinkle the water, 1 tablespoon at a time, over the flour mixture and toss together with a fork, until a dough starts to form. It will be a little sticky or tacky.
3. Form the dough into a disc shape, wrap in plastic wrap, and chill in the refrigerator for at least 30 minutes before using.


# Pâte Sucrée (Rich Pie Dough)

This French term refers to a short pastry that is sweeter and richer than *Pâte Brisée* (previous recipe) due to the addition of sugar, eggs, and a larger amount of butter. As a result, this dough maintains its shape better during baking and is suitable not only for sweet pies and tarts but for cookies as well.

**Makes 2 pounds; enough for one 9-inch double-crust pie**

> 3 cups sifted all-purpose flour
> ¼ cup granulated sugar
> ½ pound (2 sticks) cold unsalted butter, cubed
> 2 large eggs

1. Place the steel blade in the food processor bowl. Add the flour and sugar. Cover and process with on/off pulses until the mixture is combined.
2. Add the butter. Process with on/off pulses until most of the mixture is crumbly.
3. With the processor running, quickly add the eggs through the feed tube. Stop the processor when all eggs have been added, and scrape down the sides of the bowl.
4. Process with two more on/off pulses (all of the mixture may not be moistened). Remove the dough from the bowl. Form the dough into a disc shape, wrap in plastic wrap, and chill in the refrigerator for at least 1 hour before using.

# Graham Cracker Crust

The invention of graham crackers postdates the existence of City Tavern. These cookies, however, have become a traditional component of many American baked goods, including graham-cracker crusts, which serve as the base for all of the restaurant's eighteenth-century-inspired cheesecakes.

Makes 1¼ cups; enough for one 9-inch cheesecake crust

> 1½ cups finely crushed graham crackers (about 22)
> ¼ pound (1 stick) unsalted butter, melted
> ¼ cup granulated sugar

1. In a large bowl, thoroughly combine the graham crackers, butter, and sugar. Cover with plastic wrap, and store in the refrigerator.

# Rhubarb–Strawberry Crumb Pie

When preparing fruit pies, eighteenth-century bakers not only created flavorful combinations like this classic pairing of tart rhubarb and sweet strawberries but also focused on making high-quality pastry dough. From professional pâtissiers to wealthy housekeepers to domestic servants, men and women alike understood that the ability to prepare tasteful, tender pastry was a necessary skill. Whether at home or at school, a girl could learn to combine ingredients, roll the dough, and bake sweet or savory pastries to perfection. This was an art developed with pride.

The *pâte sucrée* in this recipe is a slightly sweet, tender, yet firm crust, which complements the flavor and texture of the cooked fruit.

Makes one 9-inch pie; serves 8

> 2 pounds fresh rhubarb, cleaned and chopped (about 4 cups)
> 2 pints (4 cups) fresh strawberries, hulled and quartered
> ½ cup packed light brown sugar
> ¼ cup granulated sugar
> ¼ cup cold water
> 2 tablespoons cornstarch
> ½ teaspoon freshly squeezed lemon juice
> 1 pound *Pâte Sucrée* (see page 73)
> 4 cups Streusel (see page 65)

1. Preheat the oven to 350°F. Grease one 9 x 1½-inch pie pan with butter.
2. In a large bowl, combine the rhubarb, strawberries, brown sugar, sugar, water, cornstarch, and lemon juice; mix well.
3. On a lightly floured surface, roll out the *Pâte Sucrée* into a circle about 10 inches in diameter. Ease the pastry into the prepared pie pan, being careful not to stretch the pastry. Trim the pastry to ½ inch beyond the edge of the pie pan. Fold under the extra pastry. Crimp the edge.
4. Transfer the fruit mixture to the pastry-lined pan. Top with the Streusel.
5. Bake for 35 to 40 minutes, or until the top is golden and the filling starts to bubble. Cool on a wire rack.

# Pumpkin Pie

Although pumpkins were available in Britain, they have become synonymous with American foodways. Among the many squashes the Native Americans cultivated, the pumpkin is undoubtedly the most famous, due to the serving of pumpkin pie in 1623 at the Pilgrim's second Thanksgiving celebration (Mariani 259). Records, in fact, reveal that early colonists in Connecticut postponed one of their Thanksgiving dinners because they couldn't obtain the molasses necessary for the pie (Herbst 372).

From the seventeenth century onward, Americans used pumpkin in numerous dishes besides pie. It is hardly surprising that the gourmet Thomas Jefferson included a stylish soup recipe, complete with buttered croutons, in his collection of recipes (Kimball 44).

This version of pumpkin pie is based on period recipes that, while quite simple, were flavorful and rich, due to the use of spices as well as eggs and milk.

Makes one 9-inch pie; serves 8

> 1 pound *Pâte Sucrée* (see page 73)
> 1¾ cups pumpkin purée (see Chef's Note, page 164), or about 15 ounces canned pumpkin
> 1½ cups whole milk
> ¾ cup granulated sugar
> 2 large eggs
> 2½ tablespoons all-purpose flour
> 1½ tablespoons unsalted butter, melted
> ½ teaspoon salt
> ½ teaspoon ground allspice
> ½ teaspoon grated fresh ginger
> 1 teaspoon vanilla extract
> Chantilly Cream (see page 120), for serving (optional)

1. Preheat the oven to 400°F. Grease one 9 x 1½-inch pie pan with butter.
2. On a lightly floured surface, roll out the *Pâte Sucrée* into a 10-inch-diameter circle. Ease the pastry into the prepared pie pan, being careful not to stretch it. Trim the pastry to ½ inch beyond the edge of the pie pan. Fold under the extra pastry. Crimp the edge.
3. Line the pastry with a double thickness of aluminum foil. Fill with dried beans or pie weights. Bake for 15 minutes. Remove from the oven and let cool. Reduce the oven temperature to 375°F. Carefully remove the beans and foil. Set the baked pie shell aside.
4. In a large bowl, combine the pumpkin, milk, sugar, eggs, flour, butter, salt, allspice, ginger, and vanilla extract; mix well.
5. Pour the filling into the pie shell and cover the edge with foil. Bake for about 40 minutes, or until the filling is nearly set. The top of the pie should be firm but should jiggle slightly.
6. Completely cool on a wire rack. Serve with Chantilly Cream, if desired.

In American Cookery, author Amelia Simmons's two recipes for pumpkin pie appeared among the sweet puddings—dishes that were often baked in pastry. Although they were entitled merely "Pompkin," both "No. 1" and "No. 2" are more familiar than Glasse's version. Simmons's pies differ in their ratios of milk to pumpkin, their use of sugar versus molasses, and their variety of spices, but twenty-first-century bakers would undoubtedly feel quite comfortable preparing either of these 1796 recipes (Simmons 34–35).

# Sweet Potato Pie

Sweet potato pie is generally associated with southern foodways; the cultivation of the tuber in Virginia dates to the early 1700s, if not before then, and for nearly three hundred years it has continued to appear in a wide variety of southern dishes. The sweet potato, however, originated in the tropical New World and, thanks to Christopher Columbus, was being cultivated in Spain by the end of the fifteenth century and in England by the mid-sixteenth century (Mariani 319). The tuber, therefore, was familiar to colonial Americans before they ever arrived in the New World, and dishes like sweet potato pie refer directly to traditional British foodways.

Makes one 9-inch pie; serves 8

1 pound *Pâte Sucrée* (see page 73)
1½ cups cooked sweet potatoes (about 2 medium), mashed
10 ounces (1¼ cups) sweetened condensed milk
¾ cup granulated sugar
3 large eggs
2 tablespoons unsalted butter, melted
1 teaspoon ground allspice
1 teaspoon vanilla extract
Chantilly Cream (see page 120), for serving (optional)

1. Preheat the oven to 400°F. Grease one 9 x 1½-inch pie pan with butter.
2. On a lightly floured surface, roll out the *Pâte Sucrée* into a circle about 10 inches in diameter. Ease the pastry into the prepared pie pan, being careful not to stretch the pastry. Trim the pastry to ½ inch beyond the edge of the pie plate. Fold under the extra pastry. Crimp the edge.
3. Line the pastry with a double thickness of aluminum foil. Fill with pie weights or dried beans. Bake for 15 minutes. Remove from the oven and let cool. Carefully remove the foil. Set the baked pie shell aside.
4. In a large bowl, combine the sweet potatoes, milk, sugar, eggs, butter, allspice, and vanilla extract; whisk well.
5. Carefully pour the filling into the baked pie shell. To prevent overbrowning, cover the edge of the pie with aluminum foil. Bake for 30 to 40 minutes, or until the filling is nearly set. To test for doneness, touch the top of the pie; it should be firm but should jiggle slightly.
6. Completely cool on a wire rack. Serve with Chantilly Cream, if desired.

Although recipes for sweet potato pie appear more infrequently in period cookbooks than other preparations, the tuber was certainly available and enjoyed up and down the eastern seaboard. Amelia Simmons included two recipes for "Potato Pudding" in <u>American Cookery</u>, and even though the type of potato was unspecified, it is possible that the sweet or white variety was appropriate (Simmons 33).

Even if cookbooks fail to reveal the extent to which sweet potatoes were consumed, two prominent figures, George Washington and Thomas Jefferson, were known to have cultivated and enjoyed them. Not surprisingly, Thomas Jefferson's collection of recipes included a recipe for "sweet potato pudding," which, with its addition of lemon rind, brandy, and citron, reflects the style with which Jefferson altered common dishes (Kimball 95):

> Sweet Potato Pudding No. 1: Boil 1 pound of sweet potatoes until tender. Rub them through a sieve. Add 5 well-beaten eggs, 1½ cups of sugar, 1 cup of butter, the grated rind of 1 lemon, a dash of nutmeg, and a wine-glass of brandy. Line a baking dish with pastry and our in the mixture. Sprinkle with sugar and bits of citron and bake in a slow oven until set (Kimball 95).

# Apple Pie

Apples were enjoyed for centuries in England, but it was in the New World that they flourished. Colonists planted European seeds, which grew particularly well in New England and the mid-Atlantic states, and, through grafting, they quickly discovered new varieties (Leighton 227). George Washington, Thomas Jefferson, and Benjamin Franklin were among many notable Americans to take an interest in apples, avidly corresponding with European horticulturists and cultivating numerous varieties in their own gardens.

Apples made their way into many dishes, including pie. This version is based on the apple puddings and tarts that were prepared in eighteenth-century kitchens.

Makes one 9-inch pie; serves 8

> 5 Granny Smith apples, peeled, cored, and sliced (about 1½ pounds)
> ½ cup granulated sugar
> 1 teaspoon ground cinnamon
> 2 tablespoons unsalted butter, softened
> 2 tablespoons all-purpose flour
> 2 pounds *Pâte Sucrée* (see page 73)

1. Preheat the oven to 375°F. Grease a 9 x 1½-inch pie pan with butter.
2. In a large bowl, combine the apple slices, sugar, and cinnamon. Gently toss to coat. Add the softened butter and flour. Set aside.
3. Divide the *Pâte Sucrée* in half. On a lightly floured surface, roll out each half of the pastry into a circle about 10 inches in diameter. Ease one circle of pastry into the prepared pie pan. Transfer the apple mixture to the pastry-lined pan.
4. Use the remaining circle of pastry to cover the apple mixture. Trim the pastry to ½ inch beyond the edge of the pie pan. Fold under the extra pastry. Crimp the edge. Prick the top pastry with a fork to allow steam to escape. Using a small knife, make several 1½-inch-long slits in the top crust.
5. Bake for 30 to 40 minutes, or until the top turns golden and the filling starts to bubble. Serve warm.

The popularity of apple pie and related apple desserts in the eighteenth century is revealed in the numerous variations that appear in period cookbooks. In <u>American Cookery</u>, Amelia Simmons lists three types of pie—"Apple Pie," "Dried Apple Pie," and "A buttered apple Pie"—in addition to "Apple Tarts," "Apple Pudding," and "An apple Pudding Dumplin" (Simmons 26–27, 28, 33). Thomas Jefferson's enthusiasm for apple pie is reflected in his collection of recipes as well. Among the many fruit puddings baked in a crust that he might well have enjoyed serving were "Apple Pudding," "Grated Apple Pudding," and "Sliced Apple Pudding" (Kimball 91, 97, 101).

# Apple–Almond Crumb Pie

Eighteenth-century cooks often added raisins to apple pies, puddings, and tarts. In this version, the almonds in the almond crumb topping complement the flavor and texture of the fruit.

**Makes one 9-inch pie; serves 8**

1 pound *Pâte Sucrée* (see page 73)

**Almond Crumb Topping**
1¼ cups all-purpose flour
1 cup granulated sugar
9 tablespoons (1 stick plus 1 tablespoon) cold unsalted butter, cut into cubes
½ cup blanched almonds

**Filling**
5 Granny Smith apples, peeled, cored, and sliced (about 1½ pounds)
½ cup granulated sugar
½ cup raisins
3 tablespoons freshly squeezed lemon juice (about 1 lemon)
1 teaspoon ground cinnamon

1. Preheat the oven to 375°F. Grease a 9 x 1½-inch pie pan with butter.
2. On a lightly floured surface, roll out the *Pâte Sucrée* into a circle about 10 inches in diameter. Ease the pastry into the prepared pie pan, being careful not to stretch the pastry. Trim the pastry to ½ inch beyond the edge of the pie pan. Fold under the extra pastry. Crimp the edge.
3. Prepare the Almond Crumb Topping: In the bowl of a food processor, combine the flour, sugar, butter, and almonds. Pulse until the mixture becomes just crumbly. Set aside.
4. Prepare the Filling: In a large bowl, combine the apples, sugar, raisins, lemon juice, and cinnamon. Gently toss to coat.
5. Transfer the Filling into the pastry-lined pan. Top with the Almond Crumb Topping.
6. Bake for 40 to 45 minutes, or until the top is golden and the filling starts to bubble. Let cool to room temperature; then chill in the refrigerator for at least 1 hour before serving.

# Mincemeat Pie

In late-eighteenth-century Philadelphia, this pie represented a fusion of affordable and costly ingredients. Items such as apples, flour, butter, and suet were readily available and inexpensive, while imported raisins, currants, citrus, sugar, and brandy remained luxurious foodstuffs for most of the city's inhabitants. It is likely, therefore, that only wealthy Philadelphians enjoyed this pie, eaten hot or cold, on a regular basis.

*Makes one 9-inch pie; serves 8*

12 ounces *Pâte Brisée* (see page 73), chilled overnight

**Filling**
2 tablespoons unsalted butter
2 Granny Smith apples, peeled, cored, and cut into ½-inch
   pieces
2 tablespoons all-purpose flour
1 cup dark raisins
1 cup golden raisins
1 cup currants
½ cup brandy
1 orange, zest grated and juiced
½ cup Grandma's dark molasses
½ cup honey
½ cup light brown sugar
¾ cup beef suet, chopped fine (see Chef's Note)
Maple Whipped Cream (see page 121), for serving (optional)

*Beef suet is available in many better supermarkets. Lard may be substituted if you can't find beef suet.*

1. Prepare the Filling: The day before you plan to bake the pie, in a large skillet over medium heat, melt the butter. Add the apples and cook, stirring occasionally, until they begin to soften, about 2 minutes. Sprinkle the flour over the apples, and cook until slightly thickened, about 1 minute more. Set aside in the refrigerator overnight.

2. Reduce the heat to low, and add the dark raisins, golden raisins, and currants; stir to combine. Add the brandy, orange zest, and orange juice; stir to combine.

3. Add the molasses, honey, and brown sugar, and stir to combine. Remove the mixture from the heat, and set aside.

4. Remove the apple mixture from the refrigerator, stir in the beef suet, and refrigerate overnight.

5. Grease a 9-inch-diameter, 2-inch-deep pie pan with butter, and coat lightly with flour.

6. Lightly flour your work surface and rolling pin. Roll the chilled dough into a rough circle about 12 inches in diameter. Fit the dough into the prepared pie pan. Roll the overhanging dough over itself until it rests atop the edges of the pan. Make certain the inside edges of the dough are flush with the pan. Refrigerate for 1 hour before baking.

7. Meanwhile, preheat the oven to 425°F.

8. Fill the pie shell with the chilled Filling.

9. Place the pie in the oven and immediately decrease the temperature to 375°F. Bake for 25 minutes, or until the crust turns golden and the filling bubbles. Cool the pie to room temperature before cutting it into serving portions. Serve with Maple Whipped Cream, if desired.

# Chocolate–Pecan Pie

Like many exotic foods, chocolate became fashionable in Europe before gaining popularity in colonial America. Although Columbus might have introduced the Spanish to this unusual ingredient, it wasn't until the Spanish later learned to sweeten the spicy Aztec beverage that chocolate became stylish and much in demand throughout Europe (Mariani 79). Although, like coffee and tea, chocolate was fairly expensive in late-eighteenth-century America, it was widely available in Philadelphia, sold in a variety of venues from dry goods stores to confectioners' shops.

Native to North and South America, pecans are as "American" as chocolate, although their introduction into regional foodways was arguably more direct than their Aztec counterpart. Thomas Jefferson first cultivated pecan trees in his gardens at Monticello, and his passion for the "Poccon" or "Illinois nut," as it was called, was shared by George Washington, who planted trees at Mount Vernon. Jefferson, in fact, sent the general pecan trees in January 1794 along with instructions concerning when to plant them (Mount Vernon memo 1989).

Makes one 9-inch pie; serves 8

1 pound *Pâte Sucrée* (see page 73)

**Filling**
4 large eggs
1 cup light corn syrup
1 teaspoon vanilla extract
½ cup granulated sugar
½ cup packed light brown sugar
½ teaspoon salt
½ cup (3 ounces) semisweet chocolate chips
4 tablespoons (½ stick) unsalted butter, melted
2 cups pecan halves

1. Grease a 9 x 1½-inch pie pan with butter.
2. On a lightly floured surface, roll out the *Pâte Sucrée* into a circle about 10 inches in diameter. Ease the pastry into the prepared pie pan, being careful not to stretch the pastry. Trim the pastry to ½ inch beyond the edge of the pie plate. Fold under the extra pastry. Crimp the edge. Refrigerate the pie shell for at least 1 hour before using.
3. Preheat the oven to 350°F.
4. Prepare the Filling: In the bowl of an electric mixer on medium to high speed, beat the eggs until pale yellow and thickened. Add the corn syrup and vanilla extract, and beat well.
5. In a separate bowl, combine the sugar, brown sugar, salt, chocolate chips, and melted butter; stir to mix. Add to the egg mixture and mix well.
6. Spread the pecans over the bottom of the chilled pie shell. Carefully pour in the egg-chocolate mixture.
7. Bake for 40 to 45 minutes, or until the pie puffs up slightly. To check for doneness, insert a knife into the center of the pie—it should come out clean. Completely cool on a wire rack. Refrigerate for at least 2 hours before serving.

# Cherry Pie

Wild cherries grew plentifully in early America, but, finding them too sour to eat, colonists cultivated sweeter English varieties. Cherries were enjoyed fresh during the spring and summer months, while preserved cherries, cherry wine, and cherry-flavored brandy (or kirschwasser) were consumed year-round.

Makes one 9-inch pie; serves 8

12 ounces *Pâte Brisée* (see page 73)

**Filling**
Two 20-ounce cans dark sweet cherries (4 cups)
2 vanilla beans
¾ cup granulated sugar
Pinch of ground nutmeg
3 tablespoons cornstarch
2 tablespoon kirschwasser (cherry-flavored liqueur)
2 tablespoons water
4 cups Chantilly Cream (see page 120), substituting 2 tablespoons kirschwasser for the vanilla

1. Grease a 9-inch-diameter, 2-inch-deep pie pan with butter, and coat lightly with flour.
2. Roll the chilled *Pâte Brisée* into a rough circle about 12 inches in diameter. Fit the dough into the prepared pie pan. Roll the overhanging dough over itself until it rests atop the edges of the pan. Make certain the inside edges of the dough are flush with the pan. Prick the sides and base of the dough with a fork. Refrigerate for 1 hour before baking.
3. Meanwhile, preheat the oven to 400°F.
4. Weight down the pie shell with aluminum foil and pie weights or beans. Place the shell in the oven and immediately reduce the oven temperature to 350°F. Bake the shell for about 8 minutes, until the sides are golden. Remove the shell from the oven, remove the foil, and return the shell to oven. Bake 3 to 5 minutes longer, or until evenly golden brown. Set aside to cool. Turn the oven off.
5. Meanwhile, prepare the Filling: Strain the cherries, reserving ½ cup of the canning juice. Put the cherries in a large bowl and the cherry juice in a small bowl.
6. Using a paring knife, slice the vanilla beans in half lengthwise. Scrape the beans from the pods with the back of the knife. Place the reserved cherry juice, beans, pods, sugar, and nutmeg in a small saucepan, and bring the mixture to a boil.
7. Meanwhile, in a small bowl, whisk together the cornstarch, kirschwasser, and water.
8. While the cherry juice is rapidly boiling, add the cornstarch mixture and whisk vigorously. Continue to whisk the mixture and boil until the cherry juice is thick and shiny, about 1 minute more.
9. Pour the thickened cherry juice over the cherries and, using a plastic spatula, fold the mixture to combine. Remove the vanilla pod with a spoon.
10. Transfer the hot cherry filling into the prebaked pie shell. Cover the filling directly with plastic wrap. Let cool for 1 hour at room temperature.
11. Top the cooled pie with the kirschwasser-flavored Chantilly Cream.

George Washington and Thomas Jefferson were among the renowned gardeners who grew cherries on their estates. Both cultivated the Morello cherry, a sweet and sour variety that yields dark juice (Leighton 229). In her cookbook <u>The Art of Cookery Made Plain and Easy</u>, Hannah Glasse included a recipe for preserved Morello cherries that were likely similar to the canned fruit used in this pie:

To barrel Morello Cherries.

To one pound of full ripe cherries picked from the stems, and wiped with a cloth, take half a pound of double refined sugar, and boil it to a candy height, but not a high one, put the cherries into a small barrel, then put in the sugar by a spoonful at a time, till it is all in, and roll them about every day till they have done fermenting, then bung it up close, and they will be fit for use in a month. It must be an iron-hooped barrel (Glasse 264–265).

# Maple–Buttermilk Pie

The filling of this pie is based on the many eighteenth-century puddings and custards that were flavored with spices, fruit, liqueur, and sugar and baked in pastry. The maple syrup in this recipe recalls the popularity and abundance of this sweetener in colonial America. Influenced by Native Americans, European colonists developed a fondness for American maple syrup in the early part of the century. With the implementation of the Sugar Act of 1764, which raised the price of that sweetener, maple syrup became even more popular and remained so into the nineteenth century (Mariani 197–198).

The sweet, crisp topping is the perfect complement to the pie's rich and smooth filling.

**Makes one 9-inch pie; serves 8**

12 ounces *Pâte Brisée* (see page 73)

### Filling
3 large eggs
3 large egg yolks
¼ cup granulated sugar
Pinch of salt
1 pint (2 cups) buttermilk
⅔ cup maple syrup
1 tablespoon vanilla extract
1 cup raisins, soaked in 2 tablespoons bourbon

### Topping
½ cup plus 2 tablespoons granulated sugar
½ cup plus 2 tablespoons light brown sugar
2 cups bread flour
1½ cups old-fashioned oats (not quick-cooking)
½ pound (2 sticks) cold unsalted butter, cut into ½-inch cubes
1½ cups pecans

*Baking "blind"—Prebaking a pie shell before adding the filling and baking it off is known as "blind baking," a term of English origin. This step usually involves placing aluminum foil carefully into an unbaked shell and adding pie weights to prevent the dough from puffing up while baking. If you don't have pie weights, dried beans or rice can be used for the same results.*

1.  Grease a 9-inch-diameter, 2-inch-deep pie pan with butter, and coat lightly with flour.
2.  Lightly flour your work surface and rolling pin. Roll the chilled *Pâte Brisée* into a rough circle about 12 inches in diameter. Fit the dough into the prepared pie pan. Roll the overhanging dough over itself until it rests atop the edges of the pan. Make certain the inside edges of the dough are flush with the pan. Prick the sides and base of the dough with a fork. Refrigerate for 1 hour before baking.
3.  Meanwhile, preheat the oven to 400°F.
4.  Weight down the pie shell with aluminum foil and pie weights or beans. Place the shell in the oven and immediately reduce the oven temperature to 325°F. Bake the shell for about 8 minutes, or until the crust is golden. Remove the shell from the oven, remove the foil and weights, and set aside. Turn the oven off.

5. Prepare the Filling: In a medium-size bowl, whisk together the eggs, yolks, sugar, and salt. Whisk in the buttermilk, maple syrup, and vanilla extract. Add the presoaked raisins and bourbon. Set the mixture aside.

6. Prepare the Topping: In the bowl of an electric mixer fitted with the paddle attachment, stir together the sugars, bread flour, and oats. Add the butter and pecans, and pulse until the mixture resembles coarse meal. Place in the refrigerator to chill for 1 hour.

7. Pour the Filling mixture into the prebaked pie shell. Bake for 10 minutes, or until the filling begins to firm up around the sides but is still loose in the center.

8. Remove the pie from the oven and cover it generously with the Topping. Bake the pie another 10 minutes, or until a toothpick inserted in the center comes out clean. Cool to room temperature; then transfer to the refrigerator to chill for at least 1 hour before serving.

# Coconut and Macadamia Nut Tartlets

An ancient fruit dating back to sixth-century Egypt, mention of the coconut first appeared in print in English in the mid-sixteenth century (Mariani 88). The fruit was also native to the West Indies and gained popularity in Philadelphia as well as other cities in New England and the South.

The use of coconut, nuts, and chocolate in this recipe represents the extent to which imported and exotic ingredients could have been combined if an eighteenth-century household were able to afford them.

**Makes eight 3¼ x ½-inch individual tartlets or one 9 x 1⅜-inch tart; serves 8**

### Chocolate Shortbread Dough
½ pound (2 sticks) unsalted butter, cubed and softened
1 cup granulated sugar
2 cups sifted all-purpose flour
1 cup unsweetened Dutch cocoa powder, sifted
½ teaspoon salt
2 large eggs
2 large egg yolks

### Filling
1¼ cups whole milk
2 large eggs
3 tablespoons granulated sugar
1 cup freshly grated unsweetened coconut flakes, lightly toasted
   (see Chef's Note)
1 cup macadamia nuts, toasted (see Chef's Note, page 38) and chopped

1. Prepare the Chocolate Shortbread Dough: In the bowl of an electric mixer on medium to high speed, cream the butter and sugar together until light and fluffy.
2. In a separate bowl, combine the flour, cocoa, and salt; stir to mix.
3. With the electric mixer on low, slowly add the dry ingredients to the butter-sugar mixture and beat just until combined. Add the eggs and yolks, and beat until the dough just begins to hold together. Wrap the dough in plastic wrap, and chill in the refrigerator for at least 1 hour before using.
4. Meanwhile, preheat the oven to 400°F. Grease eight 3¼ x ½-inch tartlet pans with butter, and coat lightly with flour.
5. Prepare the Filling: In a medium bowl, whisk together the milk, eggs, and sugar until well combined. Set aside.
6. Remove the dough from the refrigerator. Divide the chilled dough into 8 balls. On a lightly floured surface, roll each ball into a 6-inch-diameter circle. Ease the pastry circles into the prepared tartlet pans, being careful not to stretch the pastry. Gently press each round into the fluted side of the tart pan. Trim the pastry even with the rim of the pan. Place the tartlets on a baking pan. (Alternatively, for a single, large tart, roll out the entire dough ball into a 12-inch circle, ease the round into a greased and floured 9 x 1⅜-inch tart pan, and trim the dough to fit the pan.)

7. Line each pastry with a double thickness of foil and fill with dry beans or pastry weights to weight down. Bake for 8 minutes. Remove the foil. Bake for 4 to 5 minutes more, or until the dough is firm and set to the touch, but not browned. Reduce the oven temperature to 350°F.

8. Sprinkle each tart shell with the coconut and nuts. Carefully pour the filling into the shells.

9. Gently transfer the baking pan to the oven. Bake for 15 to 20 minutes, or until a knife inserted near the centers comes out clean.

10. Cool to room temperature on a wire rack. Refrigerate for at least 2 hours before serving.

*To toast freshly grated coconut—*
*Evenly spread out the coconut flakes*
*on a baking pan. Toast in a preheated*
*375°F oven for 5 minutes, stirring*
*about halfway through the cooking*
*time, until golden.*

# Gooseberry Tart

Gooseberries were among the most popular fruits available in the eighteenth century. Because they were not native to America, colonists imported gooseberry-bush cuttings from northern Europe and England, where they grew plentifully. Thomas Jefferson and George Washington both cultivated these jewel-like berries, which, according to the numerous recipes for preserves, creams, wine, and tarts that appear in period cookbooks, were widely available during the summer months (Leighton 231–232).

Makes one 10-inch tart; serves 10

### Filling
1 vanilla bean
2 cups whole milk
¼ cup plus 3 tablespoons granulated sugar
2 tablespoons finely chopped fresh ginger
2 tablespoons cornstarch
5 large egg yolks

1 recipe Linzertorte tart shell (see page 95), prebaked (see Chef's note, page 95)
2 pints fresh gooseberries, husked
3 tablespoons honey

1. Prepare the Filling: Using a paring knife, slice the vanilla bean in half lengthwise. Scrape the seeds from the pod with the back of the knife. In a medium-size saucepan, combine the milk, vanilla seeds and pod, ¼ cup of the sugar, and the fresh ginger; heat until the milk begins to bubble just around the edges of the pan. Remove from the heat.

2. In a large bowl, sift the cornstarch and remaining 3 tablespoons of sugar over the yolks, and whisk to combine. With a slotted spoon, remove the vanilla bean and fresh ginger from the milk. Temper the hot milk mixture into the yolk mixture by adding ¼ cup at a time of the hot liquid to the yolk mixture, whisking all the while.

3. Once all the milk has been added, return the mixture to a saucepan over medium heat. Cook the cream, whisking persistently. Bring the mixture to a boil and cook until it is thickened, about 3 minutes. Then cook 1 minute more to cook off the starch, and remove from the heat.

4. Pour the hot filling into the prebaked tart shell. Remove the gooseberries from their pods and, using a paring knife, slice them in half. Place the halved berries atop the cream. Drizzle the honey over them.

5. Return the shell to the oven and bake 10 minutes, or until the cream soufflés and the berries caramelize. Let cool for 30 minutes before serving.

In her cookbook American Cookery, Amelia Simmons included a recipe for "Gooseberry Tart" that is so simple that it was clearly intended to emphasize the quality and fresh flavor of the fruit:

"Lay clean berries and sift over them sugar, then berries and sugar, till a deep dish be filled, intermingling a handful of raisins, and 1 gill water; cover with paste No. 9, and bake some what more than other tarts" (Simmons 30).

# Citrus Tart

This tart is reminiscent of the lemon and orange puddings so commonly prepared in the eighteenth century. These elegant puff-pastry tarts contained rich fillings of imported citrus juice and zest, butter, cream, rose- or orange-flower water, eggs, and great quantities of sugar.

The use of cake flour in this orange-scented tart dough results in a delicate crust that complements the creamy, refreshing curd.

Makes one 10-inch tart; serves 10

### Tart Dough
½ pound (2 sticks) unsalted butter
½ cup granulated sugar
2 oranges, zest grated
1 large egg
1½ cups plus 3 tablespoons cake flour

### Filling
6 large eggs
6 large egg yolks
6 tablespoons sour cream
1 cup granulated sugar
2 tablespoons grated lemon zest
½ cup freshly squeezed orange juice
½ cup freshly squeezed lime juice
1 cup freshly squeezed lemon juice

1. Grease a 10-inch tart pan with a removable bottom with butter, and coat lightly with flour. Refrigerate the pan until needed.
2. Prepare the Tart Dough: In the bowl on an electric mixer fitted with the paddle attachment, on medium speed, beat the butter, sugar, and zest until smooth, scraping down the sides of the bowl, if necessary.
3. Add the egg, and mix until smooth. Scrape down the sides of the bowl.
4. Remove the bowl from the mixer and fold in the flour with a wooden spoon. Wrap the dough in plastic wrap and chill for 2 hours.
5. On a lightly floured work surface, roll the dough out evenly so that it is 12 inches in diameter.
6. Transfer the dough carefully to the chilled tart pan by draping it over a well-floured rolling pin, lifting it, and gently setting it in the pan. Mold the dough in the pan, making certain the edges are square. Chill for 1 hour. Prick the dough with a fork, and chill for 30 minutes. Meanwhile, preheat the oven to 350°F.
7. Weight down the dough with aluminum foil and beans or pie weights. Bake 10 minutes, or just until the sides of the tart shell begin to brown. Remove the shell from the oven, and set aside.
8. Prepare the Filling: In a medium-size bowl, whisk together the eggs, yolks, sour cream, sugar, and lemon zest. Whisk in the citrus juices.
9. Pour the filling into the prebaked tart shell. Bake for 25 minutes, or until the filling is firm. Cool to room temperature; then chill in the refrigerator for at least 2 hours before serving.

# Almond Anise Fig Tart

This tart well represents the eighteenth-century palate. Figs, introduced into North America centuries earlier by Spanish missionaries, had become readily available by this period (Herbst 169). As early as the 1760s, Thomas Jefferson was growing figs at Monticello, and by at least the third quarter of the century, Philadelphians were cultivating trees on their country estates (Leighton 231).

Other ingredients—including nutmeg, anise, and almonds—were also popular, albeit costly, in eighteenth-century Philadelphia and refer to the heavily spiced European foods of the sixteenth and seventeenth centuries. While nutmeg and almonds were often added to sweet dishes, anise seems to have been used rather sparingly in this period.

**Makes one 10-inch tart; serves 10**

**Filling**
1 vanilla bean
½ pound (2 sticks) unsalted butter
½ cup granulated sugar
1¼ cups sliced almonds, toasted (see Chef's Note, page 38)
2 teaspoons freshly grated nutmeg
3 large eggs
3 large egg yolks
1 tablespoon anise-flavored liqueur

¾ cup Apricot Stone Fruit Preserves (see page 243)
1 recipe Linzertorte tart shell (see page 95), prebaked (see Chef's note, page 95) and chilled for 30 minutes
2 pints black Mission figs

**Glaze**
4 tablespoons (½ stick) unsalted butter, melted
1 tablespoon honey
1 orange, zest grated
Pinch of salt

1. Preheat the oven to 350°F.
2. Prepare the Filling: Using a paring knife, slice the vanilla bean in half lengthwise. Scrape the seeds from the pod with the back of the knife. In the bowl of an electric mixer fitted with the paddle attachment, on medium speed, cream together the butter, sugar, vanilla seeds (reserving the pod for the glaze), and almonds. Scrape down the sides of the bowl often.
3. With the mixer running on low speed, add the eggs and yolks, one at a time, incorporating each after addition. Add the anisette liqueur and stir to combine. Transfer the filling to a small container and set aside at room temperature for later use.
4. Spread a thin layer of Apricot Preserves on the bottom of the prepared tart shell.
5. Fill the tart shell three-quarters full with the Filling and spread it evenly across.
6. Slice the figs in half lengthwise. Set the figs, skin side down, atop the filling.
7. Prepare the Glaze: In a small saucepan, combine the butter, honey, orange zest, reserved vanilla bean pod, and salt. Bring to a boil. Brush the figs with the hot glaze.
8. Bake the tart for 30 minutes, or until the figs caramelize, the cream sets, and the tart shell is brown. Let cool for 1 hour before serving.

# Clafouti Tart

This delicate fruit tart was inspired by the baked French pudding of the same name, traditionally from the Limousin region. Cherries are usually the fruit of choice, but others are often incorporated as well (Herbst 101). Although *clafouti* is traditionally prepared without pastry, this version is based on the eighteenth-century puddings that were commonly baked in pastry-lined pans.

**Makes one 10-inch tart; serves 10**

1 pound *Pâte Sucrée* (see page 73), chilled for at least 3 hours

**Filling**
4 large eggs
3 large egg yolks
1 cup granulated sugar
¼ cup cake flour
3 cups whole milk
1 cup sour cream or crème frâiche

4 cups red grapes
3 tablespoons granulated sugar

1. Preheat the oven to 350°F. Grease one 10 x 2-inch cake pan with butter, and coat lightly with flour.
2. Dust your countertop generously with flour. Roll out the *Pâte Sucrée* to ¼ inch thick and about 12 inches in diameter.
3. Transfer the dough to the tart pan by gently draping it over a well-floured rolling pin, lifting it, and laying it across the cake pan. Prick the dough with a fork, and chill for 30 minutes.
4. Weight down the dough with aluminum foil and beans or pie weights. Bake 10 minutes, or until the sides of the tart shell begin to brown. Remove the shell from the oven, and set aside.
5. Prepare the Filling: In a medium-size bowl, whisk together the eggs, yolks, and sugar until light and pale in color. Whisk in the flour.
6. In a separate bowl, whisk together the milk and sour cream. Add the milk mixture to the other bowl, slowly whisking all the while. Pour the filling into the prebaked shell. Arrange the grapes on top. Lightly sprinkle sugar over the top.
7. Bake until the filling is firm and soufflés, 25 to 30 minutes.
8. Cool at room temperature for 1 hour. Reheat the tart in a 325°F oven for 5 minutes. To unmold, place a plate over the top of the tart; then invert the pan and plate. Tap lightly on the bottom of the pan and then lift. Place a second plate over the tart; then invert again and remove the top plate. Cut into portions and serve.

# Berry Tart

Because this tart is made up of three basic components—tart dough, pastry cream, and fresh berries—its success depends on the high quality of each one. The berries that grew in abundance in and outside of eighteenth-century Philadelphia would have been enjoyed fresh and ripe in sweet dishes similar to this tart during the summer months. Similarly, this pastry cream not only refers to the numerous boiled and baked puddings that appear in period cookbooks but also relates to the rich French custards that were undoubtedly prepared in some of the city's confectioneries and bakery shops.

**Makes one 10-inch tart; serves 12**

> 1 pound *Pâte Sucrée* (see page 73), chilled for at least 3 hours
>
> **Pastry Cream**
> Two ¼-ounce packages unflavored gelatin
> ¼ cup water
> 2 cups whole milk
> 1 vanilla bean
> ⅛ teaspoon freshly grated nutmeg
> Pinch of salt
> ¼ cup granulated sugar
> 2 large eggs
> 1 large egg yolk
> 3 tablespoons cornstarch
> 2 tablespoons unsalted butter, softened
>
> 1 pint heavy whipping cream, whipped to medium peaks
> 1 pint each hulled strawberries, blueberries, raspberries, and blackberries
> Confectioners' sugar, for garnishing
> Fresh mint sprigs, for garnishing

1. Preheat the oven to 350°F. Grease one 10 x 2-inch tart shell with butter, and coat lightly with flour.
2. Dust your countertop generously with flour. Roll out the *Pâte Sucrée* to ¼ inch thick and about 12 inches in diameter.
3. Transfer the dough to the prepared tart pan by gently draping it over a well-floured rolling pin, lifting it, and draping it across the tart shell. Prick the dough with a fork, and chill for 30 minutes.
4. Weight down the dough with aluminum foil and beans or pie weights. Bake 10 minutes, or until the sides of the tart shell are browned. Remove the shell from the oven, and set aside. Turn off the oven.
5. Prepare the Pastry Cream: In a small metal bowl, sprinkle the unflavored gelatin over the water and whisk to combine. Let stand 10 minutes to "soften." Bring a small pot of water to a simmer.
6. In a medium-size pot, bring the milk, vanilla bean, nutmeg, salt, and sugar to a boil, stirring to combine.
7. Meanwhile, in a medium-size bowl, whisk together the eggs, yolk, and cornstarch.

8. With a slotted spoon, remove the vanilla bean from the milk mixture. Temper the hot milk mixture into the egg mixture by adding ¼ cup at a time of the hot liquid to the egg mixture, whisking continuously. Once all the milk has been added, return the mixture to the pot and cook until the cream thickens and boils. Allow the cream to boil until the starch "cooks out," about 1 minute. Add the butter and whisk to combine. Transfer the pastry cream to a plastic bowl.

9. Place the bowl of softened gelatin over the pot of simmering water, and stir until the gelatin liquefies. Add the gelatin to the pastry cream and whisk thoroughly. Cover the cream with plastic wrap, and allow it to cool to room temperature.

10. Once the pastry cream has cooled, transfer ¼ cup of the pastry cream to the whipped cream and gently stir to combine. Fold the whipped cream mixture into the pastry cream, and stir just until combined.

11. Transfer the filling to the prepared tart shell, and set the tart in the refrigerator for 1 hour. Arrange the assorted berries decoratively atop the tart. Garnish with confectioners' sugar and a sprig of mint.

# Peach Tart

This tart was inspired by some of the most popular ingredients available in eighteenth-century Philadelphia. Puff pastry was regularly prepared in bakery shops as well as in many homes; American and European varieties of peaches grew abundantly in Philadelphia gardens and were available in the city's markets; and such prized imported goods as vanilla, nutmeg, cinnamon, and raisins were sold in shops around town. This tart comes together quickly and relies on perfectly ripe peaches, which are only available during the summer months.

Makes one 9-inch tart; serves 8

### Filling
3 peaches
¼ cup raisins
¼ cup sugar
3 tablespoons cake flour
1 teaspoon dried lavender
Freshly grated nutmeg, to taste
1 teaspoon ground cinnamon

1½ pounds Puff Pastry (see page 188)
1 cup Peach Preserves (see page 243), or use store-bought version
2 large eggs, beaten with 2 tablespoons water, for egg wash
1 cup light brown sugar

1.  Grease an 11 x 17-inch baking pan with butter, and coat lightly with flour.
2.  Prepare the Filling: Slice the peaches in half and remove the pits. Cut each half in fourths. Place the peaches and raisins in a medium-size bowl and toss to combine.
3.  In a separate small bowl, stir together the sugar, flour, lavender, nutmeg, and cinnamon. Stir these dry ingredients into the fruit mixture.
4.  Lightly flour your work surface. Roll the Puff Pastry into a rough ½-inch-thick, 14-inch-diameter circle. Transfer the dough to the prepared baking pan (it's okay if it overlaps the pan since you will be folding it in) by gently draping it over a well-floured rolling pin, lifting it, and laying it across the prepared pie pan.
5.  Spread the preserves evenly across the pastry, leaving a 2-inch border uncovered. Place the filling in the center of the dough in a concise mound. Leave a 4-inch border all around.
6.  Encase the fruit with the dough, leaving a 3-inch-diameter pocket open at the top. Crimp the dough in a rustic fashion. Brush the dough with the egg wash, and refrigerate for 1 hour. Meanwhile, preheat the oven to 425°F.
7.  Brush the dough once again with the egg wash and dust with the brown sugar. Bake for 15 to 20 minutes, or until golden and the filling bubbles. Cool for at least 45 minutes on the baking pan before serving.

# Linzertorte

This simply prepared tart based on nuts and raspberry preserves or jam is a traditional dish of Linz, Austria. Almonds are most often used in Austrian linzertorte. This version, however, incorporates hazelnuts, which were not only imported into eighteenth-century Philadelphia but also cultivated there.

*Makes one 9-inch tart; serves 8*

**Tart Shell**

(4 sticks) unsalted butter, softened
1½ cups granulated sugar
2 large eggs
1 teaspoon vanilla extract
4 cups sifted cake flour
2½ cups sliced almonds, toasted (see Chef's Note, page 38) and finely ground
1 teaspoon ground cinnamon

¾ cup seedless red raspberry jam
¼ cup confectioners' sugar
Good-quality chocolate ice cream, for serving (optional)

1. Preheat the oven to 325°F. Grease a 9 x 13/8-inch tart pan with a removable bottom with butter.
2. Prepare the Tart Shell: In the bowl of an electric mixer fitted with the paddle attachment on medium-high speed, beat the butter and sugar until light and fluffy. Add the egg and vanilla extract, and beat well.
3. In a separate large bowl, combine the flour, ground almonds, and cinnamon. Add the flour mixture to the egg mixture, and beat just until a soft dough forms. Wrap in plastic wrap, and chill in the refrigerator for 30 minutes.
4. Roll 1½ to 2 cups of the dough mixture into a circle 11 inches in diameter. Ease the pastry into the pan, being careful not to stretch the pastry. Gently press the pastry into the fluted side of the tart pan and trim the edges.
5. Spread the jam evenly over the bottom of the pastry.
6. Roll the remaining dough out to ¼ inch thick, into a rectangle measuring approximate 10 x 10 inches. Cut the rectangle into ten 1-inch-wide strips.
7. Weave the strips diagonally over the jam filling to create a lattice. Press the ends of the strips into the rim of the bottom crust, trimming the ends as necessary.
8. Bake the tart for 35 to 40 minutes, or until the crust is golden brown.
9. Allow the tart to cool completely; then sift confectioners' sugar over the top. Serve alone or with chocolate ice cream, if desired.

*For recipes requiring a prebaked Linzertorte tart shell, preheat the oven to 350°F. Line the prepared tart shell with aluminum foil and fill with beans or use pie weights. Bake for 8 to 10 minutes, or until golden brown.*

# Lemon Curd Tart

Recipes for lemon tarts and lemon pudding, intended as a filling for pie dough or puff pastry, were widely published. Although citrus fruits were expensive in late-eighteenth-century Philadelphia, it is clear that the public had a great fondness for them and that cookbook authors catered to their taste. Most recipes of the time called for including not only lemon juice but lemon zest as well, thus taking full advantage of this exotic ingredient.

**Makes eight 3-inch tartlets; serves 8**

### Lemon Curd (makes 4 cups)
15 large egg yolks
2 cups freshly squeezed lemon juice (about 8 large lemons), strained
1¼ cups granulated sugar
1 cup heavy cream

### Lemon Dough
2⅔ cups all-purpose flour
¼ cup granulated sugar
¼ teaspoon salt
7 ounces (1¾ sticks) unsalted butter, cold
¼ cup freshly squeezed lemon juice (about 1 large lemon), strained
2 large egg yolks

Chantilly Cream (see page 120), for garnish (optional)

1. Prepare the Lemon Curd: In a heavy-bottomed large saucepan (to prevent scorching), combine the egg yolks, lemon juice, sugar, and cream. Cook over medium heat, whisking continuously so that the mixture does not stick to the bottom. When the mixture comes to a gentle boil, reduce the heat and stir for 1 minute more. Remove from the heat.

2. Pour the mixture into an ovenproof bowl and let cool. Cover the surface with plastic wrap to prevent a "skin" from forming on top. Chill in the refrigerator overnight before using.

3. Prepare the Lemon Dough: Place the steel blade in the bowl of a food processor. Add the flour, sugar, and salt. Cover and process briefly to combine. Add the cold butter, and process with on/off pulses until the mixture is crumbly.

4. With the processor running, quickly add the lemon juice and yolks through the feed tube. Stop the processor when all of the lemon juice and egg yolks have been incorporated. Scrape down the sides.

5. Process with two on/off pulses (all of the mixture may not be moistened). Remove the dough from the bowl. Form the dough into a disc shape, wrap in plastic wrap, and chill in the refrigerator for at least 1 hour before using.

6. Meanwhile, preheat the oven to 400°F. Set aside eight 3-inch tartlet pans.

7. Roll out the dough on a lightly floured surface until it is ⅛ inch thick. Cut the dough into squares larger than the tartlet pans. Gently place the squares of dough loosely into the pans and trim the excess dough to ½ inch beyond the edges of the pans. Prick the dough with a fork on the bottoms of the pans several times. Fold the extra dough under and crimp the edges.

8. Line each tartlet shell with aluminum foil. Fill with dried beans or pie weights. Bake for 15 minutes. Remove from the oven and let cool.

9. When ready to serve, fill the baked and cooled tartlet shells with the Lemon Curd mixture. Garnish with Chantilly Cream, if desired.

Thomas Jefferson's collection of recipes included three recipes for "Lemon Pudding" (entitled No. 1, No. 2, and No. 3), each of which was to be baked in a pan lined with pastry. The second recipe was, in fact, attributed to Philadelphia and appears to have been the most tart of the three:

> Cream 1 cup of butter with 1 cup of sugar. Beat the yolks of 6 eggs until light. Add the juice and grated rind of 2 lemons. Combine the mixtures and beat together until very light, add a pinch of salt. Pour into a baking dish lined with puff paste and bake three-quarters of an hour in a moderate oven.

> If the butter and sugar are melted together and the eggs added while warm, it will make a transparent pudding" (Kimball 92).

# Custards, Puddings & Creams

The many custards and puddings that were, for centuries, considered staples in Europe remained so as colonists continued Old World culinary traditions in America. Even in the eighteenth century, these were fairly simply prepared, frugal dishes, consisting primarily of milk, sugar, and eggs. They were not always so modest, however; period recipes commonly called for such costly ingredients as raisins, lemon or orange juice, almonds, and a variety of spices. Like other eighteenth-century desserts, the simplicity or elaborateness of these dishes often reflected the wealth of the household that produced them.

Eighteenth-century custards and puddings were similar to contemporary versions, although some of the ingredients and cooking methods have changed over time. Vanilla, so commonly used now to flavor custards and puddings, rarely appears in period recipes, perhaps due to its high cost. The absence of vanilla was countered by the frequency with which cooked fruit and vegetables flavored these dishes. Apples, pears, plums, carrots, and pumpkin were common additions to basic custards and puddings. In addition, nearly all eighteenth-century recipes called for eggs. Custards, by definition, always include them, but today's puddings are usually thickened with flour or cornstarch. Some custard and pudding recipes, however, called for both flour and eggs. One notable exception to this rule appears in recipes for Indian pudding, which were based on neither flour nor eggs but, rather, American cornmeal. As testament to the incorporation of American foodstuffs into traditionally European custards and puddings, Hannah Glasse, in her book *The Art of Cookery Made Plain and Easy*, listed two recipes for "Indian Pudding" and one for cornmeal "Mush" in a chapter entitled "Several New Receipts Adapted to the American Mode of Cooking" (137). In the eighteenth century, it was also common to bake custards and puddings with bread or pieces of cake or in pastry-lined pans. This is less common today, save for today's bread puddings, which remain virtually unchanged from their eighteenth-century predecessors.

Cooking methods have altered slightly as well. Today's custards are often thickened on the stove before baking, while in the eighteenth century this step was omitted, probably to save time. Similarly, puddings, now cooked almost exclusively on the stove, were commonly baked or boiled in cloths.

The following recipes mirror the diverse selections in period cookbooks, designed to suit a variety of households and pocketbooks.

Eighteenth-century custards and puddings were so similar that Hannah Glasse's "Rules to be observed in making Puddings &c.," which appeared in her book The Art of Cookery Made Plain and Easy, served as helpful instructions for both:

"In boiled puddings, take great care the bag or cloth be very clean, not soapy, but dipped in hot water, and well floured. If a bread-pudding, tie it loose; if a batter-pudding, tie it close; and be sure the water boils when you put the pudding in; and you should move the puddings in the pot now and then, for fear they stick. When you make a batter-pudding, first mix the flour well with a little milk, then put in the ingredients by degrees, and it will be smooth and not have lumps; but for a plain batter-pudding, the best way is to strain it through a coarse hair sieve, that it may neither have lumps, nor the treadles of the eggs: and for all other puddings, strain the eggs when they are beat. If you boil them in wooden bowls, or china-dishes, butter the inside before you put in your batter; and for all baked puddings, butter the pan or dish before the pudding is put in" (112).

# Strawberry Pudding

This elegant pudding highlights not only fresh strawberries, which many Philadelphians grew in their city and country gardens, but also lemons, which were greatly prized and costly during the period. The lemon curd, or "pudding" component of this dish, is a cross between a traditional curd and a French *sabayon*—a sauce of egg yolks, sugar, and wine (usually Marsala) whisked together until thickened. Given Philadelphians' admiration of most things French, they surely would have welcomed this pudding on their stylish dining tables.

**Makes one 2-quart casserole dish; serves 8 to 10**

**Lemon Sugar**
1 lemon
¼ cup granulated sugar

1 recipe Ladyfingers (see page 114), or use store-bought
3 pints fresh strawberries, stems hulled and cut in half
1 cup slivered almonds, toasted (see Chef's Note, page 38)

**Lemon Curd**
1 vanilla bean
5 large eggs
Pinch of salt
½ cup granulated sugar
4 lemons, zest grated and juiced
¼ cup cognac
¼ pound (1 stick) butter, melted and cooled

1. Preheat the broiler in the oven.
2. Prepare the Lemon Sugar: Grate the lemon zest over the sugar in a small bowl. Mix the zest in with your fingertips. Set aside.
3. Line the base of a shallow 2-quart baking dish with Ladyfingers. Arrange the strawberries and almonds atop the ladyfingers.
4. Prepare the Lemon Curd: Split the vanilla bean open lengthwise and scrape out the seeds with the back of a knife. Reserve.
5. Bring a medium-size saucepan of water to a simmer. In a metal medium-size bowl, add the eggs, salt, and sugar; whisk to combine. Set the bowl over the simmering water to create a double boiler, and whisk vigorously until frothy, about 30 seconds.
6. Add the vanilla seeds, pod, zest, and lemon juice to the bowl and whisk to combine. Add the cognac and continue to whisk the mixture until it is light, frothy, and tripled in volume, about 7 minutes. Add the melted butter in a thin steady stream, whisking all the while.
7. Pour the curd mixture over the strawberries and almonds. Dust the top with the Lemon Sugar.
8. Place the dish under the broiler and cook until the sauce caramelizes, about 5 minutes. Serve warm.

# Vanilla Bean Blanc Mange

*Blanc mange*, also spelled *blancmange* and *blanc manger*, dates at least to fourteenth-century Europe. Translated as "white food," this term refers to the colorless, or white, foods that became stylish in France and eventually in England as well. Early cookery books and manuscripts reveal that *blanc mange* was prepared in many varieties, both savory and sweet, relying on such colorless ingredients as poultry, fish, rice, cream, almonds, and eggs. Eighteenth-century English cookbook authors commonly offered a number of *blanc mange* recipes, all of which were essentially jellies prepared with "isinglass" (a form of gelatin), ground almonds, sugar, and very little cream. One popular variation, breaking with the "white" tradition, in fact called for spinach juice, which resulted in a bright green jelly. It wasn't until the nineteenth century that *blanc mange* became an exclusively sweet and creamy dish as it is most commonly known today.

Makes one 1-quart Bavarian mold; serves 10 to 12

> 2½ cups heavy cream
> 1½ cups whole milk
> 2 vanilla beans
> 1½ tablespoons unflavored gelatin
> 5 tablespoons dark rum
> ½ cup granulated sugar
> 3 tablespoons honey

1. In a medium-size saucepan, add the heavy cream, milk, and vanilla beans; stir to combine. Heat until the cream and milk just start to bubble around the sides of the pan, remove from the heat, and let steep 20 minutes.

2. Prepare an ice bath in a large stainless steel bowl. Bring a small saucepan of water to a simmer. In a small metal bowl, sprinkle the unflavored gelatin over the rum, and whisk to combine. Let the gelatin "soften" for 10 minutes.

3. Whisk the sugar and honey into the cream, and cook the mixture over low heat until the sugar has dissolved—do not boil.

4. Set the bowl of softened gelatin over the pan of simmering water, stirring constantly until it liquefies. Whisk the gelatin into the cream.

5. Pour the custard into a heatproof bowl, and set the bowl in an ice bath. Whisk the mixture slowly until cool. Pour it into a mold. Chill in the refrigerator overnight before serving.

Although *blanc mange* is found in the jellies and/or syllabubs chapters of most eighteenth-century cookbooks, it is telling that Elizabeth Raffald chose to list the dish in the "Table Decorations" chapter of The Experienced English Housekeeper. Like author John Farley (The London Art of Cookery), she included three variations of blanc mange: "Blancmange of Isinglass," "Green Blancmange of Isinglass," and "Clear Blancmange," which called only for "three spoonfuls of very good cream" (95–96). Each recipe was to be set in decorative molds, and Raffald suggested that the first two receive decorative garnishes: "almonds blanched and cut lengthways [and] . . . green leaves or flowers" and "red and white flowers," respectively (95). Like many eighteenth-century desserts, *blanc mange* was meant not only to celebrate the exotic flavor of almonds but to decorate the table as well.

# Indian Pudding

Based on traditional English puddings, Indian pudding was uniquely American, as it was prepared with cornmeal and often molasses. By the third quarter of the eighteenth century, American cookery books included recipes for this dish, as did English cookbooks published in America. Hannah Glasse's American edition of *The Art of Cookery Made Plain and Easy*, for example, added two "Indian Pudding" recipes to the section she referred to as "Several New Receipts Adapted To The American Mode of Cooking" (137). Similarly, Amelia Simmons published three versions of "A Tasty Indian Pudding" in *American Cookery* (31).

Inexpensive, sweet, and filling, Indian pudding quickly became a favorite of many Americans, including the esteemed George Washington and Thomas Jefferson.

**Makes one 2-quart casserole dish; serves 10 to 12**

2 cups whole milk
Two 8-ounce cans creamed corn
¾ cup Grandma's dark molasses
¾ cup coarse yellow cornmeal
2 teaspoons ground cinnamon
3 apples (Gala or Granny Smith)
4 tablespoons (½ stick) unsalted butter
¼ cup light brown sugar
1 tablespoon freshly squeezed lemon juice

1. Preheat the oven to 325°F. Butter a 2-quart casserole dish.
2. In a small saucepan, combine the milk and creamed corn and bring to a boil. Reduce the heat to low and, using a wooden spoon, stir in the molasses, followed by the cornmeal and cinnamon. Continue to cook the mixture, stirring constantly, until the mixture is thick, about 10 minutes. Set aside.
3. Peel, core, and cut the apples into ½-inch slices.
4. In a large skillet over medium heat, melt the butter; then stir in the sugar using a wooden spoon. Add the lemon juice and cook, stirring occasionally, until the sugar melts, about 1 minute. Stir in the apples and cook until they begin to soften, about 3 minutes more.
5. Pour the thickened pudding into the casserole dish, top with the sautéed apples, and bake for 15 minutes, or until set. Serve hot.

# Coconut Pudding

It is difficult to say just how prevalent coconuts were in eighteenth-century Philadelphia, but as an exotic, imported fruit, they would seem to have been not only desirable but expensive as well. Period recipes reveal that coconut was used in cookies and small cakes, so it seems likely that it could have flavored puddings as well. Coconut adds much flavor and richness to this otherwise simply prepared dessert.

**Makes one 2-quart casserole dish; serves 10 to 12**

1 coconut
1 recipe Ladyfingers (see page 114), or use store-bought
1 cup dark rum
2 cups raisins
½ cup chopped Candied Ginger (see page 235)

**Custard**
4 cups canned coconut milk (approximately 2½ cans)
2 cinnamon sticks
1 tablespoon allspice berries
1 tablespoon chopped fresh ginger
1½ cups granulated sugar
6 large eggs
2 large egg yolks

½ cup granulated sugar
1 tablespoon ground cinnamon, plus extra for dusting
4 tablespoons (½ stick) unsalted butter, melted
Confectioners' sugar
Molasses Whipped Cream (see page 121), for serving (optional)

1. Preheat the oven to 350°F. Grease a 2-quart casserole dish with butter, and lightly dust with flour.
2. Using a hammer and a Phillips head screwdriver, puncture 3 holes in the "eyes" located at the base of the coconut; strain the coconut juice. Wrap the coconut in a kitchen towel and smack it with the hammer. Use the screwdriver to carefully remove the flesh from the shell, keeping the flesh in as large of chunks as possible. Take a vegetable peeler and shave long, thin strips of coconut. You will need about 3 cups of coconut strips. Spread the coconut strips on a baking pan, and toast in the oven until golden brown, 8 to 10 minutes. Set the coconut aside to cool, and reduce the oven temperature to 300°F.
3. Arrange one layer of Ladyfingers so that they cover the bottom of the prepared casserole dish. Soak them well with rum. Sprinkle a handful of raisins, toasted coconut, and some candied ginger atop the Ladyfingers. Add another layer of Ladyfingers, and repeat the process of soaking and covering with raisins, coconut, and candied ginger until the dish is half full. Set aside while you prepare the Custard.
4. Prepare the Custard: In a medium-size saucepan, combine the coconut milk, cinnamon sticks, allspice berries, and ginger. Bring to a boil; then remove from the heat and let steep for 30 minutes.
5. Meanwhile, in a medium-size bowl, whisk together the sugar, eggs, and yolks. Strain the coconut milk mixture, return it to the saucepan, and reheat it.

6. Temper the coconut milk into the egg mixture by adding ¼ cup at a time of the hot liquid into the eggs, whisking all the while.

7. When all of the coconut milk mixture has been added to the eggs, pour the hot Custard over the Ladyfingers and let stand for 30 minutes.

8. In a small bowl, stir together the ½ cup granulated sugar and the ground cinnamon. Sprinkle the sugar topping over the dish, top with the toasted coconut, and cover the dish with aluminum foil.

9. Place the casserole dish on a large baking pan and place the tray in the oven. Fill the tray with hot water so that it comes halfway up the sides of the dish, and bake for 25 minutes. Remove the foil from the dish and bake 10 minutes more, or until the pudding is set.

10. Brush the melted butter on the pudding while it is still hot, and set aside.

11. Dust the top of the pudding with plenty of confectioners' sugar and a little cinnamon. Serve hot with Molasses Whipped Cream, if desired.

Under the heading "Puddings," Thomas Jefferson's collection of recipes included three paragraphs of basic cooking instructions and suggestions for preparing numerous varieties of the sweet dish. As was typical in the period, cake, pastry, bread, biscuits, and so forth were mentioned as suitable bases for a successful pudding. Added to this list, however, was this suggestion: "For a change with any of the above you may intermix with either fresh or dried fruits, or preserves, even plums, grated cocoanut [sic], etc." (Kimball 102). The instructions went on to give basic amounts of ingredients and a method of serving the pudding, which was certainly related to the stylish crème caramel:

When the mould is full of any of the above put into a bowl ¼ teaspoon of either ginger, cinnamon, or mixed spices, or lemon or orange peel. Beat 4 eggs. Add 4 tablespoonfuls of sugar, a pinch of salt and 3 cups of milk. Fill the pudding dish nearly to the rim. It can be either baked, boiled, or set in a saucepan ⅓ full of water, with the lid over, and let simmer for an hour, or until set. Run a knife around the edge of the dish and turn out the pudding. Pour over melted butter mixed with some sugar and the juice of a lemon, or serve with brandy sauce (102).

# Plum Pudding

Plum pudding, or Christmas pudding, as it came eventually to be known, appeared in many variations in eighteenth-century cookery books. Some recipes called for plums, while others called for raisins, currants, and candied lemon and orange peels. Some were boiled and others were baked. Some required breadcrumbs; others, pieces of bread. Sometimes the puddings were heavily spiced and flavored with liqueur, and other times only a few such ingredients were added.

What is common to most recipes, however, is the care and time that was required to produce such a rich dessert. These puddings not only demanded a lot of preparation, but they baked or boiled for hours at a time as well. In addition, until the nineteenth century, suet, rather than butter, was the fat of choice. Readily available and inexpensive, it not only added flavor but also ensured that the pudding would remain moist through hours of cooking.

Whether baked or boiled, most plum puddings were cooked in molds—some quite decorative. Like other desserts of the period, placed among a multitude of sweet and savory dishes, they were meant to add to the beauty and often luxuriousness of the dining table.

**Makes one 2-quart casserole dish; serves 12**

1 cup chopped dried pineapple
1 cup dark raisins
½ cup golden raisins
½ cup currants
½ cup dried cherries
½ cup freshly grated unsweetened coconut, toasted (see Chef's Note, page 87)
¼ cup almonds, toasted (see Chef's Note, page 38)
½ cup chopped Candied Fruit (orange, lemon, etc.; see pages 234, 236)
¼ cup finely chopped Candied Ginger (see page 235)
1 lemon, zest grated
1 lime, zest grated
1½ cups Appleton gold rum
2 cups water
2 cups chopped suet (¼-inch pieces, available at local butcher's market), or substitute lard
2 cups all-purpose flour
4 cups finely crumbled day-old Sally Lunn Bread (see page 177), or substitute any egg bread
1½ teaspoons salt
1 teaspoon ground nutmeg
1 tablespoon ground allspice
1 tablespoon ground cinnamon
Pinch of ground cloves
6 large eggs
1 cup light brown sugar
½ cup plus 2 tablespoons dark beer

1. In a large bowl, toss together the dried pineapple, dark raisins, golden raisins, currants, dried cherries, coconut, almonds, Candied Fruit, Candied Ginger, and citrus zests. Add 1 cup of the rum and the water, stir to mix, and soak overnight.

2. On a large work surface, cut the suet into the flour, running the mixture through your fingertips until a coarse meal is formed. In a large bowl, combine the flour-suet mixture with the finely crumbled Sally Lunn Bread, salt, nutmeg, allspice, cinnamon, and cloves. Stir to mix well. Add the presoaked dried fruit mixture, including any liquid in the bowl, and toss until thoroughly combined.

3. In another medium-size bowl, whisk together the eggs, brown sugar, the remaining ½ cup of rum, and the beer. Add the liquid ingredients to the dry, and mix until a smooth dough is formed. If the mixture seems too dry, add more ale until the dough is smooth.

4. Grease a 2-quart casserole dish or decorative mold with plenty of butter, and lightly dust it with flour.

5. Place the batter in the prepared casserole dish or mold, packing it well. Cover it with foil. Place the dish in a large saucepan filled with enough water to come halfway up the sides of the dish. Cover the entire pan with foil, and bring the water in the pan to a simmer. Keep the water at a simmer, and steam the pudding for 4 hours, checking the water level regularly and refilling as necessary. The pudding is done when firm and an toothpick inserted near the center comes out clean.

6. Allow the pudding to cool in the mold at room temperature for about 1 hour. Unmold and serve.

Plum puddings could be simple or elaborate depending on one's taste and the ingredients one could afford. The following recipes from American Cookery and Thomas Jefferson's collection of recipes reveal these contrasts:

### Plumb Pudding, boiled.

Three pints flour, a little salt, six eggs, one pound plumbs, half pound beef suet, half pound sugar, one pint milk; mix the whole together; put it into a strong cloth floured, boil three hours; serve with sweet sauce (Simmons 36–37).

### Wyeth's English Plum Pudding

Two pounds of best seedless raisins, 1 pound currants, 1 pound sultana raisins, 1 quart grated bread crumbs, 1 quart beef suet chopped fine, ½ pound citron cut fine, 2 ounces candied orange peel, 2 ounces candied lemon peel cut fine, 1 grated nutmeg, 1 teaspoonful of ginger, 1 of salt. Mix all well together. Beat 12 eggs and stir into the first mixture. Add 1 cup of brandy. If not moist enough add as much milk as will make it cling together. Put into tin forms and boil four or five hours. The water must be boiling when the pudding is put in. Plunge into cold water for a few minutes before turning out the pudding (Kimball 90).

# Rice Pudding

Although rice was an important southern crop, its economic significance spread north, as did its popularity as a versatile culinary staple. South Carolina became the center of New World rice production in the early eighteenth century; by 1726, the state was exporting 4,500 metric tons annually (Mariani 272). This successful campaign halted briefly during the Revolution, when the British, having taken Charleston, sent the entirety of that year's rice crop back to England (272). Thomas Jefferson clandestinely brought a variety of Italian rice back to the Carolinas in 1787, and, by the turn of the century, southern rice cultivation was again thriving (272–273).

*Makes one 2-quart baking dish; serves 6*

> 2 cups water
> ¾ cup uncooked long-grain white rice
> 2½ cups whole milk
> ½ cup granulated sugar
> 3 large eggs
> 1½ tablespoons unsalted butter, softened
> 2 teaspoons vanilla extract
> 1½ teaspoons ground cinnamon

1. Preheat the oven to 325°F.
2. In a 2-quart saucepan, bring the water to a boil, and add the rice. Simmer, covered, until the liquid is reduced by two thirds and the rice is al dente, about 15 minutes. Let stand, covered, for 5 minutes, and drain, if necessary.
3. In a separate saucepan, bring the milk to a boil. Stir in the rice and cooking water, and cook for 10 minutes more, or until the grains are soft.
4. In a large bowl, whisk together the sugar, eggs, butter, vanilla extract, and cinnamon. Gradually stir the hot rice mixture into the egg mixture.
5. Transfer to a 2-quart ovenproof glass or ceramic dish. Place the dish into a larger high-sided roasting pan, and carefully pour boiling water into the roasting pan around the dish to a depth of 1½ inches. Bake, covered, for 20 to 30 minutes, or until a knife inserted near the center comes out clean.
6. Sprinkle additional cinnamon on top as garnish. Serve hot, or cool to room temperature, according to personal preference.

Eighteenth-century cookbooks often included recipes for rice pudding. Amelia Simmons listed six versions of the dish, plus a set of special additional instructions pertaining to its preparation, in her <u>American Cookery</u>. Thomas Jefferson also obtained a rice pudding recipe for his collection, appropriately entitled "South Carolina Rice Pudding." In keeping with Jefferson's culinary panache, his version called not only for eggs but also for the whites and yolks to be beaten separately in order to create a pudding with greater lightness and volume:

> Beat the yolks of 5 eggs, add gradually 4 tablespoonfuls of sugar, and 1 pint of milk. Beat the whites of the eggs until stiff and mix with the yolks. Stir 2 tablespoonfuls of melted butter into ¾ cup of rice. Put into a baking dish and add about half the egg, a pinch of salt and milk mixture. Stir well. Pour the rest of the first mixture over it, add a piece of stick cinnamon, and bake in a moderate oven until set (Kimball 85).

# Pear Flan

Flan is a Spanish custard that can be either savory or sweet. The latter variety is closely related to the French crème caramel: a rich egg custard baked in caramel-coated molds and turned out onto a plate for presentation. This version of pear flan was inspired not only by these European dishes but also by the many varieties of fruit-based puddings prepared in eighteenth-century America.

**Makes eight 3 x ½-inch (½-cup) ramekins or 6-ounce custard cups; serves 8**

> 2 cups granulated sugar
> 2 cups whole milk
> 2 cups pear purée (or substitute frozen pears, thawed and puréed)
> 8 large eggs
> 4 large egg yolks

1. Preheat the oven to 325°F. Lightly grease eight 3 x ½-inch ramekins or 6-ounce custard cups with butter.
2. To caramelize the sugar, in a large saucepan, heat 1 cup of the sugar over medium heat, until it becomes syrupy and turns golden brown, 2 to 3 minutes, watching closely so it doesn't burn and shaking the pan occasionally to heat the sugar evenly. *Do not stir.* Once the sugar starts to melt, reduce the heat to low and cook 5 minutes more, until all of the sugar is melted and golden, stirring as needed with a wooden spoon.
3. Immediately remove the sauté pan from the heat, and pour 1 to 2 tablespoons of the caramelized sugar into the bottom of each ramekin or custard cup, being careful not to burn your skin with the caramelized sugar. Tilt each ramekin to coat the bottom evenly. Let stand 10 minutes.
4. Place the ramekins or custard cups in a large, high-sided roasting pan. Set aside.
5. To make the custard, in a medium saucepan, whisk together the milk and the remaining 1 cup of sugar, and bring to a boil. Remove from the heat and mix in the pear purée, eggs, and egg yolks.
6. Pour the custard into the prepared ramekins or custard cups. Add boiling water to the roasting pan around the ramekins or custard cups to a depth of ¼ inch.
7. Bake for 30 to 40 minutes, or until set or a knife inserted near the center comes out clean. Let the flan cool to room temperature; then cover with plastic wrap, and chill in the refrigerator for at least 4 hours, or overnight.
8. To serve, place a 7-inch plate over the top of each ramekin. Invert the plate and ramekin, gently tap the bottom of the ramekin, and then lift.

Chef's Note

*Cooking in a Water Bath—A water bath, or* bain marie, *is used to cook custard-like desserts. This technique allows delicate egg-based dishes to cook without breaking or curdling.*

# Bread Pudding

In the eighteenth century, sweet puddings of many varieties commonly called for using pieces of bread, biscuits, or cake as an enriching base for other ingredients, such as dried or fresh fruit or preserves. Bread pudding simply focused on the bread (in crumbs or pieces) and custard as primary ingredients, with the typical addition of raisins and spices.

Bread was a staple, baked at home as well as in the many bakeries operating in eighteenth-century Philadelphia, and period cookbooks suggest that bread pudding was frequently enjoyed as well. Hannah Glasse's *The Art of Cookery Made Plain and Easy* gave three recipes for the dish, as did Thomas Jefferson's collection of recipes, which also included two sweet butter sauces to accompany them (Glasse 106–108; Kimball 87–88).

**Makes one 10 x 3-inch round baking dish or 2-quart soufflé dish; serves 12**

1 cup raisins
½ cup Appleton gold rum
20 ounces white bread, crust trimmed and cut into 1-inch cubes (about 10 cups)
4 cups whole milk
15 large eggs
1½ cups granulated sugar
1 teaspoon ground cinnamon
½ teaspoon ground nutmeg
*Crème Anglaise* (see page 122), flavored with rum, for serving (optional)

1. In a small bowl, combine the raisins and rum, and soak for at least 2 hours.
2. Preheat oven to 350°F. Lightly grease a 10 x 3-inch round baking dish or 2-quart soufflé dish with butter.
3. Add the bread cubes to the prepared dish, and sprinkle the raisin-rum mixture on top.
4. In a large bowl, combine the milk, eggs, sugar, cinnamon, and nutmeg. Stir the egg mixture into the bread-raisin mixture. Cover with foil.
5. Place the baking dish in a larger high-sided roasting pan. Add boiling water into the roasting pan around the baking dish to a depth of 2 inches, and set aside for 30 minutes.
6. Bake for 45 minutes. Remove the foil. Continue baking, uncovered, for 5 minutes, or until the top is golden and the mixture is slightly puffed or until a knife inserted near the center comes out clean.
7. Cool slightly before serving. Serve with the *Crème Anglaise* flavored with rum to taste, if desired.

# Plum Fool Parfait

"Fool" refers to a variety of dishes in which cream or custard is combined with cooked fruit or fruit juice. In the eighteenth century, the terms "fool" and "cream" were used interchangeably. Like this version, these creamy desserts required a minimum of ingredients and cooking time and were served simply but beautifully in individual glasses or in one large bowl, topped with whipped cream.

Makes 6 parfaits

> 9 Stanley or Rosa plums, pitted and thinly sliced
> ½ cup red currant jelly
> ⅓ cup packed light brown sugar
> 2 teaspoons grated orange zest
> 1 stick cinnamon
> 1½ cups heavy whipping cream
> ½ teaspoon vanilla extract
> 6 fresh mint sprigs, for garnish

1. In a 2-quart saucepan, cook the plums, jelly, brown sugar, orange zest, and cinnamon stick over medium heat for 20 to 30 minutes, or until the plums are tender. Remove the saucepan from the heat and let the mixture cool to room temperature. Remove and discard the cinnamon stick.
2. In the chilled bowl of an electric mixer with the chilled whip attachment on high speed, beat the cream until soft peaks form. Add the vanilla extract, and whip for a few seconds more.
3. In a parfait glass, alternately layer the plum mixture and the whipped cream. Chill for 2 hours in the refrigerator before serving.
4. To serve, top each parfait with a fresh mint sprig for garnish.

# Orange Curd Cake

This recipe was inspired by the orange puddings, custards, and fools that were so popular in eighteenth-century colonial America. The addition of candied orange peel and almonds complements the smooth texture and refreshing citrus flavor of this light cake.

**Makes six 8-ounce ramekins; serves 6**

¼ cup almonds, toasted (see Chef's Note, page 38)
¾ cup granulated sugar
¼ cup all-purpose flour
Pinch of salt
2 tablespoons finely chopped Candied Orange Peel (see page 234)
3 large egg yolks
1 orange, zest grated
¼ cup citrus juice (half freshly squeezed lemon juice and half orange juice)
¼ cup crème fraîche, or substitute sour cream or plain, unsweetened yogurt
3 tablespoons plus 2 teaspoons melted butter
¼ cup sour cream
3 large egg whites

1. Preheat the oven to 325° F. Grease six 8-ounce ramekins with butter, and lightly dust with flour.
2. In a food processor fitted with the blade attachment, grind together the almonds, sugar, flour, salt, and orange peel.
3. In a medium-size bowl, whisk together the yolks, orange zest, citrus juice, crème fraîche, butter, and sour cream. Whisk in the mixture from the food processor.
4. In the clean bowl of an electric mixer fitted with the whip attachment on high speed, whip the egg whites to stiff peaks.
5. Add ½ cup of the base mixture to the egg whites, and gently fold together so as to not deflate them. Add the remaining base and gently fold together.
6. Divide the batter among the ramekins, filling each half full. Cover each ramekin with foil. Set the ramekins in a 2-inch-deep baking dish. Place the dish in the oven and fill it with hot water to come halfway up the sides of the ramekins.
7. Bake for 20 minutes, or until a toothpick inserted in the centers comes out clean. Serve hot.

Among the prominent Americans who enjoyed oranges were George and Martha Washington. From the 1760s until the 1790s, the general regularly ordered them in barrels of twelve or twenty-four from the West Indies, where he seems to have first been introduced to them. The couple often received the fruit as gifts as well, and by the late 1790s, oranges were growing at Mount Vernon ("Foods used in the Christmas Table Setting," Mount Vernon memo 1989).

# Crème Caramel

Crème caramel is a simple dessert made elegant by cooking a basic custard in caramel-coated molds. When served, the molds are inverted, permitting the custard to glisten with amber-colored caramel.

The fact that this dessert, like its related preparation flan, is widely available today belies its uniqueness in the eighteenth century. Although custard was commonly served, sugar not only remained expensive throughout the 1700s but also often required time-consuming refining before use. Philadelphia merchants, like those in other major cities, sold sugar in a variety of grades from coarse to fine, and it was priced according to purity.

In order to create a clear caramel like the one for this recipe, sugar would have been boiled with water, skimmed of the scum that accumulated on the surface, and passed through a sieve or flannel bag. This method appeared in most period cookbooks.

*Makes six 3 x ½-inch (½-cup) ramekins or 6-ounce custard cups; serves 6*

> 1½ cups granulated sugar
> 5 large eggs
> 2 cups light cream
> ½ cup heavy cream
> ½ teaspoon vanilla extract

1. Preheat the oven to 325°F.
2. To caramelize the sugar, in a large saucepan, heat 1 cup of the sugar over medium heat, until it becomes syrupy and turns golden brown, 2 to 3 minutes, watching closely so it doesn't burn and shaking the pan occasionally to heat the sugar evenly. *Do not stir.* Once the sugar starts to melt, reduce the heat to low and cook 5 minutes more, until all of the sugar is melted and golden, stirring as needed with a wooden spoon.
3. Immediately remove from the heat, and pour 1 to 2 tablespoons of the caramelized sugar into the bottom of each ramekin or custard cup, being careful not to burn your skin with the caramelized sugar. Tilt each ramekin to coat the bottom evenly. Let stand 10 minutes.
4. Place the ramekins or custard cups in a large, high-sided roasting pan. Set aside.
5. To make the custard, in a large bowl, whisk together the eggs and the remaining ½ cup of sugar.
6. In a small saucepan, bring the light cream, heavy cream, and vanilla extract to a boil. Slowly pour 1 cup of the hot cream mixture, whisking constantly, into the egg-sugar mixture. Whisk in the remaining hot cream and vanilla mixture. Strain the mixture through a fine sieve into an ovenproof bowl.
7. Pour the custard into the prepared ramekins or custard cups. Add boiling water into the roasting pan around the ramekins to a depth of ¼ inch.
8. Bake for 30 to 40 minutes, or until set or a knife inserted near the center of each comes out clean.
9. Remove the custards from the water bath. Cool on a wire rack. Cover with plastic wrap, and chill in the refrigerator for at least 1 hour before serving.
10. Before serving, remove the custards from the refrigerator and let stand at room temperature for 20 minutes. Run a paring knife around the edge of each custard to loosen. Turn each ramekin or custard cup over onto an individual dessert plate. The caramel will create a syrupy sauce. Serve immediately.

# Crème Brûlée

This elegant, creamy, French-titled dessert is really nothing more than basic custard (often called "English custard" or *crème anglaise*). Translated as "burnt cream," it is most often prepared by cooking cream or milk together with sugar and eggs until thickened, pouring the creamy mixture into molds, and setting them in a water bath (water-filled pan) to bake at a low temperature until just set. Once cooled, they are sprinkled with sugar and, using a torch or broiler, the sugar is cooked until caramelized. What continues to make this dessert so special is the delightful contrast between the luxurious cream and the crisp sugar layer.

**Makes six 8-ounce ramekins; serves 6**

>1 vanilla bean
>1½ quarts heavy cream
>1 cup sugar, plus additional for the topping
>10 large egg yolks
>1 large egg

1. Using a paring knife, slice the vanilla bean in half lengthwise. Using the back of your knife, scrape the seeds from the pod. Place the pod and seeds, along with the cream, in a medium-size saucepan. Bring to a boil.
2. Meanwhile, in a medium-size bowl, whisk together the sugar, egg yolks, and egg.
3. With a slotted spoon, remove the vanilla bean pod from the cream. Temper the hot cream mixture into the egg mixture by adding ¼ cup at a time, whisking all the while.
4. Chill in the refrigerator for at least 2 hours, or overnight.
5. Preheat the oven to 300°F.
6. Gently stir the cream mixture to disperse the vanilla seeds throughout. Do not whisk or stir too vigorously as this will incorporate air into the mixture.
7. Pour the batter into six 8-ounce ramekins. Place the ramekins in a large, high-sided roasting pan, and place the pan in the oven. Fill the roasting pan with hot water halfway up the sides of the ramekins.
8. Bake for 25 minutes, or until set. Turn the oven off, and allow the ramekins to cool in the oven for 30 minutes. Transfer to the refrigerator and chill for 1 hour.
9. Sprinkle ½ tablespoon sugar evenly across the top of each crème brulée . Caramelize the sugar with a blowtorch or under the broiler in the oven for 30 to 45 seconds. The sugar will melt and darken quickly, so keep a watchful eye. The caramelized sugar will harden just seconds after you remove the heat. Serve immediately.

Eighteenth-century cooks prepared custards in a variety of ways. Author John Farley offered many recipes in <u>The London Art of Cookery</u>, but his "Plain Custards" appear most similar to modern versions. He offered two methods, the first of which is nearly identical to City Tavern's recipe, although details regarding the baking are woefully absent. One can only assume he meant for them to be baked. The second method called for combining all of the ingredients without cooking them, pouring the mixture into molds, and then baking them in a water bath—a method that is still sometimes employed today. Read together, they offer an informative window into the tradition of eighteenth-century English custard preparation that continued to flourish in America:

> Set a quart of good cream over a slow fire, with a little cinnamon, and four ounces of sugar. When it has boiled, take it off the fire, beat the yolks of eight eggs, and put to them a spoonful of orange-flower water, to prevent the cream from cracking. Stir them in by degrees as your cream cools, put the pan over a very slow fire, stir it carefully one way till it be almost boiling, and then pour it into cups.

> Or you may make your custards in this manner: Take a quart of new milk, sweeten it to your taste, beat up well the yolks of eight eggs, and the whites of four. Stir them into the milk, and bake it in china basons [*sic*]. Or put them in a deep china dish, and pour boiling water round them, till the water be better than half way up their sides; but take care the water does not boil too fast, lest it should get into your cups, and spoil your custards (294).

# Charlotte Russe

This elegant French dessert of light Ladyfingers and rich Bavarian cream was surely inspired by eighteenth-century charlottes. These cakes were similar compositions of Naples biscuits (sponge cake) or pieces of bread that were spread with jam or cooked fruit and filled with sweetened, whipped egg whites or sweetened, whipped cream.

Unlike other fillings, Bavarian becomes firm as it chills due to the addition of gelatin. This charlotte is thus easy to slice and maintains its shape once plated.

*Makes one 9-inch cake; serves 10*

### Ladyfingers
1 lemon
3 tablespoons granulated sugar
1 vanilla bean
6 large egg yolks, at room temperature
1 teaspoon vanilla extract

3 large egg whites, at room temperature
½ cup plus 2 tablespoons granulated sugar
½ cup plus 2 tablespoons triple-sifted all-purpose flour
Confectioners' sugar

### Bavarian
Two ¼-ounce packets unflavored gelatin
3 tablespoons dark rum
2 cups whole milk
1 tablespoon vanilla extract
8 large egg yolks
½ cup sugar
2½ cups heavy whipping cream, whipped to medium peaks

1 cup Blueberry Preserves (see page 244)
2 pints fresh blueberries

1. Preheat the oven to 350°F. Line 2 baking pans with parchment paper. Butter and flour one 9-inch round cake pan. Fit a pastry bag with a #16 straight tip.
2. Prepare the Ladyfingers: In a small bowl, zest the lemon over the sugar.
3. Using a paring knife, slice the vanilla bean in half lengthwise. Scrape the seeds from the pod with the back of the knife, and stir the seeds into the sugar.
4. In the bowl of an electric mixer fitted with the whip attachment on high speed, whip the egg yolks, vanilla extract, and lemon-vanilla sugar until the mixture is light in color and ribbons form. Transfer the ingredients to a medium-size bowl and set aside.
5. Clean and dry the mixing bowl and whip attachment immaculately. In the electric mixer on medium speed, whip the egg whites until foam begins to form. Decrease the mixing speed to low and add the sugar, 2 tablespoons at a time, waiting until each addition incorporates before adding more. Once all the sugar has been added, increase the mixing speed to high and whip to medium peaks.

6. Transfer about 3 tablespoons of the whipped egg whites to the yolk mixture, and lightly stir to combine. Using a plastic spatula, fold the remaining whites into the lightened yolk mixture.

7. Fold the flour into the wet ingredients gently, so as not to deflate the batter.

8. Fill the 9-inch cake pan with some of the batter, to a depth of 1 inch. Bake until golden, about 7 minutes.

9. Transfer the remaining batter into the pastry bag fitted with the #16 straight tip. Pipe 3-inch-long, 1-inch-wide tubes onto the prepared baking pans. Pipe the Ladyfingers in clusters of 5. Lightly sift confectioners' sugar over the raw finger batter and let stand in the refrigerator for 5 minutes. Bake for 5 to 7 minutes, or until golden.

10. Prepare the Bavarian: Prepare an ice bath in a large stainless steel bowl. Bring a small pan of water to a simmer.

11. In a small metal bowl, sprinkle the unflavored gelatin over the rum and whisk to combine. Let the gelatin "soften" for 10 minutes.

12. In a medium-size saucepan, add the milk and vanilla extract; bring to a boil.

13. Meanwhile, in a medium-size bowl, whisk together the yolks and sugar. Temper the hot milk mixture into the yolk mixture by adding ¼ cup of the hot liquid at a time to the yolks, whisking all the while. Return the custard to the pan and cook, stirring constantly, over low heat until the mixture reaches a temperature of 185°F on a candy thermometer and is thick. Strain this mixture back into the medium-size bowl.

14. Dissolve the softened gelatin by setting the bowl over the pan of simmering water, stirring constantly until it liquefies. Whisk the gelatin into the custard.

15. Set the bowl of custard in the ice bath and whisk until the mixture is cool.

16. In a large bowl, transfer ½ cup of the cool custard into the whipped cream and fold to combine. Fold the remaining custard into the lightened whipped cream.

17. Final assembly: Spray and line a 10-inch springform pan with plastic wrap. Set the 9-inch ladyfinger round in the base of the pan. Arrange the Ladyfingers around the inside perimeter of the pan.

18. Fill the Ladyfinger-encased pan with the cool Bavarian, three fourths of the way full. Freeze for 1 hour.

19. Once the charlotte is frozen, carefully unmold it. Spread the Blueberry Preserves evenly atop the Bavarian. Top the charlotte with the fresh blueberries.

# Raspberry Charlotte Royale

This colorful dessert was inspired not only by the availability of raspberries in eighteenth-century Philadelphia but also by the elegant, molded desserts based on cream and cake that were stylish during the period. Philadelphians enjoyed raspberries fresh in the summer and preserved during the fall and winter months, when they would consume jam and whole berries cooked in sugar syrup.

The cake here also refers to the many sponge cake recipes found in eighteenth-century cookery books. This cake was a favorite of home cooks and confectioners alike, because it was, and remains, a versatile item whose subtle flavor married well with a variety of fruits and creams.

**Makes one 2-quart Bavarian mold; serves 10**

### Roulade
¾ cup all-purpose flour
¾ teaspoon baking powder
½ teaspoon salt
4 large egg yolks
½ cup granulated sugar
3 tablespoons corn syrup

½ cup framboise (raspberry-flavored liqueur)
1½ cups Raspberry Preserves (see page 244)

4 large egg whites
6 tablespoons granulated sugar

### Bavarian
Two ¼-ounce packets unflavored gelatin
3 tablespoons orange Triple Sec or Cointreau
1 tablespoon vanilla extract
½ cup granulated sugar
1 cup whole milk
3 large egg yolks
1¼ cups raspberry purée (or substitute frozen raspberries, thawed and puréed)
2½ cups heavy whipping cream, whipped to medium peaks

2 pints fresh raspberries

### Glaze
3 cups Apricot Stone Fruit Preserves (see page 243), or use store-bought kind
1 cup water

Fresh mint sprigs, for garnish

1. Preheat the oven to 400°F. Grease 2 jelly-roll pans with butter, and line with parchment paper. Grease the parchment as well.
2. Prepare the Roulade: Into a large mixing bowl, sift together the flour, baking powder, and salt three times and set it aside.
3. In the bowl on an electric mixer fitted with the whip attachment on high speed, whip the egg yolks, sugar, and corn syrup until the mixture is light in color and ribbons form. Transfer the ingredients to a medium-size bowl.

4.  Clean and dry the electric mixer bowl and whip attachment immaculately. In the electric mixer on medium speed, whip the whites until foam forms. Reduce the mixing speed to low and add the sugar, 2 tablespoons at a time, waiting until each addition incorporates before adding more. Once all the sugar has been added, increase the mixing speed to high, and whip to medium peaks.

5.  Transfer 3 tablespoons of the egg white mixture to the yolk mixture, and lightly stir to combine. Using a plastic spatula, fold the remaining whites into the lightened yolk mixture. Next, fold the reserved flour mixture in gently, so as not to deflate the batter.

6.  Divide the Roulade batter among the two pans and spread it evenly across them. Bake for 12 minutes, or until golden and the cake pulls away from the sides of the pan. Set on cooling racks to cool.

7.  Invert each cake onto the reverse side of a baking pan and remove the parchment. With a pastry brush, soak each cake with framboise liqueur. Using an angled spatula, spread an even amount of preserves on each cake.

8.  Starting with the short end, tightly roll the cake. Chill the Roulade for half an hour. Slice each roulade into thirty-six ½-inch individual jelly rolls.

9.  Line an 8-inch-wide by 6-inch-deep bowl with plastic wrap. Line the bowl with jelly rolls, starting from the base and working your way up the sides. Pack the jelly rolls tightly, leaving no gaps between them.

10. Prepare the Bavarian: Prepare an ice bath in a large stainless steel bowl. Bring a small saucepan of water to a simmer. In a small metal bowl, sprinkle the unflavored gelatin over the liqueur, and whisk to combine. Let the gelatin "soften" for 10 minutes.

11. In a medium-size saucepan, bring the vanilla extract, ¼ cup of the sugar, and the milk to a boil.

12. Meanwhile, in a medium-size bowl, whisk together the yolks and the remaining ¼ cup of sugar. Temper the hot milk mixture into the yolk mixture by adding ¼ cup at a time of the hot liquid to the yolks, whisking all the while. Return the custard to the pan and cook, stirring constantly, over low heat until the mixture reaches a temperature of 185°F on a candy thermometer and is thick. Strain this mixture back into the medium-size bowl.

13. Dissolve the softened gelatin by setting the bowl over the pan of simmering water, stirring constantly until it liquefies. Whisk the gelatin into the custard.

14. Whisk the raspberry purée into the custard.

15. Set the bowl of custard in the ice bath and whisk until the mixture is cool.

16. In a large mixing bowl, transfer ½ cup of the cool raspberry custard into the whipped cream and stir to combine. Fold the remaining custard into the whipped cream mixture.

17. Fill the jelly-roll-encased bowl with the raspberry Bavarian. Stud the Bavarian with 1 pint of raspberries by randomly dropping them into the Bavarian and letting them sink. Freeze 1 hour.

18. Prepare the Glaze: In a small saucepan, combine the Apricot Stone Fruit Preserves and water; bring to a boil. Remove from the heat and let cool for 10 minutes.

19. Unmold the charlotte onto a serving dish, and brush it with glaze. Garnish with 1 pint of fresh raspberries and a few sprigs of mint.

# Saffron–Barley Pudding

This dish not only refers to the grain-based gruels, custards, and puddings of the eighteenth century but also relates to the medieval cookery upon which these recipes were often based. Each piece of saffron is the dried stigma of a Mediterranean purple crocus. To obtain one pound of the spice, over 250,000 flowers must be harvested (Ortiz 78). Because the stigmas are still picked by hand, saffron remains the most expensive spice in the world. The saffron imported into Philadelphia in the eighteenth century was also costly, which probably explains why few shops regularly carried it. In the Middle Ages, the spice was used not only to flavor food but as a dye and for medicinal purposes as well. Again, perhaps it was because of the high cost of the spice that it almost never appears in period cookery books. Martha Washington included a passage describing "Spirit of Saffron" in her cookbook, but she did not offer a recipe. Historian Karen Hess suggests that it was omitted because all spirits of this kind were likely sold only in apothecaries (422).

In contrast, barley was widely available in the eighteenth century. Advertisements in the *Pennsylvania Gazette* (February 15, 1775; April 14, 1790) reveal that "barley sugar" (a hard, lemon-flavored candy made with barley water) and "shelled barley" (probably similar to husked barley with the outer shell removed) were among the varieties available in Philadelphia.

Makes one 1-quart casserole dish; serves 8

> ½ cup pearl barley
> Pinch of saffron
> 2 cups whole milk
> 1 teaspoon vanilla extract
> 2 cinnamon sticks
> 6 large egg yolks
> ½ cup granulated sugar
> ½ cup heavy cream

1. In a medium-size saucepan, combine the barley, saffron, milk, vanilla, and cinnamon stick; bring to a boil. Cook until the grains are soft, about 10 minutes. Discard the cinnamon stick.

2. Preheat the oven to 300° F. Grease a 1-quart casserole dish with butter.

3. In a large bowl, whisk together the egg yolks, sugar, and heavy cream. Gradually stir the hot barley mixture into the egg mixture. Transfer the mixture to the prepared casserole dish.

4. Bake the pudding for 15 to 20 minutes. Remove from the oven and cool for 2 hours before serving.

Despite the fact that Martha Washington omitted recipes flavored with saffron, she did include one entitled "To Make Gruell of French Barley," which is quite similar to this pudding. Perhaps she described the barley as "French" because the grain was exported from France:

> Take a quantety [*sic*] of french barley & boyle it in t[wo] or 3 waters till it be very tender, then boyle it in good sweet cream, & season it with a little mace & sugar, fitting yr taste, 2 eggs well beaten, & a spoonfull [*sic*] or 2 of rose water. soe serve it up (Hess 136).

# Pastry Cream

This silky, vanilla-scented cream is most often associated with French pastries, such as éclairs, cream puffs, and Napoleons. Enriched with flour and eggs, the custard has a rich texture that is also well suited as the creamy base for trifles and fruit tarts.

**Makes 3 cups**

> 2 cups whole milk
> ½ cup granulated sugar
> ¼ cup all-purpose flour
> ¼ cup cornstarch
> 3 large eggs
> ½ teaspoon vanilla extract
> 2 tablespoons unsalted butter, softened

1. In a 2-quart heavy saucepan over medium heat, bring the milk and ¼ cup of the sugar to a boil, stirring occasionally.
2. Meanwhile, in a large bowl, whisk together the flour, cornstarch, eggs, vanilla extract, and remaining ¼ cup of sugar.
3. Slowly pour the hot milk-sugar mixture into the egg mixture, whisking continuously, until combined.
4. Pour the mixture back into the saucepan, and cook, stirring constantly, until the mixture thickens and just comes to a boil. Cook for 1 minute more to "cook off" the starch.
5. Remove from the heat. Pour the mixture into a heatproof bowl and stir in the butter. Cover the surface with plastic wrap to prevent a "skin" from forming on the top, and let cool at room temperature for 30 minutes.
6. Chill in the refrigerator for at least 1 hour before using. Pastry cream will keep in the refrigerator for 4 to 5 days if sealed in an airtight container.

# Chantilly Cream

Inspired by the French *Crème Chantilly*, this term simply refers to sweetened whipped cream. It is easy to prepare and complements nearly every cake and pastry.

**Makes 4 cups**

> 2 cups heavy whipping cream
> ½ cup sifted confectioners' sugar

1. In a clean, dry bowl of an electric mixer on high speed, whip together the cream and sugar until soft peaks form.
2. Refrigerate until ready to serve. The cream will keep for 2 to 3 days covered, but you will need to rewhip it before using.

To today's cooks, whipped cream and chantilly cream are synonymous. Eighteenth-century English and colonial American versions of whipped cream, however, underscore the polarity between English and French cuisines during this period. Unlike Chantilly Cream, early English and American whipped creams were multi-flavored combinations of cream, egg whites, citrus, and spices. Published in her cookbook <u>The Art of Cookery Made Plain and Easy</u>, Hannah Glasse's recipe "To make Whipt Cream" is an example of the sort of whipped cream that certainly existed alongside simpler French versions in cosmopolitan Philadelphia:

> Take a quart of thick cream, and the whites of eight eggs beat well, with a half pint of sack; mix it together, and sweeten it to your taste, with double refined sugar. You may perfume it if you please, with a little musk or ambergrease tied in a rag, and steeped a little in the cream; whip it up with a whisk, and some lemon-peel tied in the middle of the whisk; take the froth with a spoon, and lay it in your glasses or basons. This does well over a fine tart (178).

# Maple Whipped Cream

The addition of maple syrup, orange flower water, and mace to traditional chantilly cream delicately perfumes and lightly spices this ethereal accompaniment.

**Makes 3 cups**

> 2 cups heavy whipping cream
> 3 tablespoons confectioners' sugar
> ½ cup maple syrup
> 1 teaspoon orange flower water
> Pinch of mace

1. Place the bowl of an electric mixer in the freezer until cold.
2. In the cooled bowl of an electric mixer on high speed, whip the cream and confectioners' sugar until the mixture begins to thicken and soft peaks form.
3. Reduce the speed to low, and add the maple syrup, orange flower water, and mace. Increase the speed to high and continue to whip until the mixture is thick and stiff peaks form. Refrigerate until ready to serve. The cream will keep for 2 to 3 days covered, but you will need to rewhip it before using.


# Molasses Whipped Cream

**Makes 2½ cups**

> 2 cups heavy whipping cream
> 2 tablespoon confectioners' sugar
> ¼ cup Grandma's dark molasses
> 1 teaspoon ground ginger
> 1 teaspoon ground cinnamon
> 2 tablespoons Appleton gold rum

1. Place the bowl of an electric mixer in the freezer until cold.
2. In the cooled bowl of an electric mixer on high speed, whip the cream and confectioners' sugar until the mixture begins to thicken and soft peaks form.
3. Reduce the speed to medium, and add the molasses, ginger, cinnamon, and rum. Increase the speed to high, and continue to whip until the mixture is thick and stiff peaks form. Refrigerate until ready to serve. The cream will keep for 2 to 3 days covered, but you will need to rewhip it before using.

# Crème Anglaise (Vanilla Custard Sauce)

This French term translates literally as "English cream"—a thick custard sauce, which today is most often flavored with vanilla. In keeping with eighteenth-century, English culinary fashion, however, custards of that period more commonly called for additions of nutmeg, cinnamon, rose water, almonds, and the like, rather than costly vanilla beans.

*Crème anglaise* is quite versatile. It can be baked and served as a firm custard, as it often was in the eighteenth century; flavored with a variety of spices, extracts, chocolate, or liqueurs; or served simply as a vanilla sauce, enhancing the formality and presentation of any plated dessert.

Makes 1½ cups

> 2 cups whole milk
> 4 tablespoons granulated sugar
> 1 vanilla bean, split open and seeds scraped out with the back of a knife
> 4 large egg yolks
> 2 tablespoons Appleton gold rum

1. In a 2-quart heavy saucepan over medium heat, add the milk, 2 tablespoons of the sugar, and the scraped vanilla seeds and pod; bring to a boil.
2. In a large bowl, whisk together the egg yolks and the remaining 2 tablespoons of sugar.
3. Slowly pour 1 cup of the hot milk mixture into the egg yolk-sugar mixture, whisking constantly. *Do not* pour the entire hot milk mixture into the yolk mixture, as it will curdle the eggs. Pour the tempered milk-yolk mixture back into the saucepan with the hot milk, and cook over medium heat, stirring constantly, until the mixture coats the back of a spoon. Do not boil.
4. Remove from the heat and stir in the rum. Strain the mixture through a fine sieve into a heatproof bowl. Place the sauce in an ice bath (see Chef's Note).
5. When cool, transfer the sauce to a bowl. Cover the surface with plastic wrap and chill in the refrigerator until ready to use. The sauce will keep in the refrigerator for 4 to 5 days if well sealed.

*Making an Ice Bath—If a custard mixture is not iced, the eggs will continue to cook and then scramble, making the mixture unusable. To make an ice bath, fill a large bowl with ice cubes. Insert a smaller, heatproof bowl into the large bowl. Arrange the ice cubes around the bowl. Pour the custard into the smaller bowl and stir occasionally—to allow the heat to escape—until the mixture has cooled.*

# Bavarian Cream

Bavarian Creme is a dessert based on custard or fruit, enriched with whipped cream, and stabilized with gelatin. Because it becomes firm as it cools, Bavarian cream not only is suitable as a filling for cakes and tortes but may also be decoratively molded or served in glasses, much as puddings, custards, and creams were in the eighteenth century.

Calves' hooves or calves' feet jelly was the thickener of choice in the period, but, as the nineteenth century progressed, prepared gelatin became an easier, more readily available alternative. It was in the 1800s and early 1900s as well that Bavarian cream became especially popular, due, in large part, to the culinary instruction of French gourmand Auguste Escoffier. In his <u>Guide Culinaire</u> of 1903, Escoffier explained, "There are two kinds [of Bavarian Creams]:—Bavarian with cream, and Bavarian with fruit" (791). "With cream" referred to Bavarians based on custard, while "with fruit" pertained to those based on fresh or cooked fruit. As the following recipes reveal, both types are thickened with gelatin and whipped cream.

# Vanilla Bavarian

Makes one 2-quart Bavarian mold; serves 10

> Two ¼-ounce packets unflavored gelatin
> 6 tablespoons Appleton gold rum
> 1½ cups whole milk
> 2 vanilla beans
> 10 large egg yolks
> ¾ cup granulated sugar
> 2½ cups heavy whipping cream, whipped to medium peaks

1. Prepare an ice bath in a large stainless steel bowl. Bring a small saucepan of water to a simmer.
2. In a small metal bowl, sprinkle the unflavored gelatin over the rum and whisk to combine. Let the gelatin "soften" for 10 minutes.
3. In a medium-size saucepan, add the milk and vanilla beans; bring to a boil.
4. Meanwhile, in a medium-size bowl, add the yolks and sugar, and whisk together. Temper the hot milk mixture into the yolk mixture by adding ¼ cup at a time of the hot liquid to the yolks, whisking all the while. When all of the hot liquid has been added, return the custard to the pan and cook, stirring constantly, over low heat until the mixture reaches a temperature of 185°F on a candy thermometer and is thick. Strain this mixture back into the medium-size bowl.
5. Dissolve the softened gelatin by setting the bowl over the pan of simmering water and stirring constantly until it liquefies. Whisk the gelatin into the custard.
6. Set the bowl of custard in the ice bath and whisk until the mixture is cool.
7. Fold ½ cup of the cool custard into the whipped cream. Fold the remaining custard into the whipped cream mixture.
8. Pour the Bavarian into the mold, cover with plastic wrap, and refrigerate overnight. To unmold, uncover and hold the mold over a pan of simmering water for 10 to 20 seconds to warm up. Place a large serving plate over the top of the mold, invert the plate and mold, gently tap the mold to loosen, and lift off.

# Raspberry Bavarian

Makes one 2-quart Bavarian mold; serves 10

Two ¼-ounce packets unflavored gelatin
3 tablespoons orange liqueur (such as Triple Sec or Cointreau)
1 cup whole milk
½ cup granulated sugar
1 tablespoon vanilla extract
3 large egg yolks
1¼ cups raspberry purée (or substitute frozen raspberries, thawed and puréed)
2½ cups heavy whipping cream, whipped to medium peaks

1. Prepare an ice bath in a large stainless steel bowl. Bring a small saucepan of water to a simmer.

2. In a small metal bowl, sprinkle the unflavored gelatin over the cognac, and whisk to combine. Let the gelatin "soften" for 10 minutes.

3. In a medium-size saucepan, combine the milk, ¼ cup of the sugar, and the vanilla extract; bring to a boil.

4. Meanwhile, in a medium-size bowl, add the yolks and the remaining ¼ cup of sugar, and whisk to combine. Temper the hot milk mixture into the yolk mixture by adding ¼ cup at a time of the hot liquid to the yolks, whisking all the while. When all of the hot liquid has been added, return the custard to the pan and cook, stirring constantly, over low heat until the mixture reaches a temperature of 185°F on a candy thermometer and is thick. Strain this mixture back into the bowl.

5. Dissolve the softened gelatin by setting the bowl over the pan of simmering water, stirring constantly until it liquefies. Whisk the gelatin into the custard.

6. Add the raspberry purée to the custard and whisk to combine.

7. Set the bowl of custard in the ice bath and whisk until the mixture is cool.

8. Fold ½ cup of the cool custard into the whipped cream. Fold the remaining custard into the whipped cream mixture.

9. Pour the Bavarian into the mold, cover with plastic wrap, and refrigerate overnight. To unmold, uncover and hold the mold over a pan of simmering water for 10 to 20 seconds to warm up. Place a large serving plate over the top of the mold, invert the plate and mold, gently tap the mold to loosen, and lift off.

# Chocolate Bavarian

**Makes one 2-quart Bavarian mold; serves 10**

1½ ¼-ounce packets unflavored gelatin
3 tablespoons Appleton gold rum
1½ cups whole milk
½ cup granulated sugar
1 teaspoon vanilla extract
6 large egg yolks
3 ounces semisweet chocolate, finely chopped
2½ cups heavy whipping cream, whipped to medium peaks

1. Prepare an ice bath in a large stainless steel bowl. Bring a small saucepan of water to a simmer.
2. In a small metal bowl, sprinkle the unflavored gelatin over the rum and whisk to combine. Let the gelatin "soften" for 10 minutes.
3. In a medium-size saucepan, add the milk, ¼ cup of the sugar, and the vanilla extract; bring to a boil.
4. Meanwhile, in a medium-size bowl, add the yolks and the remaining ¼ cup of sugar, and whisk to combine. Temper the hot milk mixture into the yolk mixture by adding ¼ cup at a time of the hot liquid to the yolks, whisking all the while. When all of the hot liquid has been added, return the custard to the pan and cook, stirring constantly, over low heat until the mixture reaches a temperature of 185°F on a candy thermometer and is thick. Strain this mixture back into the bowl.
5. Add the chocolate and stir until completely dissolved.
6. Dissolve the softened gelatin by setting the bowl over the pan of simmering water, stirring constantly until it liquefies. Whisk the gelatin into the custard.
7. Set the bowl of custard in the ice bath and whisk until the mixture is cool.
8. Fold ½ cup of the cool custard into the whipped cream. Fold the remaining custard into the whipped cream mixture.
9. Pour the Bavarian into the mold, cover with plastic wrap, and refrigerate overnight. To unmold, uncover and hold the mold over a pan of simmering water for 10 to 20 seconds to warm up. Place a large serving plate over the top of the mold, invert the plate and mold, gently tap the mold to loosen, and lift off.

# Coffee Bavarian

**Makes one 2-quart Bavarian mold; serves 10**

Two ¼-ounce packets unflavored gelatin
6 tablespoons Kahlúa
1½ cups whole milk
1 cup granulated sugar
¼ cup whole coffee beans, roughly ground
1 teaspoon vanilla extract
1 cinnamon stick
10 large egg yolks
2½ cups heavy whipping cream, whipped to medium peaks

1. Prepare an ice bath in a large stainless steel bowl. Bring a small saucepan of water to a simmer.
2. In a small metal bowl, sprinkle the unflavored gelatin over the Kahlua and whisk to combine. Let the gelatin "soften" for 10 minutes.
3. In a medium-size saucepan, combine the milk, ½ cup of the sugar, and the ground coffee beans, vanilla extract, and cinnamon stick; bring to a boil.
4. Meanwhile, in a medium-size bowl, add the yolks and the remaining ½ cup of sugar; whisk to combine. Temper the hot milk mixture into the yolk mixture by adding ¼ cup at a time of the hot liquid to the yolks, whisking all the while. When all of the hot liquid has been added, return the custard to the pan and cook, stirring constantly, over low heat until the mixture reaches a temperature of 185°F on a candy thermometer and is thick. Strain this mixture back into the bowl.
5. Dissolve the softened gelatin by setting the bowl over the pan of simmering water, stirring constantly until it liquefies. Whisk the gelatin into the custard.
6. Set the bowl of custard in the ice bath and whisk until the mixture is cool.
7. Fold ½ cup of the cool custard into the whipped cream. Fold the remaining custard into the whipped cream mixture.
8. Pour the Bavarian into the mold, cover with plastic wrap, and refrigerate overnight. To unmold, uncover and hold the mold over a pan of simmering water for 10 to 20 seconds to warm up. Place a large serving plate over the top of the mold, invert the plate and mold, gently tap the mold to loosen, and lift off.

# Strawberry Bavarian

**Makes one 2-quart Bavarian mold; serves 10**

> Two ¼-ounce packets unflavored gelatin
> ¼ cup water
> 1¼ cups strawberry purée (or substitute frozen strawberries, thawed and puréed)
> ½ cup granulated sugar
> 2 large egg whites
> 1 cup plus 2 tablespoons heavy whipping cream, whipped to medium peaks

1. Grease a 1-quart Bavarian mold with butter. Prepare an ice bath in a large stainless steel bowl. Bring a small saucepan of water to a simmer.
2. In a small metal bowl, sprinkle the gelatin over the water. Let the gelatin "soften" for 10 minutes.
3. n a small saucepan over medium heat, warm the strawberry purée until steam begins to rise but the purée is not yet boiling. Add ¼ cup of the sugar, and stir. Do not boil the purée. Continue to cook, stirring, until the sugar dissolves. Remove the pan from the stove and set aside.
4. Dissolve the softened gelatin by setting the bowl over the pan of simmering water, stirring constantly until it liquefies. Add the gelatin to the strawberry purée, and whisk well to combine. Set aside.
5. In a small metal bowl, add the egg whites and the remaining ¼ cup of sugar, and set over the simmering pan of water. Stir the whites and sugar until the sugar dissolves and the mixture reaches a temperature of 165°F on a candy thermometer.
6. Transfer the egg whites to the bowl of an electric mixer fitted with the whip attachment. On high speed, whip the whites until they are cool and stiff peaks form.
7. Transfer the strawberry purée to a medium-size bowl, set it in the ice bath, and whisk until cool.
8. Fold ¼ cup of the strawberry purée into the egg whites. Fold the lightened meringue into the remaining strawberry purée.
9. Fold ½ cup of the meringue-purée mixture into the whipped cream. Fold the remaining purée into the whipped cream mixture.
10. Pour the Bavarian into the mold, cover with plastic wrap, and refrigerate overnight. To unmold, uncover and hold the mold over a pan of simmering water for 10 to 20 seconds to warm up. Place a large serving plate over the top of the mold, invert the plate and mold, gently tap the mold to loosen, and lift off.

# Cookies

In the eighteenth century, the use of the word "cookie" was rare. In fact, Amelia Simmons seems to have been one of the few authors to use the term, including in her cookbook *American Cookery* recipes for "Cookies" and "Another Christmas Cookey" [*sic*] (45, 46). She titled the remaining recipes in this category, however, in the style of her contemporaries: primarily as biscuits, drops, and cakes. Some of these cookies remain familiar in America, such as gingerbread and macaroons, while others, with their English roots, are less so, including Naples biscuits, ratafia drops, Savoy cakes/drops, and Shrewsbury cakes.

Despite the differences in their shapes and textures, most of these cookies were similarly flavored with a variety of spices and other concentrated ingredients, such as rose water and orange and lemon zests. Cinnamon, nutmeg, mace, and cardamom, some of the most celebrated spices of the Middle Ages, continued to be popular in eighteenth-century American baking. Like other imported items, spices were expensive. So desirable were they, however, that home cooks and confectioners alike discovered ways to prudently combine them with American dairy products, fruits, and nuts so as to satisfy the European-influenced, eighteenth-century palate.

Just as cookies are today, colonial American cookies were prepared for special holiday and social occasions as well as daily treats, and were enjoyed with a variety of beverages, including wine, punch, cider, tea, coffee, and hot chocolate.

# Apricot Tea Cookies

Apricots were much appreciated in the eighteenth century, perhaps because of their limited availability. They were cultivated more successfully in the South's temperate climate than in the North. Both George Washington and Thomas Jefferson included apricot trees in their orchards, and they, like many of their contemporaries, must have enjoyed the fruit not only fresh in season but preserved year-round as well (Leighton 228-229).

These German-inspired confections are filled with the sweet-tart flavor of apricots; preserves are incorporated into the dough and jam is spooned decoratively on top of each cookie.

**Makes 3 dozen cookies**

> 1 pound (4 sticks) unsalted butter, softened
> ¾ cup granulated sugar
> 2 large eggs
> 5 cups sifted all-purpose flour
> 2 teaspoons baking powder
> ½ teaspoon salt
> 1 cup sliced almonds, toasted (see Chef's Note, page 38)
> ½ cup apricot preserves
> ¼ cup grated, unsweetened coconut, toasted (see Chef's Note, page 87)
> ½ cup apricot jam

1. In the bowl of an electric mixer fitted with the paddle attachment on medium speed, beat the butter and sugar until light and fluffy, scraping down the sides of the bowl often. Add the eggs and beat well.
2. In a separate bowl, combine the flour, baking powder, and salt.
3. Add the almonds, preserves, and coconut to the mixer bowl, and beat well. Add the flour mixture and mix until just combined.
4. Wrap the dough in plastic wrap and chill in the refrigerator for at least 1 hour, or until easy to handle.
5. Meanwhile, preheat the oven to 350°F.
6. Shape the chilled dough into 1-inch balls. On an ungreased cookie sheet, place the dough balls 1 inch apart.
7. Press your thumb into the center of each ball. Place ½ teaspoon of jam in the center of each impression.
8. Bake for 12 to 15 minutes, or until the edges are lightly browned. Transfer the cookies to a wire rack and let cool.

# Anise Biscotti

Biscotti are Italian cookies with which some eighteenth-century colonists, particularly those who had traveled through Italy, were most likely familiar. They are related in name to the French *biscotte* and the English "rusk"—often referred to in period cookbooks as "French Bisket" (Hess 338)—although the latter two varieties are yeast-raised cookies, whereas biscotti rely on chemical leaveners, such as baking powder and baking soda. In addition, biscotti achieve their crispness through twice baking, while *biscottes* and rusks are often only baked once after the dough rises.

For centuries, anise has been one of the most traditional additions to biscotti, and it was certainly a popular spice in the eighteenth century. Like many other imported spices and foodstuffs, anise seeds were readily available in local markets.

**Makes about twenty-four 3 x ½-inch biscotti**

> 1¾ cups granulated sugar
> ¾ cup vegetable oil
> 2 large eggs
> ½ cup sour cream
> 1 teaspoon vanilla extract
> 4½ cups sifted all-purpose flour
> 1 teaspoon baking powder
> 1 teaspoon baking soda
> ½ teaspoon salt
> ½ teaspoon crushed anise seed

1. Preheat the oven to 350°F. Place parchment paper on a cookie sheet, and grease lightly with butter.
2. In the bowl of an electric mixer fitted with the paddle attachment on medium to high speed, beat the sugar, oil, and eggs until combined, scraping down the sides of the bowl often. Add the sour cream and vanilla extract, and beat well.
3. In a separate bowl, sift together the flour, baking powder, baking soda, and salt. Stir in the anise seed. With the mixer on low, slowly add the dry ingredients to the wet ingredients.
4. Transfer the dough to a lightly floured surface, and knead the dough with your hands for 1 minute.
5. Shape the dough into a 12-inch roll, about 3 inches in diameter, and place the roll in the center of the prepared cookie sheet.
6. Bake for 20 to 25 minutes, or until light golden brown.
7. Remove from the oven. Cool on the cookie sheet for about 25 minutes. Using a serrated-edge knife, cut the log into ½-inch-thick diagonal slices.
8. Arrange the slices, flat sides down, on the same cookie sheet, and put back into the oven for 5 minutes. Turn each slice over and bake 5 minutes more, or until the biscotti are just toasted. *Do not overbake.*
9. Transfer the biscotti to a wire rack and let cool. To store, transfer them to a tightly covered container and keep at room temperature.

# Walnut–Orange Biscotti

Nuts and citrus fruit were common additions to eighteenth-century baked goods. Walnuts were among the most popular nuts available, and oranges were prized for their juice, the tart marmalade they produced, and their peels, which added concentrated citrus flavor to confections like these biscotti.

**Makes about twenty-four 3 x ½-inch biscotti**

> 1¼ cups granulated sugar
> 6 ounces (1½ sticks) unsalted butter, softened
> 4 large eggs
> 2 tablespoons grated orange zest
> 1 teaspoon orange extract
> 3¾ cups sifted all-purpose flour
> 2 tablespoons baking powder
> 1 teaspoon ground cinnamon
> ¼ teaspoon salt
> 1½ cups chopped walnuts

1. Preheat the oven to 350°F. Place parchment paper on a cookie sheet, and coat lightly with butter.
2. In the bowl of an electric mixer fitted with the paddle attachment on medium to high speed, beat the sugar and butter until light and fluffy, scraping down the sides of the bowl often. Add the eggs, zest, and orange extract; beat well.
3. In a separate bowl, sift together the flour, baking powder, cinnamon, and salt. With the mixer on low, slowly add the dry ingredients to the wet ingredients. Add the nuts and mix well.
4. Shape the dough into a 12-inch roll, about 3 inches in diameter.
5. Place the roll in the center of the prepared pan. Bake for 20 to 25 minutes, or until light golden brown.
6. Remove from the oven. Cool on a cookie sheet for 1 hour, or until cool to the touch. Using a serrated knife, cut the roll into ½-inch-thick diagonal slices.
7. Arrange the slices, flat sides down, on the same cookie sheet, and put back into the oven for 5 minutes. Turn each slice over and bake 5 minutes more, or until the biscotti are just toasted. *Do not overbake.*
8. Transfer the biscotti to a wire rack and let cool. To store, transfer them to a tightly covered container and keep at room temperature.

# Lemon–Lavender Biscotti

These cookies celebrate the eighteenth-century fondness for lemons as well as lavender, which was valued for its perfume and its medicinal qualities. Only a small amount of lavender is required to flavor these biscotti and complement the refreshing flavors of the lemon zest and juice.

**Makes twenty 3 x ½-inch biscotti**

> 1¼ cups granulated sugar
> 2 lemons
> 1½ teasspoons dried lavender
> Freshly grated nutmeg, to taste
> 4¼ cups bread flour
> 1 teaspoon baking powder
> 5 ounces (1¼ sticks) unsalted butter, cubed into ½-inch pieces and very cold
> 2 large eggs
> 2 tablespoons freshly squeezed lemon juice
> 1 tablespoon vanilla extract
> 2 large eggs beaten with 1 tablespoon water and pinch of salt, for egg wash

1. In a small bowl, add the sugar. Grate the zest of the lemons over the sugar. Add the lavender and nutmeg, and stir to combine.
2. In the bowl of an electric mixer fitted with the paddle attachment on low speed, mix together the flour and baking powder. Add the cold cubed butter and the sugar mixture, and beat on medium speed until the mixture resembles coarse meal.
3. In a large bowl, whisk together the eggs, lemon juice, and vanilla extract. Transfer the coarse meal mixture to the same bowl, and knead the dough by hand until it is well combined. The dough should feel grainy.
4. Line 2 cookie sheets with parchment paper.
5. Shape the dough into 3 logs, about 1 inch thick and 8 inches long. Arrange the logs on the prepared cookie sheets, and brush the logs with the egg wash. Chill in the refrigerator for 1 hour.
6. Preheat the oven to 350°F.
7. Brush the logs with egg wash again, and bake for 15 minutes, or until golden. Remove the trays from the oven, and cool completely on the cookie sheets.
8. Slice the logs diagonally, ½ inch thick. Arrange the slices, flat side down, on the same cookie sheets. Bake 3 minutes; then turn the biscotti over and bake 3 minutes more on the other side, until light golden on all sides. Do not overbake.
9. Cool completely on the sheets on wire racks. To store, transfer them to a tightly covered container and keep at room temperature.

# Coconut Cookies

The creamy white flesh of coconuts imported from the West Indies was enjoyed fresh and dried in the eighteenth century. Coconut pudding recipes based on fresh coconut appeared frequently in period cookbooks; Thomas Jefferson's collection of recipes included two variations. Cookies, such as this version, were more likely to call for dried coconut, which cooks prepared themselves after purchasing the fresh fruit.

**Makes 3 dozen cookies**

> 5 ounces (1¼ sticks) unsalted butter, softened
> 1 cup granulated sugar
> 1 large egg
> 1 cup sifted all-purpose flour
> 1½ cups grated, unsweetened coconut, toasted (see Chef's Note, page 87)

1. Preheat the oven to 375°F. Lightly grease a cookie sheet with butter.

2. In the bowl of an electric mixer fitted with the paddle attachment on medium speed, beat the butter and sugar until light and fluffy, scraping down the sides of the bowl often. Add the egg and beat well.

3. Slowly add the flour and coconut, and beat well, until the dough becomes stiff. Wrap the dough in plastic wrap and refrigerate for 30 minutes, or until chilled.

4. Shape the chilled dough into 1-inch balls. Place them 1 inch apart on the prepared cookie sheet.

5. Bake about 15 minutes, or until the edges are lightly browned. Transfer the cookies to a wire rack and let cool.

In her cookbook of 1770, Harriott Pinckney Horry included a recipe for "Cocoa Nut Puffs," which is remarkably similar to this version of coconut cookies. Its flavorful simplicity suggests that confections like these puffs were enjoyed in many cities, including Philadelphia.

## Cocoa Nut Puffs

Take a Cocoa Nut and dry it well before the fire, then grate it and add to it a good spoonfull [sic] of Butter, sugar to your tast [sic], six Eggs with half the whites and 2 spoonfulls of rose water. Mix them all together and they must be well beat before they are put in the Oven (Hooker 71).

# Spritz Cookies

Buttery flavor and fanciful shapes define these cookies of Northern European origin. The soft dough is pushed through a special cookie press—hence the name, which refers to *spritzen*, German for "to squirt or spray." This press may be fitted with a variety of decorative templates, enabling one to easily create festive cookies so typical of Germany and Scandinavia.

Many varieties of butter cookies existed in the American colonies. The large German population in Philadelphia certainly continued to enjoy this version reminiscent of Old World foodways.

**Makes 2 dozen cookies**

> 1 pound (4 sticks) unsalted butter, softened
> 1½ cups granulated sugar
> 4 large egg yolks
> 2 teaspoons vanilla extract
> 5 cups sifted all-purpose flour
> 4 teaspoons baking powder
> 1 teaspoon salt

1. Preheat the oven to 350°F.
2. In the bowl of an electric mixer fitted with the paddle attachment on medium speed, beat the butter and sugar until light and fluffy, scraping down the sides of the bowl often. Add the yolks and vanilla extract, and beat well.
3. In a separate bowl, sift together the flour, baking powder, and salt. With the electric mixer on low speed, slowly add the dry ingredients and beat until just combined.
4. Shape the dough into 2-inch, finger-shaped logs. Place the logs 1 inch apart on an ungreased cookie sheet. Alternatively, you may use a cookie press (spritzer) to form the decorative cookies—fill the cookie press and shape cookies as per the manufacturer's directions.
5. Bake for 15 minutes, or until the edges are firm and golden but not brown. (If you are baking cookies you formed with a cookie press, you will probably need to reduce the baking time accordingly; again, see the manufacturer's directions.) Transfer the cookies to a wire rack and let cool.

# Spice Cookies

Most eighteenth-century cookies, or "cakes" as they were called in the period, were flavored with spices. Whole or ground caraway and coriander seeds ranked among the most popular, but others were frequently used as well. As in these cookies, nutmeg, ginger, and cinnamon were added to a variety of baked goods to add a taste of the exotic and depth of flavor to simple preparations. This recipe recalls the crisp Shrewsbury cakes and numerous varieties of gingerbread (more closely related to cookies than cake) that filled the kitchens and shelves of many colonial American homes and bake shops.

**Makes about 3 dozen cookies**

½ pound (2 sticks) unsalted butter, softened
¾ cup granulated sugar
½ cup Grandma's dark molasses
2 large egg yolks
1 teaspoon vanilla extract
2⅓ cups sifted all-purpose flour
2 teaspoons ground cinnamon
1½ teaspoons ground ginger
½ teaspoon salt
¼ teaspoon ground nutmeg

**Lemon Glaze**
1 cup confectioners' sugar
1½ tablespoons freshly squeezed and strained lemon juice

1. Preheat the oven to 350°F.
2. In the bowl of an electric mixer fitted with the paddle attachment on medium speed, beat the butter and sugar until light and fluffy, scraping down the sides of the bowl often. Add the molasses, egg yolks, and vanilla extract; beat well.
3. In a separate bowl, sift together the flour, cinnamon, ginger, salt, and nutmeg. With the electric mixer on low speed, add the dry ingredients to the wet ingredients, and mix just until combined.
4. Drop the dough by teaspoonfuls 1 inch apart onto an ungreased cookie sheet.
5. Bake for 15 to 20 minutes, or until golden.
6. Transfer the cookies to a wire rack and let cool about 15 minutes.
7. Prepare the Lemon Glaze: In a small bowl, whisk together the confectioners' sugar and lemon juice until smooth. When the cookies are cool, use a small spoon to drizzle the glaze over each cookie top.

Many shops that stood in the vicinity of City Tavern carried a variety of imported foodstuffs that were incorporated into the dishes served at this stylish establishment. On April 14, 1790, for example, Cadwalader & David Evans advertised in the Pennsylvania Gazette that "At their Store, the south side of Market street, the second door below Fifth street" they had for sale imported "Pepper, alspice [sic], ginger, cinnamon [and] cloves," as well as the ever-popular "Anniseed."

# Oatmeal–Raisin Cookies

Numerous markets and shops in eighteenth-century Philadelphia featured raisins in their advertisements, testament to the popularity and high demand of this dried fruit once considered exotic, sugary jewels. When raisins are combined with the spices and oatmeal in this recipe, the result is a sweet, chewy cookie that is satisfying and comforting.

**Makes about 28 cookies**

> 12 ounces (3 sticks) unsalted butter, softened
> 1½ cups granulated sugar
> 1½ cups packed light brown sugar
> 4 large eggs
> 4 teaspoons vanilla extract
> 4 cups old-fashioned rolled oats
> 2 cups sifted all-purpose flour
> 1 teaspoon baking soda
> ½ teaspoon ground cinnamon
> ¼ teaspoon ground nutmeg
> 1½ cups raisins

1. Preheat the oven to 375°F.
2. In the bowl of an electric mixer fitted with the paddle attachment on medium speed, beat the butter, sugar, and brown sugar until light and fluffy, scraping down the sides of the bowl often. Add the eggs and vanilla extract, and beat well.
3. In a separate bowl, add the oats, flour, baking soda, cinnamon, and nutmeg; stir to combine. With the mixer on low speed, gradually add the dry ingredients to the wet ingredients, and beat just until combined.
4. Add the raisins and beat well.
5. Using a 2-inch ice cream scoop, drop the dough 2 inches apart onto an ungreased cookie sheet.
6. Bake about 15 minutes, or until the edges of the cookies are golden.
7. Transfer the cookies to a wire rack and let cool.

Not only is George Washington known to have cultivated grapes at Mount Vernon, which he possibly dried to produce raisins, but he also frequently imported the dried fruit. Between 1758 and 1798, Washington ordered jars of raisins from England. Although specialty foods of this sort regularly arrived in America, they sometimes spoiled in transit, thus making their desirability that much greater. In a letter to his agent in England in November 1762, Washington, in fact, placed an order for what were called "best Raisons [*sic*]," adding that "those sent last year were good for nothing." The general must have finally received some acceptable raisins by 1795, however, when, in addition to "puddings, jellies, oranges, apples, nuts, and figs," he served the fruit at a congressional dinner in Philadelphia (Mount Vernon memo 1989).

# Macaroons

These modest-looking cookies date at least to the seventeenth century and appear in nearly every eighteenth-century cookbook available in Philadelphia and abroad. Often also appearing as "mackroons," "mackeroons," "maccaroons," and "macarons" (the French spelling), they were simple combinations of a few flavorful ingredients. A cookery book from 1611 described them as sweetmeats "compounded of Sugar, Almonds, Rosewater, and Muske, pounded together, and baked with a gentle fire" (Hess 341). With the occasional substitution of orange water for rose water, eighteenth-century macaroons remained nearly identical to their medieval predecessors. "[T]hese cookies are," as historian Karen Hess writes, "simply baked puffy marchpane [marzipan]," and, as such, they satisfied the eighteenth-century palate's fondness for almonds (341).

Makes 2 dozen cookies

> ½ cup sliced almonds, toasted (see Chef's Note, page 38)
> ½ cup Almond Paste (see page 40), or 5¼ ounces store-bought almond paste
> 3 large egg whites
> 1 cup granulated sugar

1. Preheat the oven to 425°F. Line two cookie sheets with parchment paper. Fit a pastry bag with a #16 round tip.
2. Grind the cooled toasted almonds in a food processor, and set aside.
3. In the bowl of an electric mixer fitted with the paddle attachment, on low speed, mix the Almond Paste with 1 tablespoon of the egg whites until soft, scraping down the sides of the bowl often. Add the sugar and mix until light. With the mixer on medium speed, *slowly* add the remaining egg whites, and mix until smooth.
4. With a rubber spatula or wooden spoon, fold in the ground almonds.
5. Fill the pastry bag one-quarter full with the macaroon batter. Pipe 1-inch rounds of batter, a few inches apart, on the prepared cookie sheets, or drop the batter by the tablespoonful.
6. Put the macaroons in the oven and *immediately* reduce the oven temperature to 375°F. Bake for 7 to 10 minutes, or until light golden. Remove from the oven and let cool completely before removing from the cookie sheets.

Hannah Glasse's recipe "To make Mackeroons," published in The Art of Cookery Made Plain and Easy, is just one example of how medieval culinary traditions continued to influence eighteenth-century foodways. This recipe is little changed from those of centuries earlier:

> Take a pound of almonds, let them be scalded, blanched, and thrown into cold water, then dry them in a cloth, and pound them in a mortar, moisten them with orange-flower water, or the white of an egg, lest they turn to oil, afterwards take an equal quantity of fine powder sugar, with three or four whites of eggs, and a little musk, beat all well together, and shape them on a wafer-paper, with a spoon round. Bake them in a gentle oven on tin plates (168).

# Shortbread Triangles with Apple Chutney

Shortbread, a traditionally Scottish holiday treat, is here served with a fragrant, spicy chutney that combines some of the most flavorful ingredients available to eighteenth-century Philadelphians. Molasses, ginger, cinnamon, and raisins were all imported from the West Indies and were available in local shops.

**Makes 6 servings**

### Vanilla Shortbread

¾ pound (3 sticks) unsalted butter, softened
1 cup sifted confectioners' sugar, plus extra for dusting
½ teaspoon vanilla extract
3 cups sifted all-purpose flour
½ teaspoon salt

### Apple-Chutney Filling

½ pound (1 stick) unsalted butter, softened
½ cup packed dark brown sugar
¼ cup Grandma's dark molasses
¼ teaspoon salt
2 sticks cinnamon
2 teaspoons grated fresh ginger
4 Granny Smith apples, peeled, cored, and cubed
1 medium lime, zest grated and juiced (strained)
½ cup raisins
½ cup chopped walnuts, lightly toasted (see Chef's Note, page 38)

1½ teaspoons granulated sugar, for garnish
Store-bought caramel or butter-pecan ice cream, for serving (optional)

1. Prepare the Vanilla Shortbread: In the bowl of an electric mixer fitted with the paddle attachment on medium speed, beat the butter, confectioners' sugar, and vanilla extract until light and fluffy.
2. In a separate bowl, combine the flour and salt. With the mixer on low, slowly add the dry ingredients to the butter-sugar mixture, and beat just until the dough begins to hold together. Form the dough into a disc shape, wrap in plastic wrap, and chill in the refrigerator for at least 1 hour before using.
3. Preheat the oven to 325°F. Line a cookie sheet with parchment paper.
4. Prepare the Apple-Chutney Filling: In a large saucepan over medium heat, melt the butter. Stirring constantly, add the brown sugar, molasses, and salt. Add the cinnamon sticks and ginger, and bring the mixture to a boil.
5. Reduce the heat to low and add the apples, lime zest, and lime juice. Cook just until the apples start to soften, 3 to 5 minutes.
6. Add the raisins and walnuts, and remove from heat. Set aside.
7. On a lightly floured surface, roll out the shortbread to ¼ inch thick.
8. Cut the dough into eighteen 3-inch triangle shapes and place them 1 inch apart on the prepared cookie sheet. Sprinkle the granulated sugar over the top of each triangle.
9. Bake for 15 to 20 minutes, or until golden brown around the edges. Cool on a wire rack.

10. Assemble the triangles: When the triangles are cool, spoon ½ cup of the warm Apple Chutney onto each of six triangles. Top each with another triangle and more chutney. Top with a third triangle. You should have a total of six 3-layer triangles.

11. Dust the serving plates with confectioners' sugar and, if desired, serve with purchased ice cream.

One month before City Tavern opened for business, Moses Cox advertised his new grocery store, located two blocks west of the Tavern at Second and Spruce Streets, in the Pennsylvania Gazette. Like many shops in Philadelphia at that time, Cox sold a variety of merchandise, from foodstuffs to household goods. Among the items he was offering in November 1773 "at the lowest prices" were "cinnamon . . . melasses . . . raisins, currants . . . [and] ginger" (November 17, 1773).

# Coconut Macaroons

It is unclear just how available coconuts were in the colonies. It appears that greater quantities of the fruit were imported in later years, for although it is mentioned in only a few eighteenth-century cookbooks, coconut appears in numerous nineteenth-century publications. It is also uncertain, therefore, just when coconut macaroons became popular. Those prepared with almonds had been enjoyed for centuries, and it seems only logical that the coconut variety developed as the fruit became more available. This, in fact, seems to have been the case. Eliza Leslie's *Directions for Cookery, in Its Various Branches*, published in Philadelphia in 1837, included no less than eight coconut cake, pudding, cookie, and macaroon recipes. It should be mentioned, however, that her recipe for "Cocoa-Nut Jumbles" closely resembles Harriott Pinckney Horry's 1770 recipe for "Cocoa Nut Puffs" (Leslie 353; Hooker 71). Prepared with sugar, rose water, butter, and whole eggs rather than simply sweetened egg whites, these cookies seemingly were earlier, buttery versions of what became coconut macaroons.

**Makes 2 dozen cookies**

> 2 tablespoons honey
> 2 limes
> 6 large egg whites, at room temperature
> Pinch of salt
> 1 cup granulated sugar
> 2 cups grated unsweetened coconut, toasted (see Chef's Note, page 87)

1. Preheat the oven to 425°F. Line two cookie sheets with parchment paper. Fit a pastry bag with a #16 star tip.

2. To a small bowl, add the honey. Grate the zest of the lime into the bowl of honey. Squeeze the juice from the limes into the honey, and mix to combine.

3. In an immaculately clean bowl of your electric mixer on low speed, whip the egg whites and salt until soft peaks begin to form.

4. Increase the mixer speed to medium speed, and slowly add the sugar in a thin steady stream. Once all the sugar has been added, turn the mixer on high and whip the egg whites to medium peaks.

5. Reduce the mixer speed to low, and add the honey mixture. Whip to stiff peaks. With a rubber spatula or wooden spoon, fold in the toasted coconut.

6. Fill the pastry bag half full with the batter. Pipe 1-inch rosettes, 2 inches apart, on the lined cookie sheets, or drop the batter by the tablespoonful.

7. Transfer the cookie sheets to the oven, and immediately reduce the oven temperature to 350°F. Bake for 7 to 10 minutes, or until light golden. Remove from the oven and let cool completely before removing from the cookie sheets.

# Rosewater–Almond Cookies

These delicate cookies refer to the many eighteenth-century varieties perfumed with rose water and almonds. With their relatively loose dough, they are similar to today's "tuile cookies" and are a cross between the "ratafia cakes" and "butter drops" that appear in period cookbooks.

**Makes 2 dozen cookies**

> 6½ tablespoons unsalted butter
> 1 tablespoon amaretto (almond-flavored) liqueur
> 1 tablespoon rose water
> ½ cup ground, toasted almonds (see Chef's Note, page 38)
> 1 cup granulated sugar
> ½ cup pastry flour
> 1 tablespoon honey
> 6 large egg whites

1. Butter and flour 2 miniature muffin pans (12 muffins each) and place them in the refrigerator for later use. Preheat the oven to 400°F.
2. To make brown butter (*beurre noisette*), fill a stainless steel bowl with ice water. In a small saucepan over medium heat, melt the butter. Continue to cook the butter until it begins to brown; then remove from the heat and immediately place the pan in the ice bath. Carefully add the amaretto and rose water—the mixture may spatter. Stir to combine. Set the brown butter aside, at room temperature, for later use.
3. In the food processor, grind together the toasted almonds, sugar, flour, and honey until it forms a coarse meal. Transfer the mixture to a stainless steel bowl.
4. In a separate bowl, whip the egg whites for a few seconds to loosen them. In a steady stream, stirring constantly, slowly add the whites to the ground almond mixture.
5. Add the brown butter to the batter and stir to combine. Cover, and chill the batter for at least 1 hour.
6. Fill the muffin pan molds just above half full. Bake in the preheated oven, with the door propped open, for 10 minutes, or until light golden. Cool the pans on wire racks and unmold.

These cookies are similar to eighteenth-century ratafia cakes (prepared with egg whites and almonds) as well as butter drops (made with eggs, butter, and rose water). The following recipe for ratafia cakes appeared in Elizabeth Raffald's cookbook <u>The Experienced English Housekeeper</u>:

"Take one pound and a half of sweet almonds and half a pound of bitteralmonds, beat them as fine as possible with the whites of two eggs. Then beat the whites of five eggs to a sugar beat and sifted very fine. Drop them in little drops the size of a nutmeg on cap paper, and bake them in a slack oven."

# Pine Nut Cookies

These cookies are yet another variation of the many butter cookies baked in the eighteenth century. It is unclear just when Americans began cooking and baking with pine nuts. Today they are harvested from pine cones, which grow on pine trees in "China, Italy, Mexico, North Africa, and the southwest United States" (Herbst 351). It is possible that these nuts were imported from Europe or Asia during the eighteenth century.

**Makes 2 dozen cookies**

> 2 cups pine nuts
> ½ cup plus 2 tablespoons Almond Paste (see page 40), or 6½ ounces store-bought almond paste
> 6 tablespoons honey
> 8 ounces (2 sticks) unsalted butter, cubed, at room temperature
> ½ cup granulated sugar
> 4 large eggs
> 4 large egg yolks
> 1¼ cups plus 2 tablespoons sifted all-purpose flour
> 1 cup finely ground, toasted almonds (see Chef's Note, page 38)

1. Preheat the oven to 325°F. Line 2 cookie sheets with parchment paper.
2. Place the pine nuts on a baking pan, and toast in the oven for 5 minutes, checking frequently, until light golden. Set aside to cool completely.
3. In the bowl of an electric mixer fitted with the paddle attachment on low speed, mix the Almond Paste with the honey until soft and smooth. Scrape down the sides of the bowl.
4. With the mixer still running on low speed, add the butter by the cube. Scrape down the sides of the bowl when half the butter has been added. Once all the butter has been added, scrape down the sides of the bowl, add the sugar, and mix on medium speed until smooth.
5. With the mixer still on medium speed, add the eggs and yolks, one at a time. Mix until smooth. Scrape down the sides of the bowl.
6. Shut the mixer off; add the flour, ground almonds, and toasted pine nuts; and pulse just the mixture until it comes together. Scrape down the sides of the bowl, making sure the mixture is homogenous.
7. Drop the batter by the tablespoonful, 1 inch apart, onto the prepared cookie sheets.
8. Bake for 7 to 8 minutes, or until the sides just begin to turn light golden. Cool on the cookie sheets for 10 minutes. Store in airtight containers at room temperature for up to 1 week.

# Financiers

Like many of the dry sweetmeats of the eighteenth century, financiers are a cross between little cakes and cookies. Usually prepared with almonds, this recipe may be varied to use pistachios, which Thomas Jefferson cultivated for some years, most likely having purchased the trees from Italy or elsewhere in Europe (Leighton 236). Flavored with orange, vanilla, utmeg, and liqueur, these cookies would have appealed to the eighteenth-century palate.

Makes 2 dozen cookies

> 6 tablespoons (¾ stick) unsalted butter, cubed
> 2 tablespoons vanilla extract
> 2 tablespoons orange liqueur (such as Cointreau or Triple Sec)
> 1 cup almonds, toasted (see Chef's Note, page 38)
> 1 cup all-purpose flour
> 1⅔ cups granulated sugar
> 1 orange, zest grated
> Pinch of ground nutmeg
> 5 large egg whites
> Pinch of salt

1. Preheat the oven to 425°F. Butter and flour 24 financier molds (available at specialty kitchenware stores) or miniature muffin pans, and refrigerate for later use.
2. To make brown butter (*beurre noisette*): Fill a stainless steel bowl with ice water. Cube the butter, and melt it in a small saucepan over medium heat. Continue to cook the butter until it begins to brown. When the butter begins to brown, remove it from the heat and shock the pan in the ice water bath. Carefully mix in the vanilla extract and orange liqueur—the mixture may spatter. Set aside the brown butter, at room temperature, for later use.
3. In the bowl of a food processor, add the toasted almonds, flour, 1 cup of the sugar, the orange zest, and nutmeg; process until finely ground. Set aside.
4. In the immaculately clean bowl of your electric mixer fitted with the whip attachment on medium speed, whip the egg whites and salt until they begin to foam. Slowly add the remaining ⅔ cup of the sugar in a thin steady stream. Once all the sugar has been added, increase the mixer to high, and whip the meringue to medium peaks. Transfer the meringue to a separate bowl.
5. Check to make sure the brown butter is cool—if not, place it in the refrigerator for a few minutes. Fold a quarter of the almond-flour mixture into the egg whites. Fold a third of the cooled brown butter into the whites. Proceed with another quarter of the flour mixture and a third of the brown butter until the mixtures are complete and the batter is thoroughly combined and smooth. Chill the batter for 2 hours.
6. Fill the prepared molds halfway with the batter, put them in the oven, and immediately reduce the oven temperature to 375°F. Bake 7 minutes, or until golden. Cool briefly on wire racks, and unmold the financiers while still warm.

# Orange Shortbread

This flavorful shortbread is based on original recipes that call for baking the rich butter-cookie dough in round pans. In keeping with the eighteenth-century affinity for nuts, spices, and citrus, this version is flavored with almonds, orange zest, orange extract, nutmeg, and orange marmalade. The result is a rich and refreshing butter cookie suitable for tea or dessert.

**Makes 2 dozen cookies**

### Shortbread
¾ cup almonds, toasted (see Chef's Note, page 38)
1 orange
1 cup granulated sugar
Pinch of ground nutmeg
10 ounces (2½ sticks) unsalted butter, cubed, at room temperature
2 large eggs
1 large egg yolk
1 tablespoon vanilla extract
1 teaspoon orange extract
2 cups sifted all-purpose flour

2 cups Orange Marmalade (see page 247), or use store-bought kind
4 cups sliced almonds
Confectioners' sugar, for dusting (optional)

1. Preheat the oven to 375°F.
2. Transfer the almonds to the bowl of a food processor, and process until finely ground. Set aside
3. In a small bowl, grate the orange zest over the sugar and nutmeg.
4. In the bowl of an electric mixer fitted with the paddle attachment, on medium speed, beat the orange-sugar mixture and the butter. Scrape down the sides of the bowl.
5. To the mixer bowl while still on medium speed, add the eggs and yolk, one at a time. Scrape down the sides of the bowl. Add the ground almonds, and mix to combine. Add the vanilla and orange extracts, mix to combine, and scrape down the sides of the bowl.
6. Remove the bowl from the mixer, and fold in the flour with a rubber spatula or a wooden spoon.
7. Chill the dough for at least 3 hours, or overnight.
8. Turn over 2 jelly-roll pans, grease the bottoms with butter, and coat lightly with flour. Set the upside-down pans in the refrigerator until needed. Dust your countertop and rolling pin generously with flour. Roll the dough out ¼ inch thick. Cut the dough into two similarly sized pieces to fit on the prepared pans.
9. Transfer the dough to the cold pans by gently draping it over a well-floured rolling pin, lifting it, and laying it across the back of each tray.
10. Prick the dough with a fork, and chill for 30 minutes in the refrigerator.
11. Preheat the oven to 375°F.
12. Bake the dough for 3 to 5 minutes, or until it just begins to color. Remove it from the oven and let it cool slightly.

13. Assemble the cookies: Carefully spread the Orange Marmalade over the prebaked almond dough. Sprinkle 2 cups of almonds per tray evenly atop the marmalade. Return the pans to the oven and bake until the marmalade bubbles.

14. Remove the tray from the oven and allow to cool slightly, about 5 minutes. With a chef's knife, cut the cookie sheets into 3-inch squares. Return the squares to the oven for 30 seconds to rewarm and make cutting them easier. Cut the squares diagonally in half, making triangles.

15. Allow to cool, and dust lightly with confectioners' sugar, if desired.

# Pistachio Crescents

Buttery crescent-nut cookies exist in numerous cultures and were introduced into America as immigrants arrived throughout the centuries. This version is simply and richly flavored with ground pistachios, vanilla, and butter and delicately ornamented with confectioners' sugar.

**Makes 32 crescents**

> ½ cup shelled pistachio nuts
> 1¾ cup plus 2 tablespoons all-purpose flour
> 1 vanilla bean
> One 1-pound box confectioners' sugar
> ½ pound (2 sticks) unsalted butter, cubed, at room temperature
> 3 large egg yolks

1. Preheat the oven to 350°F.
2. Arrange the pistachios in a single layer on a cookie sheet. Toast in the oven for about 5 minutes. Remove from the oven, and let cool for about 10 minutes. Transfer the pistachios to the bowl of a food processor, add 2 tablespoons of the flour, and process until finely ground. Turn off the oven.
3. Slice the vanilla bean in half lengthwise. Using the back of a knife, scrape the seeds from each half. In a small bowl, combine ¾ cup of the confectioners' sugar and the vanilla seeds.
4. In the bowl of an electric mixer fitted with the paddle attachment on medium speed, beat the butter and vanilla-confectioners' sugar mixture until smooth. Scrape down the sides of the bowl.
5. With the mixer on medium speed, add the yolks one at a time, beating after each addition. Scrape down the sides of the bowl.
6. Remove the bowl from the mixer, and with a rubber spatula or wooden spoon, fold in the remaining 1¾ cups of flour and the ground pistachios.
7. Scrape the dough onto a lightly floured countertop, and knead a few times until smooth. Roll the dough into three 1-inch-thick by 12-inch-long logs. Wrap the logs in plastic wrap, and chill in the refrigerator for 2 hours.
8. Preheat the oven to 350°F.
9. Lightly dust the countertop with flour, and unwrap the cookie dough. Using a chef's knife or bench scraper, cut each log into 2-inch-long pieces. With your left and right index fingers, roll out each piece slightly and taper the edges somewhat. Bend the edges in, creating a half moon. It is easier to work with cold dough, so if the dough becomes difficult to work with, return it to the refrigerator to chill for a few minutes—try to avoid using too much dusting flour because this will dry out the cookies.
10. Line up the cookies on two cookie sheets, 1 inch apart. Transfer the cookie sheets to the refrigerator to chill for 30 minutes.
11. Transfer the chilled cookie sheets to the oven, and bake for 8 minutes, or until light golden. Let the cookies cool slightly.
12. While the cookies are in the oven, fill a bowl with the remaining confectioners' sugar from the 1-pound box. While the cookies are still warm, roll them in the bowl of confectioners' sugar, covering them well.
13. On cooling racks, allow the cookies to cool completely; then dust again with confectioners' sugar.

# Madeleines

These French cookies resemble the small sponge cakes prepared so frequently in eighteenth-century America. They are traditionally shell shaped and coated with confectioners' sugar after baking.

**Makes 2 dozen cookies**

¼ cup granulated sugar
1 lemon
1 tablespoon lemon thyme, or substitute regular dried thyme
4 large egg yolks
¼ pound (1 stick) unsalted butter, melted
3 large egg whites
¼ cup sifted all-purpose flour

1. Grease a madeleine tray, and coat lightly with flour. Preheat the oven to 375°F.
2. In a small bowl, add the sugar and grate the lemon zest over it. Add the lemon thyme and stir to combine.
3. In the bowl of an electric mixer fitted with the whip attachment on medium speed, whip the egg yolks and lemon thyme-sugar mixture until the mixture triples in volume and ribbons form. Slowly mix in the butter.
4. Transfer the whipped yolks to a medium-size stainless steel bowl.
5. Clean the electric mixer bowl and whip attachment and dry thoroughly. Add the egg whites, and whip to stiff peaks.
6. In a medium-size bowl, sift the flour 3 times. Fold the flour into the yolk mixture, about 1 tablespoon at a time.
7. Transfer one third of the yolk mixture into the whipped egg whites. Fold the egg white mixture into the yolk mixture, being careful not to deflate the batter. With a delicate hand, fold the remaining flour into the batter.
8. Fill the madeleine molds half full.
9. Bake for 5 to 7 minutes, or until golden and puffed (doubled in size). Unmold the madeleines immediately and cool to room temperature.

# Poppy Seed Squares

These bar cookies pay tribute to the affinity eighteenth-century Americans and Europeans had for exotic, Eastern foodstuffs. For centuries, poppy seeds have been harvested from the opium poppy cultivated in the Middle East and used in sweet and savory dishes throughout Europe (Ortiz 91). Some period recipes for "surfeit waters" (medicinal waters) call for poppy flowers, but of the "Corn-Rose or wilde [*sic*]" variety rather than the Eastern opium sort. Although these red poppies were renowned for treating headaches, bad breath, and flatulence, they also had a slight sedative effect (Hess 417).

Rather than for any medicinal effect, poppy seeds are used in these cookies to add flavor and texture to the rich filling of nuts, citrus, and honey.

Makes 24 squares

**Cookie Dough**
½ pound (2 sticks) unsalted butter
½ cup granulated sugar
1 large egg
1½ cups all-purpose flour

**Poppy Seed Filling**
½ cup poppy seeds
1 cup whole milk
¼ cup honey
½ cup heavy cream
1 lemon, zest grated
1 teaspoon cornstarch
2 tablespoons orange liqueur (such as Cointreau or Triple Sec)
3 tablespoons unsalted butter
¼ cup ground walnuts
1 large egg

1.  Grease an 11 x 17-inch baking pan, coat it lightly with flour, and refrigerate it.
2.  Prepare the Cookie Dough: In the bowl on an electric mixer fitted with the paddle attachment on medium speed, beat the butter and sugar until smooth. Scrape down the sides of the bowl. Add the egg and beat until smooth. Scrape down the sides of the bowl.
3.  Remove the bowl from the mixer, and with a rubber spatula or wooden spoon, fold in the flour.
4.  Wrap the dough in plastic wrap, and chill in the refrigerator for 2 hours.
5.  On a lightly floured work surface, roll the dough evenly out so that it is 12 x 18 inches.
6.  Transfer the dough carefully to the prepared baking pan by draping it over a well-floured rolling pin, lifting it, and gently setting it in the pan. Mold the dough into the baking pan, making certain the edges are square. Don't fuss over the dough if it breaks—simply patch together the dough inside the pan. Chill in the refrigerator for 1 hour.
7.  Prepare the Poppy Seed Filling: In a medium-size saucepan, stir together the poppy seeds, milk, and honey, and let the ingredients soak for 1 hour.
8.  Preheat the oven to 350°F.

9. Add the heavy cream and lemon zest to the poppy seed mixture. Place the saucepan over medium-low heat and cook, stirring constantly, until the mixture boils. Continue to cook the mixture, stirring occasionally, until the poppy seeds absorb half the milk and the mixture begins to thicken, about 15 minutes.

10. Meanwhile, in a small bowl, whisk together the cornstarch and liqueur.

11. When the milk-poppy seed mixture begins to boil, add the cornstarch mixture, stirring continuously to prevent clumping, and cook for 30 seconds.

12. Remove the pan from the heat, add the butter and ground walnuts, and mix well to combine. Stir vigorously until the mixture cools slightly, and add the egg.

13. Pour the warm filling into the chilled, dough-lined cookie sheet. Bake for 15 minutes, or until the filling puffs slightly and is firm and the sides brown.

14. Let cool to room temperature, and cut into 2¼-inch squares.

Like Martha Washington, who included medicinal beverages entitled "To Make Surfit [*sic*] Water of Poppies" and "To Make the Surfit Water" in her cookbook, Hannah Glasse published "To make Cordial Poppy Water" in her book <u>The Art of Cooking Made Plain and Easy</u> (Hess 416-417; Glasse 281-282). It is similar to Washington's waters—spicy, sweet, and strong:

Take two gallons of very good brandy, and a peck of poppies, and put them together in a wide-mouthed glass, and let them stand forty-eight hours, and then strain the poppies out; take a pound of raisins of the sun, stone them, and an ounce of coriander-seed, an ounce of sweet-fennel seeds, and an ounce of liqueurice [*sic*] sliced, bruise them all together, and put them into the brandy, with a pound of good powder sugar, and let them stand four or eight weeks, shaking it every day; and then strain it off, and bottle it close up for use.

# Lemon Bars

These refreshing cookies celebrate the eighteenth-century fondness for buttery cookies and small cakes as well as for lemons, which were imported and therefore costly. When baked, this filling takes on the consistency of custard, and its sweet and refreshing flavor complements the buttery crust.

**Makes 16 Squares**

### Cookie Dough
¾ cup confectioners' sugar
2 lemons
½ pound (2 sticks) unsalted butter, at room temperature
1 large egg
1¾ cups all-purpose flour

### Lemon Filling
1 large egg
1 large egg yolk
½ cup granulated sugar
1 cup freshly squeezed lemon juice
2 tablespoons grated lemon zest
2 tablespoons sour cream

2 large eggs whisked with 1 tablespoon water and pinch of salt, for egg wash

1. Grease an 11 x 17-inch baking pan with butter, and coat lightly with flour. Chill the pan in the refrigerator.
2. Prepare the Cookie Dough: In the bowl of an electric mixer fitted with the paddle attachment, add the sugar. Grate the zest of the 2 lemons over the sugar.
3. Add the butter to the mixer bowl, and beat on medium speed until the ingredients are smooth. Scrape down the sides of the bowl.
4. Add the egg and beat until smooth. Scrape down the sides of the bowl. Remove the bowl from the mixer, and, with a rubber spatula or wooden spoon, fold in the flour.
5. Wrap the dough in plastic wrap and chill in the refrigerator for 2 hours.
6. On a lightly floured work surface, roll the dough evenly out so that it is 12 x 18 inches. Transfer the dough carefully to the chilled baking pan by draping it over a well-floured rolling pin, lifting it, and gently setting it in the pan. Mold the dough in the baking pan, making certain the edges are square. Don't fuss over the dough if it breaks—simply patch together the dough inside the pan. Chill the dough in the refrigerator for 1 hour.
7. Preheat the oven to 350°F.
8. Prepare the Lemon Filling: In a medium-size mixing bowl, add the egg, egg yolk, and sugar, and whisk together. Add the lemon juice, lemon zest and sour cream; whisk to combine. Set aside.
9. Weight the chilled and molded dough with foil and raw beans or pie weights, and partially bake the dough for 7 minutes, or until it begins to color. Remove the foil and weights, and brush the dough with the egg wash. Return the dough to the oven and bake for 5 minutes more, or until golden.

**10.** Remove the dough from the oven, and pour the filling into the shell. Return the pan to the oven, reduce the oven temperature to 300°F, and bake for about 8 minutes, or until the filling is set.

**11.** Let the bars cool to room temperature. Then chill for 1 hour in the refrigerator, unmold, and cut into 2½-inch squares.

# Hamantaschen

These filled cookies refer to the many varieties of rich, buttery cookies and cakes prepared in the eighteenth century. A traditional Jewish confection, these cookies are triangular in shape, recalling the hats of Haman (a Persian prime minister who planned to exterminate Persian Jews), after which they were named. Hamantaschen are commonly filled with preserves and/or nuts and are served during Purim, which celebrates Haman's failed murderous attempt on the Jewish people. Of course, these cookies refer not only to Jewish foodways but also to the German traditions many Jews acquired once they settled in northern Europe. The preparation of hamantaschen is just one example of how Philadelphia's eighteenth-century Jewish community, like many others, continued to express their diverse heritage through the foods they prepared.

**Makes 2 dozen cookies**

### Cookie Dough
4½ cups all-purpose flour
¾ cup granulated sugar
12 ounces (3 sticks) unsalted butter, cubed, at room temperature
4 ounces cream cheese, cubed, at room temperature
2 large eggs
4 teaspoons vanilla extract

### Plum Prune Filling
4 tablespoons (½ stick) unsalted butter
2 cups prunes, chopped
3 plums, pitted and cut into ½-inch cubes
¼ cup light brown sugar
1½ teaspoons freshly squeezed lemon juice
1 cup Orange Marmalade (see page 247), or use store-bought kind
½ cup raisins

3 large eggs, beaten with 2 tablespoons water, for egg wash

1. Prepare the Cookie Dough: In the bowl of an electric mixer with the paddle attachment, on medium speed, mix together the flour, sugar, butter, and cream cheese until smooth. Add the eggs and vanilla extract, and mix until combined. Chill in the refrigerator for 2 hours.

2. Prepare the Plum Prune Filling: In a medium-size saucepan, melt the butter over medium heat. With a wooden spoon, stir in the prunes and plums. Add the brown sugar and lemon juice. Cook the mixture until the sugar dissolves, the mixture thickens, and the fruit begins to break down.

3. Stir in the Orange Marmalade and raisins. Cook the mixture until it boils; then remove from the heat, and allow the mixture to cool to room temperature.

4. To shape the hamantaschen, roll the dough to a ¼-inch thickness. Using a 5-inch fluted biscuit cutter, cut 12 rounds from the dough. Brush the dough rounds with the egg wash.

5. Place 2 tablespoons of the filling in the center of each round. Fold the dough in thirds over the filling, leaving the center uncovered and forming a triangle-shaped pastry. Brush the folded edges with the egg wash.

6. Transfer the hamantaschen to a cookie sheet. Chill the cookies in the refrigerator for 1 hour.
7. Preheat the oven to 375°F.
8. Bake the hamantaschen for 15 minutes, or until golden. Cool completely on the cookie sheets on wire racks.

The first permanent Jewish settlement in colonial America began in 1654 with the arrival of twenty-three Jews who had sailed from Brazil to New Amsterdam (now New York). Thus began an immigration that continued into the early nineteenth century (Faber 4). Jews from Poland, Germany, Spain, and Portugal first relocated to England and Holland and a generation or two later moved again to make their homes not only in New York but also in New England (Newport, Rhode Island, and New Haven, Connecticut), in the South (Charleston, South Carolina, and Savannah, Georgia), and elsewhere in the mid-Atlantic, particularly in Philadelphia and Lancaster (26, 4). In eighteenth-century America, Jews made up less than one percent of the population (4). Yet, holding firm to many of their rich, varied traditions, they influenced the regions in which they lived and contributed to the diversity that ultimately shaped and defined the new nation.

# Gingerbread Cookies

Nearly every eighteenth-century cookbook included recipes for gingerbread cookies, even though they were simply titled "Gingerbread." Recipes for cake-like gingerbread appeared occasionally as well, but less frequently. In fact, even "gingerbread cake" recipes usually referred to plain cookies or those pressed into decorative molds before baking.

Period cookbooks that listed multiple gingerbread recipes often included "molasses" or "culler'd" types as well as "white" versions, which were sweetened with sugar alone rather than with molasses (Simmons 49; Hess 346–347). These lighter-colored cookies were also highly spiced and often flavored with wine and rose water. It seems that white gingerbreads were baked ¼ inch thick or less, while those with molasses were rolled thicker. As Martha Washington's recipe for the former stated: "[T]he prints of white ginger bread are used much thinner then the cullerd [*sic*], which is commonly made allmoste [*sic*] halfe an Intch [*sic*] thick, or a quarter of an intch at ye least" (Hess 347).

**Makes 16 cookies (depends on the size of the cutter)**

¼ pound (1 stick) unsalted butter
½ cup dark brown sugar
¼ cup granulated sugar
2 tablespoons chopped fresh ginger
4 cups bread flour
2¼ cups pastry flour
2¼ teaspoons baking soda
1 tablespoon ground ginger
1 teaspoon ground allspice
½ teaspoon ground cloves
½ teaspoon ground nutmeg
½ teaspoon ground cardamom
Pinch of ground mace
½ cup plus 2 tablespoons apple cider
2 tablespoons rose water
½ cup Grandma's dark molasses
¼ cup honey
¼ cup maple syrup

1. In the bowl of an electric mixer fitted with the paddle attachment on medium speed, beat the butter, brown sugar, granulated sugar, and fresh ginger until light and fluffy, scraping down the sides of the bowl often.
2. In a large bowl, sift together the bread flour, pastry flour, baking soda, ground ginger, allspice, cloves, nutmeg, cardamom, and mace. In a small bowl, whisk together the cider and rose water.
3. In another small bowl, whisk together the molasses, honey, and maple syrup. Add the cider-rosewater mixture, and whisk to combine. With the mixer running on medium speed, add half the syrup mixture to the butter mixture in a thin steady stream. Scrape down the sides of the bowl. Add the remaining syrup in the same manner.
4. Transfer the butter mixture to a large bowl. Add the sifted dry ingredients, and mix with your hands until combined.

5. Transfer the dough to a lightly floured countertop and knead until smooth. Wrap the dough in plastic wrap and chill in the refrigerator for several hours, or overnight.
6. Preheat the oven to 375°F. Line 2 cookie sheets with parchment paper, and grease the parchment with butter.
7. Roll out the dough to ¼ inch thick and, using a medium-size cookie cutter of choice, cut into desired shapes.
8. Bake the cookies about 12 minutes, or until set. Cool completely on the pans on wire racks.

Although gingerbread cookies were enjoyed year-round in the eighteenth century, it appears that those which were decoratively printed or molded were deemed especially appropriate for the holidays. In her cookery book, Martha Washington instructed that once the dough was prepared, "[M]ake it into prints or rouls [*sic*] as you like them best, or cakes, but prints is moste [*sic*] used after the second course in christmas [*sic*]" (Hess 347).

# Quick Breads

It is unclear just when the term "quick bread" became part of American culinary vocabulary. What is certain, however, is that in the eighteenth century these breads were popularly referred to as cakes and biscuits, some of which were prepared with "emptins" (a fermented leavener based on flour and ale). Unlike yeast breads, which require numerous hours of kneading and fermentation, quick breads rely on fast-acting leaveners, including baking powder, baking soda and, in the case of light batters, eggs. Although chemical leaveners were not widely available until the nineteenth century, eighteenth-century bakers used pearl ash or pot ash (early forms of baking soda) to ensure that their cakes and biscuits would rise quickly.

Indeed, in texture and flavor, quick breads resemble cakes more than yeast breads. Perhaps one of the earliest examples of how cake and bread became linked in name, if not in concept, is Eliza Leslie's 1848 recipe for "Bread Cake," published in *Directions for Cookery, in Its Various Branches*. It called for a combination of wheat-bread dough—"as much of it as would make a twelve cent loaf"—and cake ingredients, including "confectioners' sugar . . . butter . . . milk . . . [and] a beaten egg" (350). Unlike eighteenth-century yeast-leavened breads, cakes, and biscuits, this recipe required only half an hour of rising. As the availability of baking soda and powder increased throughout the nineteenth century, the need for using bread dough and/or yeast in such recipes grew obsolete, and quick breads that resembled eighteenth-century cakes and biscuits became easier than ever to prepare.

# Thomas Jefferson's Sweet Potato Biscuits

In the eighteenth century, sweet potatoes were plentiful in the southern states, and Thomas Jefferson participated as enthusiastically in their cultivation as other farmers. George Washington, in fact, was one of his compatriots in this venture (Mount Vernon memo). This root vegetable makes a number of appearances in Jefferson's collection of recipes and, consequently, inspired this recipe (Kimball 95, 100). Sweet potatoes contribute a sweet flavor and light texture to these biscuits and are complemented by the addition of one of this renowned gardener's other favorite foods, pecans.

**Makes about 2 dozen biscuits**

> 5 cups all-purpose flour
> 1 cup packed light brown sugar
> 2 tablespoons baking powder
> 1½ teaspoons ground cinnamon
> 1 teaspoon salt
> 1 teaspoon ground ginger
> ½ teaspoon ground allspice
> 1 cup vegetable shortening
> 2 cups cooked, mashed, and cooled sweet potato (about 2 large potatoes)
> 1 cup heavy cream
> ½ cup coarsely chopped pecans

1. Preheat the oven to 400°F.
2. In a large mixing bowl, add the flour, brown sugar, baking powder, cinnamon, salt, ginger, and allspice; stir to combine.
3. Add the shortening, and cut in with two knives until crumbly.
4. Add the sweet potato, and mix well with a wooden spoon. Add the cream and pecans, and stir just until moistened.
5. Turn the dough out onto a lightly floured surface. Roll out the dough to 1½ inches thick. Cut out biscuits with a 2-inch floured biscuit cutter. Place the biscuits 1 inch apart on ungreased baking pans.
6. Set the pans in the oven, reduce the oven temperature to 350°F, and bake for 25 to 30 minutes, or until golden brown. Serve warm or let cool on a wire rack to room temperature.

**Chef's Note**

*The biscuit dough freezes beautifully unbaked. Just layer the dough between wax paper and store for up to 3 months. Defrost the dough and follow the baking directions. It pays to make a double batch of these biscuits and freeze half for later.*

# Almond–Buttermilk Biscuits

This recipe was inspired by the many varieties of biscuits featured in period cookbooks. Some were simple combinations of flour, butter, egg, milk, and occasionally spices or fruit. Others were leavened with yeast or emptins—a mixture of "fermenting ale . . . [and] flour"—whose sourdough-like flavor resembled the tartness that buttermilk imparts to these biscuits (Simmons 69). The addition of sliced almonds complements their mild sweetness and moist texture.

**Makes 12 biscuits**

> 2¼ cups all-purpose flour
> ½ cup granulated sugar
> 1½ teaspoons baking powder
> ¾ teaspoon baking soda
> ¼ teaspoon salt
> 6 tablespoons (¾ stick) unsalted butter, chilled and cubed
> 1¼ cups buttermilk
> 1 large egg yolk
> 1 teaspoon vanilla extract
> 1 cup sliced almonds
> Chantilly Cream (see page 120), for serving (optional)
> Fresh berries, for serving (optional)

1. Preheat the oven to 400°F.
2. In a large mixing bowl, stir together the flour, sugar, baking powder, baking soda, and salt.
3. Add the butter to the flour mixture, and cut in with 2 knives until crumbly.
4. In a small mixing bowl, combine 1 cup of the buttermilk, the egg yolk, and the vanilla extract. Add to the butter-flour mixture, and stir just until moistened.
5. Turn the dough out onto a lightly floured surface, roll out the dough until 1 to 1¼ inches thick. Cut out biscuits with a 3-inch floured biscuit cutter. Place the biscuits 1 inch apart on ungreased baking pans.
6. Brush the tops of the biscuits with the remaining buttermilk, and sprinkle with the sliced almonds.
7. Reduce the oven temperature to 350°F, and bake for 15 to 20 minutes, or until golden brown.
8. Transfer the biscuits to a wire rack and cool to room temperature. If desired, serve with the Chantilly Cream and berries. If storing the biscuits, wrap in plastic wrap and keep at room temperature for up to 2 days.

# Lemon-Poppy Seed Bread

This bread represents the intermingling of cultures and foodways that took place throughout the American colonies and especially in cosmopolitan Philadelphia. Lemons were imported from Spain and Portugal, and poppy seeds represent the exotic foodstuffs from Europe and the Orient (the Middle East and India) that influenced stylish eighteenth-century dishes.

Like oranges, lemons are frequently characterized as an elite fruit, so expensive that only the wealthy could afford to display and cook with them. Although their high cost is undisputed, the use of lemons appears to have been fairly widespread. Period cookbooks, even those whose authors focused specifically on domestic frugality, contained numerous recipes that called for lemon juice, peel, oil, and syrup, sometimes in great quantities. If a home cook chose to purchase rather than prepare her own lemon sweetmeats, they were widely available in local shops as well. According to Philadelphia advertisements, "lemmon chips" (candied lemon peel) were among the most popular items sold in confectioners' stores (*Pennsylvania Gazette*, August 9, 1775).

Makes two 8-inch loaves

> 1¼ pounds (5 sticks) unsalted butter, at room temperature
> 2 cups granulated sugar
> 9 large eggs
> ¼ cup freshly squeezed lemon juice (about 1 large lemon), strained
> 2 teaspoons grated lemon zest
> 1 teaspoon vanilla extract
> 4 cups all-purpose flour
> 2 tablespoons poppy seeds
> 2 teaspoons baking powder
> 1 teaspoon salt

1. Preheat the oven to 325°F. Grease two 8½ x 4½ x 2½-inch loaf pans with butter.
2. In the bowl of an electric mixer on medium speed, beat together the butter and sugar until light and fluffy, 2 to 3 minutes.
3. Beat in the eggs one at a time. Add the lemon juice, lemon zest, and vanilla extract; beat until combined.
4. In a medium-size bowl, stir together the flour, poppy seeds, baking powder, and salt. Add the egg mixture to the flour mixture, and mix on low speed just until moistened.
5. Divide the batter between the prepared pans. Bake about 1 hour, or until golden brown and a toothpick inserted in the center comes out clean.
6. Cool in the pans on wire racks for 10 minutes. To remove the breads, flip the pans on their sides and gently pull out the bread. Serve warm, or let cool to room temperature.

# Cornbread

To Europeans, "corn" has always been a generic name for all grains, and "maize," from the American Indian *mahiz*, has referred specifically to what Americans know as corn. The colonists associated this native grain not only with the New World but also with the Indians who introduced them to it; they, therefore, referred to the grain frequently as "Indian corn" to differentiate it from other varieties.

Not only was cornbread included in period cookbooks, but related corn recipes appeared frequently as well, including baked and boiled indian pudding, mush, and Johny or Johnny cakes, also known as journey and hoe cakes. These mildly sweet (if they were sweetened at all) dishes called for cornmeal (or Indian), whole corn, or even, as in the case of Thomas Jefferson's "Corn Pudding" recipe, green (unripened) corn (Kimball 89).

Like this version of cornbread, these recipes were flavorful and quick to prepare. In addition, as they were frequently served alongside European-inspired dishes on eighteenth-century dining tables, cornbread and its related preparations certainly represented distinctively American foodways.

**Serves 10 to 12**

> 2 cups coarse yellow cornmeal
> 2 cups all-purpose flour
> ½ cup granulated sugar
> 2 tablespoons baking powder
> 1 teaspoon salt
> 2 cups whole milk
> ¼ pound (1 stick) unsalted butter, melted
> 2 large eggs, lightly beaten

1. Preheat the oven to 400°F. Grease two 8½ x 4½ x 2½ loaf pans with butter.
2. In a large mixing bowl, add the cornmeal, flour, sugar, baking powder, and salt; stir to combine.
3. In a medium-size mixing bowl, combine the milk, butter, and eggs. Add to the dry ingredients, and stir just until moistened.
4. Pour the batter into the prepared pans. Bake for 30 to 35 minutes, or until golden brown and a wooden toothpick inserted near the center comes out clean.
5. Let cool in the pan for 30 minutes (to prevent crumbling).

# Lemon–Blueberry Bread

This sweet, tart bread exemplifies the cultural and culinary fusion that shaped eighteenth-century Philadelphia. The combination of lemons and blueberries represents the merging of European and Native American cultures and foodways, respectively. The result is more than simply symbolic, however; the clear lemony glaze complements the tender blueberry bread, resulting in a refreshingly sweet treat.

**Makes one 8-inch loaf**

### Bread

1 cup granulated sugar
6 tablespoons (¾ stick) unsalted butter, at room temperature
2 large eggs
2 teaspoons grated lemon zest
1½ cups all-purpose flour
1 teaspoon baking powder
¼ teaspoon salt
½ cup sour cream
1½ cups fresh blueberries

### Lemon Glaze

⅓ cup granulated sugar
3 tablespoons freshly squeezed and strained lemon juice

1.  Prepare the Bread: Preheat the oven to 325°F. Grease an 8½ x 4½ x 2½-inch loaf pan with butter.
2.  In the bowl of an electric mixer fitted with the paddle attachment on medium speed, beat together the sugar and butter until light and fluffy, 2 to 3 minutes.
3.  Add the eggs and lemon zest, and beat until combined.
4.  In a small mixing bowl, add the flour, baking powder, and salt; stir to combine. Fold the dry ingredients into the butter mixture in thirds, alternating with the milk.
5.  With a rubber spatula or wooden spoon, gently fold in the blueberries.
6.  Pour the batter into the prepared pan. Bake for 50 to 60 minutes, or until golden brown and a toothpick inserted near the center comes out clean.
7.  Cool in the pan on a wire rack for 10 minutes. To remove the bread, flip the pan on its side and gently pull out the bread. Serve warm, or let cool to room temperature on a wire rack.
8.  Prepare the Lemon Glaze: In a small saucepan, bring the sugar and lemon juice to a boil, stirring to dissolve the sugar. Remove from the heat. Drizzle over the cooled bread loaf.

# Cranberry Bread

In the eighteenth century, cranberries were often preserved or baked in tarts and puddings, most likely because, as Lydia Maria Child explained in *The American Frugal Housewife*, "They need a great deal of sweetening" (68). Mrs. Child also recommended that "[a] little nutmeg, or cinnamon, improves them," and Amelia Simmons similarly suggested that after stewing and sweetening the fruit, one should "add spices till grateful" (Child 68; Simmons 29).

This recipe calls for a minimal amount of sugar and fresh, rather than cooked, fruit. Even Child and Simmons would agree, however, that the bread is "gratefully," and successfully, flavored with the additions of orange zest and pecans.

**Makes one 8-inch loaf**

> 4½ ounces (1 stick plus 1 tablespoon) unsalted butter, at room temperature
> ¾ cup granulated sugar
> 4 large eggs
> 2⅓ cups sifted cake flour
> 1 tablespoon baking powder
> 1 teaspoon salt
> ¾ cup whole milk
> 2 cups fresh cranberries
> ½ cup chopped pecans
> 2 teaspoons grated orange zest

1. Preheat the oven to 350°F. Grease an 8½ x 4½ x 2½-inch loaf pan with butter.
2. In the bowl of an electric mixer fitted with the paddle attachment on medium speed, beat together the butter and sugar until light and fluffy, 2 to 3 minutes.
3. Add the eggs one at a time, and beat until combined.
4. In a medium-size mixing bowl, add the flour, baking powder, and salt; stir to combine. Fold the dry ingredients into the butter mixture in thirds, alternating with the milk.
5. In a medium-size mixing bowl, combine the cranberries, pecans, and orange zest. With a rubber spatula, gently fold into the batter.
6. Pour the batter into the prepared pan. Bake about 45 minutes, or until golden brown and a toothpick inserted near the center comes out clean.
7. Remove the pan from oven, and let cool for 10 minutes. To remove the bead, flip the pan on its side and gently pull out the bread.

# Zucchini–Nut Bread

Although many varieties of squash were familiar to Native Americans and early European settlers, zucchini was introduced to Americans only in the early twentieth century (Mariani 309, 358). Similar in texture and flavor to cake, this recipe recalls not only eighteenth-century cake recipes but also the sweet puddings of the period that incorporated vegetables.

**Makes two 8-inch loaves**

> 3 large eggs
> 2½ cups grated zucchini
> 1¾ cups granulated sugar
> 1 cup vegetable oil
> 1 tablespoon vanilla extract
> 3 cups all-purpose flour
> 2 teaspoons ground cinnamon
> 1 teaspoon baking soda
> ½ teaspoon baking powder
> ¼ teaspoon salt
> 1 cup chopped walnuts

1.  Preheat the oven to 350°F. Grease two 8½ x 4½ x 2½-inch loaf pans with butter.
2.  In the bowl of an electric mixer on medium speed, beat the eggs until the yolks are broken. Add the zucchini, sugar, oil, and vanilla extract; beat until well combined.
3.  In a medium-size mixing bowl, add the flour, cinnamon, baking soda, baking powder, and salt; stir to combine. With a rubber spatula or wooden spoon, fold the dry ingredients into the zucchini mixture. Gently fold in the walnuts.
4.  Divide the batter between the prepared pans. Bake about 1 hour, or until golden brown and a toothpick inserted near the center comes out clean.
5.  Cool in the pans on a wire rack for 10 minutes. To remove the breads, flip the pans on their sides and gently pull out the bread. Serve warm, or let cool to room temperature on wire racks.

# Pumpkin–Raisin Bread

This simple but flavorful bread represents the fusion of the New and Old Worlds. Pumpkins grew plentifully in North America and were cultivated first by Native Americans and later by the colonists. Pumpkin, or "pompion," as Americans and Europeans often called it, was not only commonly incorporated into puddings and pies but was also candied, as Harriet Pinckney Horry's recipe "To make Pompion Chips" illustrates (Hooker 66). In contrast, raisins were imported to urban areas like Philadelphia, where they were sold as specialty items in local shops among such other exotic ingredients as nutmeg, cinnamon, and chocolate.

**Makes two 8-inch loaves**

> 2 cups pumpkin purée (see Chef's Note)
> 1 cup vegetable oil
> ⅔ cup water
> 4 large eggs
> 3⅓ cups sifted all-purpose flour
> 3 cups granulated sugar
> 2 teaspoons baking soda
> 1½ teaspoons salt
> 1 teaspoon ground nutmeg
> 1 teaspoon ground cinnamon
> ½ cup raisins

1. Preheat the oven to 350°F. Grease two 8½ x 4½ x 2½-inch loaf pans with butter.
2. In a medium-size mixing bowl, add the pumpkin purée, oil, water, and eggs; stir to combine.
3. In a large mixing bowl, add the flour, sugar, baking soda, salt, nutmeg, and cinnamon; stir to combine. Fold the egg mixture into the dry ingredients.
4. With a rubber spatula or wooden spoon, gently fold the raisins into the batter.
5. Divide the batter between the prepared pans. Bake about 1 hour, or until the top springs back when touched or pulls away from the sides of the pan and a toothpick inserted near the center comes out clean.
6. Cool in the pans on a wire rack for 10 minutes. To remove, flip the pans on their sides and gently pull out the bread. Let cool to room temperature on a wire rack. Slice when completely cool.

**Chef's Note**

*Puréeing Fresh Pumpkin—Preheat the oven to 400°F. Cut off the top of a medium pumpkin. Remove and discard the seeds. Cut the pumpkin in half and place both pieces, pulp sides down, on a greased baking pan. Bake about 1 hour, or until the inside is soft. Remove from the oven and cool. Remove the skin, place the pulp in a food mill or food processor bowl, and purée until smooth.*

# Almond–Lemon Bread

In the eighteenth century, almonds and lemons were among the most luxurious foodstuffs available in shops that featured imported goods. Almonds were not common here until the 1850s, when they were imported from the port of Seville. George Washington and Thomas Jefferson both cultivated almonds (Leighton 236), and period cookbooks feature recipes calling for the nuts, as well as for the juice and rind of lemons, testament to the popularity of these foods despite their cost.

Makes two 8-inch loaves

> ¾ pound (3 sticks) unsalted butter, at room temperature
> 2 cups granulated sugar
> 6 large egg yolks
> ½ teaspoon ground cloves
> 1 teaspoon ground cinnamon
> 2 teaspoons grated lemon zest
> 1½ cups all-purpose flour
> 1½ cups cake flour
> 1½ cups sliced almonds, toasted (see Chef's Note, page 38)

1. Preheat the oven to 350°F. Grease two 8½ x 4½ x 2½-inch loaf pans with butter.
2. In the bowl of an electric mixer on medium speed, beat together the butter and sugar until light and fluffy, 2 to 3 minutes.
3. Add the egg yolks, cloves, cinnamon, and lemon zest; beat until well combined.
4. In a medium bowl, add the all-purpose flour, cake flour, and almonds; stir to combine. Add the flour mixture to the butter mixture, and stir just until moistened.
5. Divide the batter between the prepared pans. Bake for 50 to 55 minutes, or until the top springs back when touched and a toothpick inserted near the center comes out clean.
6. Remove the pans from oven, and let cool for 30 minutes. To remove the breads, flip the pans on their sides and gently remove the bread. Slice when completely cool.

# Chocolate–Almond Swirl Bread

Although chocolate remained costly throughout the eighteenth century in America, it was widely available in various forms in confectioners' shops and stores specializing in imported dry goods and foodstuffs. The panache of chocolate seems to have equaled that of such foods as exotic mustards, whose seeds were in high demand; shopkeepers, in fact, often advertised the two together. Chocolate was sold alongside other imported goods as well. Francis Daymon, on May 14, 1777, advertised in the *Pennsylvania Gazette* that he had many items available "JUST imported in the brig Little Julia." Apropos to this recipe, he listed one after the other "sweet almonds" and "sweeted [*sic*] chocolate."

In this recipe, almond paste complements semisweet chocolate to make a moist and delightfully sweet treat.

**Makes one 8-inch loaf**

> 3 ounces roughly chopped semisweet chocolate
> 1 cup Almond Paste (see page 40), or 10½ ounces store-bought almond paste
> ½ pound (2 sticks) unsalted butter, at room temperature
> 6 large eggs
> 1½ teaspoons vanilla extract
> ½ cup sifted all-purpose flour

1. Preheat the oven to 350°F. Grease an 8½ x 4½ x 2½-inch loaf pan with butter.
2. In a small, dry metal bowl set over barely simmering water, heat the chocolate, stirring occasionally, until melted. Reserve.
3. In the bowl of an electric mixer fitted with the paddle attachment on medium speed, beat the Almond Paste until light and fluffy. Add the butter gradually, and beat until combined.
4. Add the eggs and vanilla extract to the butter mixture, and beat until combined. Add the flour, and stir just until moistened.
5. Fold about one-third of the batter into the melted chocolate.
6. Pour the plain batter into the prepared pan. Spoon the chocolate batter over the top. Gently swirl the batter to marbleize.
7. Bake for 45 to 55 minutes, or until the loaf is firm on top and pulls away from the sides of the pan and a toothpick inserted near the center comes out clean.
8. Cool the bread in the pan on a wire rack for 30 minutes. To remove the bread, flip the pan on its side and gently pull out the bread. Slice and serve warm.

# Apple–Walnut Bread

Apples and walnuts were two foodstuffs that, stored properly, would have remained fresh over extended periods of time in the eighteenth century. In warm months, apples were kept in root cellars, while walnuts required cool, dry pantries or cupboards and were stored whole in burlap. The applesauce in this recipe recalls that prepared in colonial America as the base for rich fruit puddings, similarly flavored with aromatic spices. Applesauce not only lends a subtle sweetness to this bread but also helps to maintain a moist texture, which is nicely complemented by the walnuts.

**Makes two 8-inch loaves**

> 2 cups granulated sugar
> 1 cup vegetable shortening
> 4 large eggs
> 3¼ cups unsweetened, natural-style applesauce
> 4 cups sifted all-purpose flour
> 2 teaspoons baking powder
> 2 teaspoons baking soda
> 1½ teaspoons ground allspice
> 1½ teaspoons ground cinnamon
> 1 teaspoon salt
> ½ teaspoon ground nutmeg
> ½ teaspoon ground cloves
> ½ cup whole milk
> 1½ cups chopped walnuts, lightly toasted (see Chef's Note, page 38)

1. Preheat the oven to 350°F. Grease two 8½ x 4½ x 2½-inch loaf pans with butter.
2. In the bowl of an electric mixer fitted with the paddle attachment on medium speed, beat together the sugar and shortening until light and fluffy, 2 to 3 minutes.
3. Add the eggs to the shortening-sugar mixture, one at a time, beating after each addition. Add the applesauce and beat until combined.
4. In a large bowl, add the flour, baking powder, baking soda, allspice, cinnamon, salt, nutmeg, and cloves; stir to combine. Fold the dry ingredients into the egg mixture in thirds, alternating with the milk.
5. With a rubber spatula or wooden spoon, gently fold in the walnuts.
6. Divide the batter between the prepared pans. Bake for 55 to 60 minutes, or until the top springs back when touched and a toothpick inserted near the center comes out clean.
7. Cool the bread in the pans on a wire rack for 30 minutes. To remove the bread, flip the pans on their side and gently pull out bread. Slice and serve warm.

# Blueberry Muffins

Blueberries were abundantly available to the colonists, who undoubtedly enjoyed them fresh, preserved, and in baked goods. Muffins were included in period cookbooks, especially those dating to the nineteenth century. Resembling English muffins, they were, however, quite different from the sweet little cakes that are so popular today. These light little breads were leavened with yeast and browned on a griddle either free form or in muffin rings, which held their shape.

**Makes 24 standard muffins**

½ pound (2 sticks) unsalted butter, at room temperature
1¾ cups granulated sugar
5 large eggs
2 cups whole milk
1 teaspoon vanilla extract
3¾ cups all-purpose flour
3 tablespoons baking powder
½ teaspoon salt
2 cups fresh blueberries

1. Preheat the oven to 375°F. Grease twenty-four ½-cup muffin cups with butter.
2. In the bowl of an electric mixer fitted with the paddle attachment on medium speed, beat together the butter and sugar until light and fluffy, 2 to 3 minutes.
3. Beat in the eggs one at a time. Add the milk and vanilla extract, and beat until combined.
4. In a medium-size mixing bowl, add the flour, baking powder, and salt; stir to combine. With the mixer on low speed, add to the wet ingredients in the mixer bowl, and stir just until combined.
5. With a rubber spatula or wooden spoon, gently fold in the blueberries.
6. Divide the batter among the prepared muffin cups. Bake for 20 to 30 minutes, or until golden brown.
7. Cool in the pan on a wire rack for about 10 minutes. Remove the muffins from the muffin cups, and serve warm.

*Vanilla Bavarian (page 123)*

*Raspberry Charlotte Royale (page 116)*

*Martha Washington's Chocolate Mousse Cake (page 30)*

*Left to right: Oatmeal-Raisin Cookies (page 136), Poppy Seed Squares (page 148), Anise Biscotti (page 130), Spritz Cookies (page 134) topped with Raspberry Preserves (page 244), Spice Cookies (page 135), Financiers (page 143), and Pistachio Crescents (page 146)*

*Clockwise from bottom center: Anadama Bread (page 178), Thomas Jefferson's Sweet Potato Biscuits (page 157), and Sally Lunn Bread (page 177)*

*Crème Caramel (page 111)*

*Apple-Cranberry Strudel (pages 202–204)*

*Left: Pumpkin Pie (page 75), Right: Linzertorte (page 95)*

*Peach Tart (page 94), garnished with blackberries*

*Poached Pears (page 239), shown here without Chocolate Sauce*

*Crème Brûlée (page 112)*

*Vol-au-Vent with Berries (page 196)*

*Apple-Cranberry Cobbler (page 68)*

# Banana–Nut Muffins

For nearly five hundred years, bananas have been cultivated in the West Indies and similar tropical climates, but the fruit remained unfamiliar to Americans until well into the nineteenth century. In fact, at the 1876 Philadelphia Centennial Exhibition, bananas were still considered new and "exotic" (Mariani 17–18).

Had bananas been known to colonial Americans, however, they would have likely been incorporated into dishes much like cooked sweet potatoes or apples were. The walnuts in this recipe complement the flavor and texture of these muffins.

**Makes twelve 3 x 1½-inch muffins**

> 2 cups all-purpose flour
> ¼ cup granulated sugar
> 1 tablespoon baking powder
> ½ teaspoon salt
> 1 cup whole milk
> 1 cup water
> ¾ cup mashed, ripe banana (about 2 bananas)
> ⅓ cup vegetable oil
> 1 large egg
> ½ cup chopped walnuts, toasted (see Chef's Note, page 38)

1. Preheat the oven to 400°F. Grease twelve 3 x 1½-inch muffin cups with butter.
2. In a large mixing bowl, add the flour, sugar, baking powder, and salt; stir to combine.
3. In a medium-size mixing bowl, add the milk, water, banana, oil, and egg; stir to combine. Add the milk mixture to the dry ingredients, and stir just until moistened.
4. With a rubber spatula or wooden spoon, gently fold in the walnuts.
5. Divide the batter among the prepared muffin cups, filling each cup about half full. Bake for 15 to 20 minutes, or until golden brown.
6. Cool the muffins in the pans for 5 minutes; then turn out while still warm. If they stick, carefully run a paring knife around the sides. Cool on a wire rack.

# Buttermilk Scones

A traditional Scottish bread, scones were originally prepared with oats and cooked on a griddle (Herbst 414). This version resembles the many variations of yeast-leavened biscuits that appeared in eighteenth-century cookbooks. Some of those yeasts not only helped the bread to rise but also contributed a pleasantly tart flavor to the finished product. In this recipe, that flavor, as well as a tender texture, is achieved through the addition of buttermilk, while the baking powder gives the biscuits a pleasant lightness.

**Makes about 1 dozen scones**

½ pound (2 sticks) unsalted butter, at room temperature
6 tablespoons granulated sugar
3 large egg yolks
2½ cups sifted cake flour
2½ cups sifted bread flour
2¼ tablespoons baking powder
1½ cups buttermilk
1 cup raisins

1. Preheat the oven to 400°F.
2. In the bowl of an electric mixer fitted with the paddle attachment on medium speed, beat together the butter and sugar until light and fluffy, 2 to 3 minutes. Add the egg yolks one at a time, and beat until combined.
3. In a large mixing bowl, add the cake flour, bread flour, and baking powder; stir to combine. Fold the dry ingredients into the butter mixture in thirds, alternating with the buttermilk.
4. With a rubber spatula or wooden spoon, gently fold in the raisins.
5. Turn the dough out onto a lightly floured surface. Roll out the dough to 1½ inches thick.
6. Cut out the scones with a 2-inch floured biscuit cutter. Place the scones 2 inches apart on ungreased baking pans. Any leftover dough should be chilled for 30 minutes before rolling out again, to prevent overworking and toughening the dough. Reduce the oven temperature to 350°F, and bake for 30 to 40 minutes, or until golden brown.
7. Transfer the scones to a wire rack to cool for 10 to 15 minutes. Serve warm.

Although most eighteenth-century biscuit recipes were leavened with yeast, some were simply prepared with flour, milk, and butter, creating a dense, hearty bread. Mary Randolph's recipe for "Cream Cakes" is one such example. In addition, rather than baking the cakes/biscuits in an oven, she grilled them over direct heat:

> Melt as much butter in a pint of milk as will make it rich as cream, make the flour into a paste with this, knead it well, roll it out frequently, cut it in squares, and bake on a griddle (171).

# Ginger-Raisin Scones

Both ginger and raisins were commonly imported into urban centers like Philadelphia, where the demand for such exotic items was high. Not only were they incorporated into a variety of baked goods, but they were used to prepare specialty items as well. In her book *The Art of Cookery Made Plain and Easy*, for example, Hannah Glasse included recipes for "Ginger Tablets" (a sort of candied ginger) and "The best way to make Raisin Wine" (243, 252). Many eighteenth-century cookery books offered similar instruction, but if home cooks preferred, they could purchase ginger (fresh, preserved, powdered, or candied) as well as jars of raisins in local shops.

Makes eight 2-inch scones

> 2 cups all-purpose flour
> ⅓ cup packed dark brown sugar
> 1 tablespoon baking powder
> ¾ teaspoon ground cinnamon
> ½ teaspoon ground ginger
> ⅛ teaspoon ground cloves
> 6 tablespoons (¾ stick) unsalted butter, at room temperature
> ¼ cup whole milk
> 3 tablespoons Grandma's dark molasses
> 1 large egg
> 1 teaspoon vanilla extract
> ⅔ cup raisins
> Chantilly Cream (see page 120), for serving (optional)

1. Preheat the oven to 375°F.
2. In a large mixing bowl, add the flour, brown sugar, baking powder, cinnamon, ginger, and cloves; stir to combine.
3. In a medium-size mixing bowl, combine the butter, milk, molasses, egg, and vanilla extract. Add the egg mixture to the dry ingredients, and stir just until moistened.
4. With a rubber spatula or wooden spoon, gently fold in the raisins.
5. Turn the dough out onto a lightly floured surface. Roll out the dough to 1 to 1½ inches thick. Cut out the scones with a 2-inch floured biscuit cutter. Place 2 inches apart on an ungreased baking pan.
6. Bake about 25 minutes, or until golden brown.
7. Serve warm with Chantilly Cream, if desired, or butter.

On November 9, 1785, just two blocks from City Tavern "in Second street, eight doors below Arch street," Joseph Walker was selling "A NEAT and GENERAL ASSORTMENT of GROCERIES." Among the English wares he offered, including "best London pewter, tin plates in boxes, glass and queens ware," Mr. Walker also sold exotic foodstuffs from Europe and the Orient. On his shelves, one could find such goods as "Fine and coarse salt," "Coffee in barrels and bags," "Hyson, souchong & bohea teas," and "Cocoa," as well as "Raisins in barrels and kegs" and "Ginger" (Pennsylvania Gazette).

# Popovers

British colonists brought recipes for these light, golden breads to North America, where they gained particular favor in the mid-Atlantic and New England. Popovers are native to Yorkshire, England, and are so named because the thin batter "pops over" the edges of the individual tins or cups during baking, creating a bread with great height and a hollow center. Coating these baking dishes with roasted meat drippings before pouring in the batter and flavoring the latter with herbs or extracts, as in this version, were purely American interpretations of the traditional, simply flavored British recipe (Mariani 249).

**Makes 8 popovers**

> Granulated sugar, for coating the pan
> 1 cup whole milk
> 3 large eggs
> 3 tablespoons unsalted butter, melted
> 1 teaspoon extract (lemon, vanilla, or almond)
> 1 cup all-purpose flour
> ¼ teaspoon salt

1. Preheat the oven to 400°F. Grease a popover pan or muffin tin with butter, and dust the cups with the sugar, discarding any excess.
2. In a blender container, combine the milk, eggs, melted butter, and extract; blend well. Add the flour and salt, and blend until smooth.
3. Divide the batter between the prepared cups, filling each cup three-fourths full. Bake for 40 to 50 minutes, or until puffed up and golden brown.
4. Serve immediately with flavored butters and preserves.

# Soda Bread

The name of this bread derives from the addition of baking soda, which, in the presence of acidic buttermilk, causes it to rise. Eighteenth-century versions of this bread would likely have relied on leaveners such as yeast or pearl ash/pot ash (early forms of baking soda), and many would have included caraway seeds as well—a spice often added to cakes, breads, and cookies of the period.

Makes one 9-inch round loaf

> 3½ cups all-purpose flour
> 2 tablespoons caraway seeds
> 1 teaspoon baking soda
> ¾ teaspoon salt
> 1⅔ cups buttermilk

1. Preheat the oven to 400°F. Grease a large baking pan with butter.
2. In a large mixing bowl, add the flour, caraway seeds, baking soda, and salt; stir to combine. Add the buttermilk, and stir just until moistened.
3. Turn the dough out onto a lightly floured surface. Knead until the dough holds together.
4. Shape the dough into a 9-inch circle, and cut an X on top of the bread. Place the dough on the prepared baking pan.
5. Bake for 25 to 30 minutes, or until golden brown and the bread sounds hollow when tapped on the bottom.
6. Remove the bread from the baking pan, and cool on a wire rack for 15 minutes before slicing.

In her cookbook The Experienced English Housekeeper, Elizabeth Raffald included a recipe entitled, "To make a common Seed Cake," which is remarkably similar to this soda bread. Notice that plain milk and barm (or yeast) are used rather than the more modern buttermilk and baking soda:

> Take two pounds of flour, rub into it half a pound of powder sugar, one ounce of carraway [sic] seeds beaten. Have ready a pint of milk with half a pound of butter melted in it, and two spoonfuls of new barm. Make it up into a paste, set it to the fire to rise, flour your tin and bake it in a quick oven (138).

# Yeast Breads

If there is one type of item absent from many period cookery books, it is yeast bread. Eighteenth-century authors gave detailed instructions pertaining to numerous cakes, pies, tarts, and biscuits, many of which relied on leaveners, including yeast. Yet the preparation of bread appears to have been viewed as a baking skill separate from the others. Perhaps this is because in an urban center like Philadelphia bread was sold daily in many bakeries throughout the city. Home cooks could affordably purchase their family's bread while focusing on the preparation of other items that would have been more expensive to buy at local shops, including preserves, puddings, and pastries.

Advertisements from the *Pennsylvania Gazette* ultimately yield more information on bread baking than do period cookery books. Although many confectioners made and sold numerous varieties of baked goods, they specialized in cakes, pastry, and preserved fruits, rather than breads. Some bakeries that specialized in bread, however, also made cakes, although perhaps not as fine as those available in confectioners' shops. In October 1771 an advertisement read, "TO BE SOLD, TWO Brick Houses, each two Stories high, with two Story Brick Kitchens, each House has an Oven, proper for the Baking of Loaf Bread and Cakes, and is very suitable for that Business, which has been carried on there for many Years" (October 10, 1771).

Also telling is an advertisement placed in September 1767 by a woman seeking a position as "House keeper and LadyMaid" [*sic*]. In it she listed her abilities, describing herself as "capable of setting off all Kinds of Meat Dishes, and Pastry, in the genteelist [*sic*] Manner; can preserve and pickle, and make any Kind of Collar Beef or Brawn; is well acquainted with all Sorts of Needlework, and can wash and do up any Sort of Lace or Gauze. She has lived in some of the best Families in London, and in this Country, in that Station" (*Pennsylvania Gazette*, September 17, 1767). With all of this experience, the absence of her skill as a bread baker is striking. One can only assume that she failed to list this ability because it was unnecessary for her to know how to make bread. With the many bakeries in London and in Philadelphia, she could purchase her family's bread and focus on other culinary and domestic duties.

The breads included here vary from dense and substantial to delicate and sweet. They draw on the many varieties that were available in an eighteenth-century Philadelphia that welcomed European baking traditions and offered them opportunities to flourish.

# Rosemary Bread

Aptly meaning "dew of the sea," rosemary has grown wild in the soil around the Mediterranean for over 2,500 years (Ortiz 46). This herb is a member of the mint family and was often used medicinally to reduce the effects of illnesses associated with memory loss and the digestive and nervous systems (Hess 208, 424; Herbst 393). Of course, rosemary also flavored a variety of savory dishes, such as roasted meats or sausage, as well as sweet preparations. In her cookbook, Martha Washington called for rosemary in a custard recipe, "To Make French Curds," and rosemary flowers in those entitled "To Make Conserue [*sic*] of Rosemary Flowers," "To Candy Rosemary Flowers," and "Spirits of Rosemary Flowers" (Hess 152–153, 277, 281, 424–425).

Fresh or dried rosemary adds a fragrant aroma and delicately herbaceous flavor to this light-textured bread.

**Makes one 12-inch-long loaf**

> 1 package (2¼ teaspoons) active dry yeast
> 2 cups warm water (110° to 115°F)
> ¼ cup vegetable oil
> 1 tablespoon finely chopped fresh rosemary, or 1 teaspoon dried
> 1 teaspoon salt
> 5 cups bread flour

*When substituting dried herbs for fresh herbs in recipes from this book, use one third as much dried herbs as fresh.*

1. In a large mixing bowl, dissolve the yeast in the warm water. Let stand about 10 minutes, until foamy.
2. Stir in the oil, rosemary, and salt. Mix in the bread flour, 1 cup at a time, to make a soft dough.
3. Turn out the dough onto a lightly floured surface. Knead for 6 to 8 minutes, until smooth and elastic, adding only enough flour to prevent sticking.
4. Transfer the dough to a large bowl coated with vegetable oil, and turn the dough to coat all surfaces. Cover with a slightly damp towel. Let rise in a warm place, free from drafts, for 45 minutes to 1 hour, until doubled in size.
5. Punch down the dough. Cover and let rest for 10 minutes.
6. Lightly grease a 15 x 10 x 1-inch baking pan with butter. Preheat the oven to 375°F.
7. Roll the dough into a 12 x 8-inch rectangle. Starting at a long side, tightly roll up the dough, jelly-roll style. Pinch the seam to seal. Taper the ends. Place the 12-inch loaf, smooth side up, on the prepared baking pan. Cover, and let rise for 30 to 45 minutes, until almost doubled in size.
8. Bake the loaf for 20 to 25 minutes, or until golden and the bread sounds hollow when tapped on the bottom.
9. Remove the bread from the baking pan, and cool on a wire rack for 45 minutes before serving.

# Rye and Caraway Seed Bread

Native to Asia and the Middle East, caraway seeds have flavored food and been used to aid digestion for millennia. Europeans eventually developed a palate for this strong spice, which came to characterize a variety of English cakes and breads. The seeds, however, are most closely associated with German and Austrian baked goods (Ortiz 74).

Rye flour, too, has been used for centuries in Northern European countries, where it is combined with white flour to make dense brown breads. Colonial American versions of brown bread existed as well. They, however, often combined rye flour with cornmeal, or Indian meal, distinguishing them as uniquely American. Despite the addition of yeast, these breads must have been dense indeed, as rye flour, like cornmeal, contains very little gluten. This recipe, therefore, calls for rye flour as well as high-gluten bread flour to ensure a traditionally dense but properly leavened loaf. With the addition of caraway seeds, this brown bread recalls the Old World versions that inspired it.

**Makes 2 small loaves**

> One ¼-ounce package (2¼ teaspoons) active dry yeast
> 2 cups warm water (110° to 115°F)
> 4 ounces (1 stick) unsalted butter, at room temperature
> 1 tablespoon caraway seeds
> 1 teaspoon salt
> 2 cups rye flour
> 3 cups bread flour
> Cornmeal, to coat baking pan

1. In a large mixing bowl, dissolve the yeast in the warm water. Let stand about 10 minutes, until foamy.
2. Using a wooden spoon, beat in the butter, caraway seeds, and salt. Mix in the rye flour, 1 cup at a time, followed by the bread flour, to make a moderately stiff dough.
3. Turn the dough out onto a lightly floured surface. Knead for 6 to 8 minutes, until smooth and elastic, adding only enough flour to prevent stickiness.
4. Transfer the dough to a large bowl coated with vegetable oil, and turn the dough to coat all surfaces. Cover with a slightly damp towel. Let rise in a warm place, free from drafts, for 45 minutes to 1 hour, until doubled in size.
5. Punch down the dough. Turn out onto a lightly floured surface. Divide the dough in half. Cover and let rest for 10 minutes.
6. Preheat the oven to 425°F. Lightly grease a large baking pan with butter and sprinkle it with cornmeal.
7. Shape each half of the dough into a ball. Place the balls, smooth sides up, on the prepared baking pan. Flatten each ball into a 6-inch round loaf. Cover, and let rise for 30 to 45 minutes, until almost doubled in size.
8. Bake the loaves for 35 to 40 minutes, or until golden and the bread sounds hollow when tapped on the bottom.
9. Remove the breads from the baking pans, and cool on wire racks for 45 minutes before serving.

# Sally Lunn Bread

This golden, rich bread is said to have been named for an eighteenth-century baker, Sally Lunn, of Bath, England, who sold buttery tea cakes to a wealthy clientele. Originally popular in the South, this bread eventually acquired a following in the mid-Atlantic and New England by the nineteenth century (Mariani 280). Sally Lunns are traditionally baked as large, individual breads and served with clotted cream (a thick cream from Devonshire, England) (Herbst 402). This version, prepared in a single, large decorative mold, celebrates the bread's luxurious richness with a fanciful appearance. The slices may be served with clotted cream or, for a lighter but equally elegant accompaniment, with Chantilly Cream (see page 120).

**Makes two breads**

> One ¼-ounce package (2¼ teaspoons) active dry yeast
> 2 cups warm water (110° to 115°F)
> ½ cup granulated sugar
> 4 tablespoons (½ stick) unsalted butter, at room temperature
> ¼ cup whole milk
> 2 large eggs, lightly beaten
> 1 teaspoon salt
> 6½ cups all-purpose flour

1. Generously grease 2 Bundt pans or two 7-cup tube molds with butter. Reserve.
2. In the bowl of an electric mixer, whisk together the yeast and warm water with a hand-held whisk. Let stand about 10 minutes, until foamy.
3. Fit the mixer with the dough hook attachment, and beat in the sugar, butter, milk, eggs, and salt. Mix in the flour, 1 cup at a time, to make a soft dough. Turn the dough out onto a lightly-floured surface, and knead for 5 minutes, or until smooth.
4. Transfer the dough to a large bowl coated with vegetable oil, and turn the dough to coat all surfaces. Cover the dough with a slightly damp towel. Let rise in a warm place, free from drafts, for 45 minutes to 1 hour, until doubled in size.
5. Stir the batter to deflate. Divide the dough between the prepared pans. Cover, and let rise in a warm place for 40 to 45 minutes, until almost doubled in size.
6. Preheat the oven to 400°F.
7. Bake for 30 to 35 minutes, or until golden and the bread sounds hollow when tapped on the bottom.
8. Remove the breads from the pans. Serve the bread warm, or cooled and toasted.

# Anadama Bread

This soft, comfortingly sweet, cornmeal-and-molasses bread has a colorful history. For years, New Englanders have passed down two stories that attempt to explain the meaning of this bread's unique name. Both revolve around a fishing village household. The first tells of a Gloucester, Massachusetts, fisherman, whose wife, Anna, prepared nothing for him to eat but a bowl of cornmeal and molasses. Desirous of something different to eat, one day he added yeast and flour to his daily gruel, in an attempt to create a tasteful bread. So frustrated was he in this endeavor that he grumbled, "Anna, damn her!" (Mariani 6).

A similar but more endearing story tells of a sea captain whose wife, Anna, was quite a good baker and renowned for her cornmeal-and-molasses bread. New England lore suggests that upon her death her gravestone read, "Anna was a lovely bride, but Anna, damn 'er, up and died" (Mariani 6).

**Makes 2 loaves**

Two ¼-ounce packages (4½ teaspoons) active dry yeast
2 cups warm water (110° to 115°F)
¾ cup coarse yellow cornmeal, plus extra for coating pan
½ cup Grandma's dark molasses
6 tablespoons (¾ stick) unsalted butter, at room temperature
1 teaspoon salt
5½ cups bread flour

1. In a large mixing bowl, dissolve the yeast in the warm water. Let stand about 10 minutes, until foamy.
2. Using a wooden spoon, beat in the cornmeal, molasses, butter, and salt. Mix in the flour, 1 cup at a time, to make a moderately stiff dough.
3. Turn the dough out onto a lightly floured surface. Knead for 6 to 8 minutes, until smooth and elastic, adding only enough flour to prevent sticking.
4. Transfer the dough to a large buttered bowl or a bowl coated with vegetable oil, and turn the dough to coat all surfaces. Cover with a slightly damp towel. Let rise in a warm place, free from drafts, for 1 to 1½ hours, until doubled in size.
5. Punch down the dough. Turn out onto a lightly floured surface. Divide the dough in half. Cover, and let rest for 10 minutes.
6. Preheat the oven to 375°F. Lightly grease a large baking pan with butter; sprinkle with cornmeal.
7. Shape each half of the dough into a ball. Place the balls, smooth sides up, on the prepared baking pan. Flatten each ball into a 6-inch round loaf. Cover and let rise for 30 to 45 minutes, until almost doubled in size.
8. Bake for 25 to 30 minutes, or until almost doubled in size.
9. Remove the breads from the baking pan, and cool on wire racks.

# Braided Easter Bread

Rich yeast breads like this version are found in the culinary traditions of nearly every European culture. These breads are usually served during religious holidays and hold significant symbolic meaning for those who prepare and consume them. For many Catholic immigrants to the New World, Easter remained the most holy day of the Christian calendar, as revealed by the traditional foods they continued to prepare.

The richness of this bread celebrates the great joy of Christ's resurrection following the solemnity of His suffering. The Crucifixion epitomized this dark period and is also represented here in the round shape, which symbolizes the crown-of-thorns Christ wore. In addition, colored eggs are often set decoratively into this braid before baking and also symbolize the resurrection.

**Makes two 14-inch braided loaves**

> Two ¼-ounce packages (4½ teaspoons) active dry yeast
> 2 cups warm water (110° or 115°F)
> 2 large eggs
> 4 ounces (1 stick) unsalted butter, at room temperature
> 1 teaspoon salt
> 7 to 8 cups all-purpose flour
> 2 large eggs, lightly beaten, for egg wash

1. In a large mixing bowl, dissolve the yeast in the warm water. Let stand about 10 minutes, until foamy.
2. Using a wooden spoon, beat in the eggs, butter and salt. Mix in the flour, 1 cup at a time, adding just enough to make a soft dough.
3. Turn the dough out onto a lightly floured surface. Knead for 6 to 8 minutes, until smooth and elastic, adding only enough flour to prevent sticking.
4. Transfer the dough to a large bowl coated with vegetable oil, and turn the dough to coat all surfaces. Cover with a slightly damp towel. Let rise in a warm place, free from drafts, for 1 to 1½ hours, until doubled in size.
5. Punch down the dough. Turn out onto a lightly floured surface. Divide the dough into sixths. Cover, and let rest for 10 minutes.
6. Preheat the oven to 375°F. Lightly grease 2 large baking pans with butter.
7. Shape each portion of dough into a 14-inch-long rope (6 ropes total). Place 3 ropes on each prepared baking pan, 1 inch apart.
8. Braid the dough: Starting in the middle of the ropes, loosely braid by bringing the left rope over the center rope. Next, bring the right rope over the new center rope. Repeat to the end; then flip the braid over. On the other end, braid by bringing alternate ropes over the center rope from the center to the end. Using the palms of your hands, roll the ends of the dough against the table to taper them. Brush one end with the beaten egg wash; then place the other end on top of it. Pinch the ends together to seal.
9. Cover the braids and let rise for 30 to 40 minutes, until almost doubled in size.
10. Brush the braids with the beaten egg wash. Bake for 25 to 30 minutes, or until golden and the breads sound hollow when tapped on the bottom.
11. Remove the breads from the baking pans, and cool on wire racks.

# Orange Bread with Orange Glaze

This light bread perfumed with orange recalls the many eighteenth-century breads and cakes that were flavored with the imported fruit. As costly as oranges were, period recipes frequently called for them, and Philadelphia shopkeepers and confectioners often advertised their availability.

**Makes two 9-inch round loaves**

> One ¼-ounce package (2¼ teaspoons) active dry yeast
> 2 cups warm whole milk (110° to 115°F)
> 4 tablespoons (½ stick) unsalted butter, at room temperature
> ¼ cup grated orange zest (about 2 medium oranges)
> 1 teaspoon salt
> 6 cups all-purpose flour
> 1 large egg, lightly beaten, for egg wash
>
> **Orange Glaze**
> 2 cups sifted confectioners' sugar
> ½ cup orange juice

1. In a large mixing bowl, dissolve the yeast in the milk. Let stand about 10 minutes, until foamy.
2. Using a wooden spoon, beat in the butter, orange zest, and salt. Mix in the flour, 1 cup at a time, to make a soft dough.
3. Turn the dough out onto a lightly floured surface. Knead for about 5 minutes, until elastic and smooth, adding only enough flour to prevent sticking.
4. Transfer the dough to a large bowl coated with vegetable oil, and turn the dough to coat all surfaces. Cover with a slightly damp towel. Let rise in a warm place, free from drafts, for 45 to 50 minutes, until doubled in size.
5. Punch down the dough. Turn out onto a lightly floured surface. Divide the dough in half. Cover and let rest for 10 minutes.
6. Preheat the oven to 425°F. Lightly grease 2 large baking pans with butter.
7. Shape each half of the dough into a ball. Place each ball on a prepared baking pan. Flatten each ball into a 9-inch round loaf. Cover and let rise 30 to 40 minutes, until almost doubled in size.
8. Brush the tops of the loaves with the egg wash. Bake for 30 to 35 minutes, or until golden and the breads sound hollow when tapped on the bottom.
9. Remove the breads from the baking pans, and cool on wire racks for at least 45 minutes before glazing.
10. Prepare the Orange Glaze: In a small bowl, stir together the confectioners' sugar and orange juice until smooth. If too thick, add a few drops of additional orange juice. Drizzle the glaze decoratively over the tops of the loaves. Let stand for 30 minutes, until the glaze is set.

# Kugelhopf

Native not only to Austria but also to Alsace, Germany, and Poland, *kugelhopf* is one of the many rich egg and butter yeast breads found throughout Europe that made their way to the Americas in the eighteenth century. It is often prepared with candied fruit and nuts, but this version focuses on the delicious simplicity of the unadorned bread. Baked in special, decorative *kugelhopf* ring molds, this bread not only would have added elegance to the eighteenth-century table but would have made a statement about the strong influence of northern European cultures—especially Germany—in cosmopolitan Philadelphia.

Makes 1 *kugelhopf* mold or one 1-quart Bundt pan mold

### Sponge
2 tablespoons active dry yeast
1 cup plus 2 tablespoons whole milk, at room temperature
1 cup high-gluten flour (see Chef's Note)

### Dough
1¼ cups high-gluten flour (see Chef's Note)
½ cup granulated sugar
3 large eggs
1 tablespoon salt
½ pound (2 sticks) unsalted butter, at room temperature

*If you can't find high-gluten flour in your area supermarkets, King Arthur Flour makes a product called Sir Lancelot Hi-Gluten Flour (see Sources, page 252).*

1. Grease a *kugelhopf* mold or 1-quart Bundt pan, and coat lightly with flour.
2. Prepare the Sponge: In a large mixing bowl, whisk together the yeast and milk. Add the flour and stir, using your hand (it's too stiff to use a spoon), until smooth. Transfer the dough to a large bowl. Cover and let stand at room temperature for 30 minutes, until the sponge has tripled in volume and begins to sag.
3. Prepare the Dough: In the bowl of an electric mixer fitted with the paddle attchment, add the Sponge, flour, sugar, eggs, and salt. Mix on low speed for 3 minutes.
4. With the mixer still running on low speed, add the butter 2 tablespoons at a time. Once all the butter has been added, mix on low speed for an additional 3 minutes.
5. Transfer the dough to the prepared mold. Although the dough will be wet and sticky, try to avoid using extra flour when handling it. Let the dough rise at room temperature for 1 hour, until it has nearly doubled in volume.
6. Meanwhile, preheat the oven to 450°F.
7. Place the *kugelhopf* in the oven, and immediately turn the temperature down to 375°F. Bake for 20 minutes, or until golden and a toothpick inserted near the center comes out clean. Let the bread cool in the pan, and unmold.

# Baguettes

Baguettes—long, slim breads with crisp, golden crusts and tender interiors—not only epitomize the French bread-baking tradition but also represent French foodways as a whole. As French bakers opened shops in cities like Philadelphia, patrons, who were enamored with French fashion and culture, certainly must have quickly become aware of their great artistry and appreciated the high quality of their products. As for French visitors to America in the eighteenth century, many commented on how little bread Americans consumed and criticized the quality of breads they tasted in American cities. One visitor noted that although "[d]inner . . . is generally . . . composed of a great quantity of meat . . . [Americans] eat very little bread." Another visitor, named Beaujour, remarked, "In France each individual . . . consumes a pound of bread a day and a half a pound of meat . . . An American consumes hardly half a pound of bread, but on the other hand, at least a pound of meat" (Sherrill 99). And yet another visitor, known as Du Bourg, explained that in American cities "they often substitute for bread little biscuits that are easily made and cooked in half an hour." According to historian Charles Sherrill, "Our bread was one of the few American products of which the French consistently vouchsafe no word of praise—for them it was always bad" (100).

Regardless of what the French thought about the American breads that were heartily enjoyed in homes and public eateries like City Tavern, it is undeniable that skillfully prepared baguettes must have been as much appreciated in the eighteenth century as they continue to be today. Note, however, that because they are prepared without any fat, they go stale very quickly and are best consumed the day they are made.

**Makes three 14-inch loaves**

### Sponge
1 teaspoon active dry yeast
2 cups water
1 cup plus 2 tablespoons bread flour
Pinch of cumin

### Baguette
4¾ cups bread flour
2 teaspoons salt
One ¼-ounce package (2¼ teaspoons) active dry yeast
2 cups plus 3 tablespoons warm water

1. Prepare the sponge: In a mixing bowl, add the yeast, water, bread flour, and cumin; stir to combine. Let stand at room temperature for 12 to 15 hours, covered, until the mixture has tripled in volume and begins to sag. For this recipe, use only ½ cup. The rest can be stored in the refrigerator.
2. Prepare the Baguette: In the bowl of an electric mixer fitted with the dough hook attachment, add the flour and salt; stir to combine.
3. In a separate bowl, whisk together the yeast and water. Whisk in the half the Sponge.
4. Add the Sponge mixture to the flour, and mix on low speed for 4 minutes. Turn the dough out onto a floured surface and knead until smooth and elastic.
5. Transfer the dough to a large bowl coated with vegetable oil, and turn the dough to coat all surfaces. In a cool place, allow the dough to double in volume, about 1 hour.

6. Punch the dough down. Cover and allow the dough to double in volume again, about 45 minutes.
7. Preheat the oven to 400°F.
8. Transfer the dough to a lightly floured work surface and punch down. Divide the dough into 3 equal portions. Shape each portion into a round and cover with a damp cloth. Let the dough relax for 20 minutes.
9. Roll each round of dough into a 14-inch-long cylinder. Place the baguettes onto a parchment-coated and lightly floured baking pan, or set them in a greased baguette pan. Allow each baguette to double in volume, about 45 minutes.
10. Bake the loaves for 20 minutes, or until golden. Cool on wire racks for 45 minutes before serving.

*The extra "sponge" (leavener) can be stored for 2 to 3 days in the refrigerator, but you must "feed" it half of each quantity of water and bread flour six to eight hours before using, and then let it sit at room temperature.*

# Potato Bread with Onions and Dill

Although it appears that many Philadelphians purchased their bread in bakeries in the eighteenth century, others did indeed choose to prepare it at home. Potato bread would have been a good choice for home cooks, for it utilized not only pantry foodstuffs, such as flour and yeast, but potatoes and occasionally onions from root cellars as well.

Root cellars were vital to the eighteenth-century kitchen, particularly in the winter, when fresh garden vegetables were unavailable. Because these cellars were often damp and filled intermittently with water, root vegetables risked freezing in the winter. Vermin threatened them as well. The cellars, therefore, received a thorough cleaning in the summer, and the vegetables were usually stored in layers of sand. Potatoes were among the most oft prepared root vegetables at George Washington's Mount Vernon. Hundreds of bushels of potatoes were stored in his cellars during the late eighteenth century. In 1794, his slaves "Put In the Cellar 730 Bushels of potatoes That grew In the Mansion house Lot" (Thompson 4).

Flavored with coriander (which was most likely purchased from shops) and dill from the herb garden, this soft bread would have flavorfully accompanied the many savory dishes that appeared on the eighteenth-century dining table.

**Makes 2 loaves**

> 2 large baking potatoes
> 5 ounces (1¼ sticks) unsalted butter, at room temperature
> 1 medium-size Spanish onion, roughly chopped
> 1 teaspoon ground coriander
> 1 tablespoon active dry yeast
> 4 cups high-gluten flour (see Chef's Note)
> 4 tablespoons honey
> 2 teaspoons salt
> ¼ cup roughly chopped fresh dill

1. Peel the potatoes. To a large pot of water, add the potatoes. Bring to a boil and cook at a simmer until fork tender, about 20 minutes. Strain the potatoes and set aside, reserving 2 cups of the potato cooking liquid.

2. In a large skillet over medium heat, melt 2 tablespoons of the butter. Add the onion and cook, stirring, until translucent and soft, about 5 minutes.

3. Transfer the hot onions to the food processor. Add the coriander and potatoes, and process until smooth. Allow the mixture to cool.

4. In the bowl of an electric mixer fitted with the dough hook attachment, whisk together the yeast and the reserved cooking water. With the mixture on medium speed, stir in 2 cups of the flour and 2 tablespoons of the honey; mix until smooth. Scrape down the sides of the bowl, cover the bowl with plastic wrap, and allow the mixture to double in volume, about 45 minutes.

5. In the bowl of the mixer fitted with the dough hook attachment, add the remaining 2 cups flour, 2 tablespoons honey, and 1 stick of butter, the salt, and the mashed potato mixture. Mix on medium speed until combined. Add the dill, and mix on low speed until it is incorporated. Turn out onto a floured work surface, and knead until smooth and elastic.

6. Cover the bowl with plastic wrap or a damp cloth. In a cool place, allow the dough to double in volume, about 1 hour.

7. Punch the dough down, cover, and allow the dough to double in volume again, about 35 minutes.

8. Preheat the oven to 400°F.

9. Transfer the dough to a lightly floured work surface and punch down. Divide the dough into 2 equal portions. Shape the dough into rounds. Transfer the dough rounds to parchment-lined baking pans. Allow the loaves to double in volume, 30 to 45 minutes.

10. Transfer the baking pans to the oven, and bake for 20 minutes, or until golden. Cool the breads on wire racks for 45 minutes before serving.

*If you can't find high-gluten flour in your area supermarkets, King Arthur Flour makes a product called Sir Lancelot Hi-Gluten Flour (see Sources, page 252).*

# Pastries

As mentioned in the Pies and Tarts chapter, the skills associated with the preparation of pastry were much admired in the eighteenth century. Home cooks as well as professional bakers were familiar with many doughs and "pastes" and knew just which pastry was suitable for which dish. Not only do the following recipes feature elaborate "pastes" and the desserts made with them, but they are also based on other preparations, such as *pâte à choux*, meringue, and pancake and fritter doughs.

Although many of the eighteenth-century desserts prepared in Philadelphia reflected the influence of European traditions, pastries of the period seem to have particularly done so. The artistry of German and French pâtisserie was especially evidenced in Philadelphia pastry due to the strong cultural influence these groups maintained in the city. Additionally, in keeping with the food produced in Philadelphia (and perhaps inspiring it), cookery books published in America and in England included numerous German and French pastry recipes. Fried breads, such as fritters and pancakes, were often associated with German traditions, while desserts based on meringue, puff pastry, and *pâte à choux* were most often based on time-honored French preparations. William Verral's *A Complete System of Cookery*, published in London in 1757, was virtually a treatise on French culinary arts, with each recipe printed in French and English. Similarly, Eliza Smith's *The Compleat Housewife*, published in London in 1758, offered readers a combination of English and French dishes. Despite her apparent dislike of French fashion, Smith clearly acknowledged the importance of including French-inspired recipes, as she discussed in her preface:

> WHAT you will find in the following Sheets, are Directions generally for dressing after the best, most natural and wholesome Manner, such Provisions as are the Product of our own Country; and in such a Manner as is most agreeable to English Palates; saving that I have so far temporized, as, since we have, to our Disgrace, so fondly admired the French Tongue, French Modes, and also French Messes, to present you now and then with such Receipts of the French Cookery as I think may not be disagreeable to English Palates.

Like the large quantity of pie and tart recipes included in eighteenth-century cookery books, pastry preparations also often numbered in the dozens. In keeping with many of her contemporaries, Eliza Leslie, in fact, published a total of forty pastry recipes in her *Directions for Cookery, in Its Various Branches*. Versions of these often elegant and time-consuming dishes were available to most Philadelphians, whether prepared at home or in confectionery shops. It is clear that traditional, skillfully prepared pastries were appreciated and admired as much then as they are today.

# Mille-Feuille

French for "a thousand leaves," *mille-feuille* is a dessert traditionally consisting of three layers of puff pastry and two layers of whipped cream or pastry cream. The top piece of pastry is often decoratively finished with a liberal sprinkling of confectioners' sugar or a thin coating of fondant (white icing).

Most eighteenth-century, English puff pastry desserts were essentially pies and tarts. *Mille-feuille*, however, is undeniably French. Each component is prepared separately and used to build the final, stylishly elegant form. As French pâtisseries arrived in colonial America, they shared their culinary artistry with enthusiastic patrons, many of whom had experienced varieties of French pastry while traveling abroad.

Serves 4

> 3 pounds Puff Pastry (see page 188), or use store-bought sheets
> Beaten egg whites, for brushing
> Granulated sugar, for dusting
> 6 cups Pastry Cream (see page 119)
> Confectioners' sugar, for dusting

1. Preheat the oven to 325°F.
2. Divide the Puff Pastry dough into three portions. Roll each portion into a ½-inch-thick, roughly shaped rectangle about 12 inches long by 6 inches wide. Prick each sheet of Puff Pastry with a fork, and transfer them to 3 separate parchment-lined baking pans.
3. Brush the tops of each sheet lightly with egg whites and dust evenly with granulated sugar.
4. Bake for 15 minutes, or until golden brown. Let the pastry sheets cool; then remove from the pans.
5. Spread about a tablespoon of Pastry Cream on the inverted side of a clean baking tray to act as a "glue." Set one pastry sheet atop the baking tray, smooth side down. Spread an even 1-inch-thick layer of pastry cream atop the first pastry sheet. Place the rough side of the second sheet directly atop the cream. Chill the sandwiched layers for 20 minutes.
6. Spread an even 1-inch-thick layer of pastry cream atop the second sheet. Top with the third pastry layer, rough side down. Freeze for 20 minutes.
7. Using a serrated knife, square off the edges of the pastry. Hold the knife at a 45-degree angle and make short choppy strokes when sawing the pastry.
8. Cover the top of the *mille-feuille* generously and evenly with confectioners' sugar. Chill 20 minutes, cut into 4 portions, and serve.

### Variation: Strawberry *Mille-Feuille*

> 2 cups Berry Preserves (see page 244), using stemmed strawberries
> 2 pints fresh strawberries, stemmed and sliced

1. Follow the procedure for making *Mille-Feuille*, except spread an even layer of preserves atop each sheet of pastry before adding the Pastry Cream.
2. Finish by spreading pastry cream atop the final sheet of pastry. Arrange sliced strawberries nicely atop.

# Puff Pastry

Preparing traditional puff pastry is a rewarding and worthwhile but time-consuming task that requires several hours of work. Chilled butter and a flour-and-water dough are rolled and folded together in thirds at least six times, creating hundreds of delicate layers that expand during baking. The process is a long one, because the pastry must remain very cold and rest in the refrigerator in between "turns" (the term for the rolling and folding procedure).

As a time-saving alternative, high-quality, frozen puff pastry is available in supermarkets as well.

**Makes 3 pounds; enough for 12 meat turnovers or potpie lids**

2 cups plus 2 tablespoons bread flour
1 pound (4 sticks) plus 6 tablespoons (¾ stick) unsalted butter
1 teaspoon salt
1 cup less 2 tablespoons water
2 large egg yolks
2 tablespoons cake flour

1. In the bowl of an electric mixer fitted with the paddle attachment, combine 2 cups of the bread flour, 1 pound of butter, and the salt. Mix until the mixture becomes fine and crumbly. Remove the paddle attachment and replace with the dough hook.

2. In a separate mixing bowl, whisk together the water and the egg yolks. Make a well in the center of the flour mixture, and add the egg mixture. Mix on low speed just until a dough forms, about 5 minutes.

3. Remove the dough from the bowl, and roll it out into an 11 x 17-inch rectangle. Wrap in plastic wrap and refrigerate for 30 minutes.

4. Meanwhile, in a medium-size mixing bowl, add the remaining 2 tablespoons bread flour, the remaining 6 tablespoons butter, and the cake flour. Stir to combine, making sure that the butter is well incorporated into the flour and that there are no lumps of butter in the mixture.

5. Line an 11 x 17-inch baking pan with parchment paper. Grease two thirds of the parchment with butter; then refrigerate for about 20 minutes to chill the butter.

6. Coat a work surface generously with flour. Lay out the chilled dough. Spread the butter mixture on top of the dough, covering the left two thirds of the dough, and leaving a 1-inch border of dough uncovered around the edges (see Illustration #1).

7. Fold the unbuttered third of the dough over, from right to left (Illustration #2); then fold the butter-covered third over, from left to right (Illustration #3). Seal all of the edges so that no butter is showing.

8. Turn the dough so that the seam is facing away from you; then, using a rolling pin, roll the dough out to 33 x 17 inches. Fold the dough in thirds, using the same method as used when folding in the butter. Place the folded dough on a baking sheet, cover with plastic wrap, and refrigerate for another 30 minutes.

9. Coat a work surface generously with flour. Lay out the chilled dough so that the seam is facing away from you. Using a rolling pin, roll the dough out to 33 x 17 inches again. Fold the left half of the dough in, and then fold the right half of the dough in, so that they touch in the middle of the dough (Illustration #4). Then fold the two halves together as if closing a book (Illustration #5). Cover with plastic wrap, and refrigerate for 30 minutes.

10. Repeat step #8; then cover and refrigerate for another 30 minutes.
11. Repeat step #9; then cover and refrigerate for another 30 minutes.
12. Repeat step #8 again; then cover and refrigerate for 1 hour before use. The final size of the puff pastry sheet will be 11 x 17 inches. The puff pastry will last 3 to 4 days in the refrigerator but can be frozen for up to 2 weeks and defrosted 1 day before use.

**Variation:**
To make Spiced Puff Pastry, in step #5, add ½ teaspoon allspice,
2 teaspoons ground cardamom, and a pinch of ground cloves to the butter mixture.

Inspired by their European counterparts, colonial Americans admired the skill required to prepare fine pastry. Amelia Simmons, certainly aware of the significance pastry played in the meal, offered readers no less than eight different puff pastry recipes in her cookbook <u>American Cookery</u> (37–38).

# Cream Puffs

Cream puffs, luxurious combinations of delicate pastry and rich cream filling, are yet another type of confection that combines British and French baking traditions. It is difficult to say where pastry cream first developed, although it seems to have roots in English pudding and custard preparation. *Pâte à choux*, however, also called "choux paste" and "cream-puff pastry," appears to derive from French pastry traditions. It translates as "cabbage paste," perhaps because as the dough rises in the oven it resembles little cabbages. Although few eighteenth-century English cookery books included this sort of dough, one influential text did so: William Verral's *A Complete System of Cookery*, published in London in 1759. In his introduction to the facsimile edition entitled *The Cook's Paradise*, published in 1948, R. L. Megroz explained that "Verral's treatise was designed as an introduction to French cookery. . . . [T]he book is really a tribute to French culinary art" (Verral 9). Eighteenth-century Philadelphians almost assuredly had access to Verral's work and therefore would have been exposed to his French recipes, including that entitled "French paste"—undoubtedly *pâte à choux*. The author suggested filling the pastry with cherry conserve, much in the manner in which cream puffs are filled with pastry cream. The full title of Verral's recipe is "Des bignets [*sic*] de cerises au four" or "Cherries in a French paste"; the recipe reads:

> [Y]our paste make as follows; take half a pint of water, put to it a morsel of fine sugar, a grain of salt and a bit of lemon-peel, an ounce of butter, and boil it a minute or two, take it from your fire, and work in as much fine flour as it takes to a tender paste, put one egg at a time and mould it well till it comes to such a consistence as to pour with the help of a spoon out of the stewpan upon a tin or cover, covered with flour; scrape it off in lumps upon tin with the handle of a large key, and bake them of a nice colour and crispness, cut a hole in the bottom, and fill up with your conserve, sift some sugar over, and dish up. If you make this paste according to the rule before you, it will swell very large and hollow, and makes a genteel "entremets" (Verral 116).

**Makes 20 Cream Puffs**

### *Pâte à Choux*
½ cup plus 2½ tablespoons bread flour
1 cup whole milk
¼ pound (1 stick) unsalted butter, softened at room temperature
1 tablespoon granulated sugar
¼ teaspoon salt
Pinch of nutmeg
5 large eggs
1 large egg yolk
6 cups Pastry Cream (see page 119)

### Chocolate Sauce
1 cup whole milk
8 ounces finely chopped semisweet chocolate
4 tablespoons (½ stick) unsalted butter, softened
1 cup heavy cream

1. Preheat the oven to 450°F. Line an 11 x 17-inch baking pan with parchment paper. Fit your mixer with the paddle attachment. Fit a pastry bag with a #16 straight tip.

2. Prepare the *Pâte à Choux*: Into a large mixing bowl, sift the flour three times.

3. In a medium-size, heavy-bottomed saucepan, combine the milk, butter, sugar, salt, and nutmeg; bring to a boil. Briefly whisk the mixture for a few seconds. Remove the pot from the heat, and stir in the flour with a sturdy wooden spoon. Return the pot to high heat, and cook the mixture, stirring constantly, until the mixture pulls away from the sides of the pan and is satiny in appearance, 2 to 3 minutes.

4. Immediately transfer the dough to the electric mixer bowl, and beat on low speed until the bowl of the mixer is cool to the touch.

5. With the mixer running on medium speed, add 4 of the eggs, one at a time—make sure each egg is completely incorporated before adding the next. Turn the mixer off, and run your index finger through the batter. The batter should be wet, but your finger should leave a trail that will pull back on itself to half its original width. Day to day, the *Pâte à Choux* recipe is subject to variation due to weather changes and the flour's absorbency properties. If the batter is too dry, add the remaining egg and yolk.

6. To prepare the pastries, fill your pastry bag one quarter full with the batter. With the bag held at a 75-degree angle 1 inch above the parchment-lined baking sheet, pipe rounds 1 inch wide by ¼ inch high. Allow the batter to fall on top of itself. Appling even pressure to the bag, a quick count to two will leave you with the right size. When you achieve the desired size, stop applying pressure and quickly pull up and away to the right.

7. Transfer the baking sheet to the oven, and immediately reduce the temperature to 375°F. Bake until golden and puffed, about 15 minutes. The cream puffs will sound hollow when tapped on their bases. Remove the pans from the oven, and set aside on wire racks to cool.

8. Prepare the Chocolate Sauce: In a medium-size saucepan, bring the milk to a boil, stirring to avoid scorching the bottom. Immediately reduce the heat to low. Add the chopped chocolate, and stir until the chocolate has completely melted.

9. Remove the pot from the heat. Add the butter and cream, mix to combine, and let cool to room temperature.

10. Using a paring knife, poke a small hole in the sides of each cream puff. Fit a pastry bag with a #10 straight tip. Fill the bag a third of the way with Pastry Cream.

11. Hold a cream puff in your nondominant hand and the pastry bag in your dominant hand. Insert the tip of the pastry bag just inside the Cream Puff. Fill the puff with cream by applying steady pressure. When the puff feels heavy and full, stop applying pressure and remove the tip from the puff, pulling quickly down and away from it.

12. Dip the top of each cream puff in the Chocolate Sauce and set aside while you finish the rest.

# Pears in Puff Pastry with Gloucester Cheese, Walnuts, and Raisins

This recipe was inspired by the eighteenth-century penchant for combining sweet and savory ingredients and pays tribute to the popularity of fruit, cheese, and nuts. Cheese not only was a staple but could also be a stylish delicacy—especially imported varieties available in cosmopolitan cities like Philadelphia. The *Pennsylvania Gazette* frequently printed advertisements listing cheese. Most of the shops that carried housewares also sold foodstuffs, including chocolate, spices, wine, and a "Quantity of excellent cheese" (December 8, 1773). In 1786, "Fisher and Roberts" announced that "at their Store, on the South side of Market street Wharff" they had available "double Gloucester Cheese of the best Quality" (July 5, 1786).

Gloucester cheese, also known as double Gloucester, was originally made from the milk of Gloucester cows (presently on the verge of extinction) (Herbst 198). It is a smooth, yellow cheese with a mild flavor that is enjoyable on its own or as part of a cheese tray accompanied by fruit, nuts, and wine. It is, therefore, perfectly suited to this dish, in which all of these elements are combined.

**Serves 4**

> ½ cup dried cherries
> ¼ cup raisins
> 1 cup dark rum
> 1 cup cake crumbs, preferably from Gingerbread (see page 29)
> 6 tablespoons light brown sugar
> 1 cup grated double Gloucester cheese (or Edam or Cheddar)
> ½ cup walnuts, toasted (see Chef's Note, page 38) and roughly chopped
> 2 lemons, zest grated and juiced
> 2 teaspoons ground cinnamon
> 6 ounces (1½ sticks) unsalted butter, melted
> 1½ pounds Spiced Puff Pastry (see Variation, page 188–189), or use store-bought sheets
> 4 Bartlett pears
> ¼ cup granulated sugar
> 2 teaspoons ground star anise
> 3 large eggs, beaten with 1 tablespoon water and pinch of salt, for egg wash

1. In a small bowl or container, add the dried cherries and raisins, and add enough rum to cover. Allow to soak for at least 8 hours, or overnight. Strain the raisins and cherries, and reserve the rum.

2. Preheat the oven to 425°F. Line a baking pan with parchment paper.

3. In a large bowl, add the cake crumbs, brown sugar, cheese, walnuts, lemon zest, cinnamon, and the soaked dried cherries and raisins; stir to combine. Moisten the mixture with ½ cup of the melted butter and 2 tablespoons of the reserved rum, and stir to combine well.

4. In a large bowl, add a few cups of water and the lemon juice; stir to combine. Peel the pears, remove the stems, and trim the top lobes (top part) of each pear. Roughly chop the top lopes into ½-inch cubes. Add the chopped pear to the filling mixture, and stir to combine. Using a melon baller, hollow out a ¾-inch hole in the center of each pear. Set the hollowed pears aside in the bowl of lemon water.

5. Roll the Puff Pastry out to ¼-inch thickness and, using a paring knife, cut into four 6-inch squares.

6. In a small bowl, stir together the granulated sugar and star anise. Remove the pears from the water and pat them dry. Lightly brush each pear with the remaining ¼ cup of melted butter, and dust lightly with some of the anise sugar.

7. Place 1 pear in the center of each puff pastry square. Generously pack each pear tightly with the filling.

8. Lightly brush the exposed corners of the pastry with the egg wash. Bring each corner of the pastry to the top center of each pear, encasing the pears in pastry, and pinch the corners together to create a seal.

9. Brush the pears in puff pastry with the egg wash, and dust generously with anise sugar. Place the pears in the oven and immediately reduce the temperature to 375°F. Bake for 20 minutes, or until golden. Serve warm.

Most eighteenth-century cookery books included a chapter in which the author discussed ingredients and how to purchase those of the best quality. Some, like John Farley in his *The London Art of Cookery*, entitled this section "Marketing." Writing in detail about many items, he included a treatise on cheese as well. He advised the reader to "Observe the coat of your cheese before you purchase it; for if it be old, with a rough and ragged coat, or dry at top, you may expect to find little worms or mites in it. If it be moist, spongy or full of holes, it will give reason to suspect that it is magotty [sic]. Whenever you perceive any perished places on the outside, be sure to probe to the bottom of them; for, though the hole in the coat may be but small, the perished part within maybe considerable" (Farley 29).

# Rice Custard and Fig–Stuffed Apples in Puff Pastry

This dish refers to some of the most basic and commonly enjoyed of eighteenth-century foods: rice pudding or custard, baked fruit, and flaky pastry. Each component was frequently prepared in homes and shops around Philadelphia and frugally made use of readily available ingredients. Fruit baked alone or stuffed was as practical as it was delicious and healthful. Because it was served cooked, the fruit did not have to be perfectly free of blemishes or pristinely fresh. In addition, the pastry here further overcomes any visible imperfections the fruit might have, cloaking the apples in a golden exterior. Spicy, sweet, and warm, this dessert is especially suited to fall menus.

Serves 4

### Custard
1 cup dried figs, roughly chopped
½ cup golden raisins
2½ cups water, plus extra for lemon water
¼ cup brandy
1 lemon, zest grated and juiced
4 Granny Smith apples
2 cups heavy cream
2 cinnamon sticks
1 vanilla bean
1 cup short-grain white rice (such as arborio)
¾ cup Madeira wine
3 large eggs
¼ cup granulated sugar

1½ pounds Puff Pastry (see page 188), or use store-bought sheets
3 large eggs, beaten with 1 tablespoon water and pinch of salt, for egg wash
4 tablespoons (½ stick) unsalted butter, melted

### Cinnamon Sugar
½ cup granulated sugar
1 tablespoon ground cinnamon
⅛ teaspoon ground nutmeg

1. Prepare the Custard: In a medium-size bowl, soak the dried figs and golden raisins in 1 cup of the water and the brandy for at least 8 hours, or overnight. Strain the figs and raisins.

2. In a large bowl, add a few cups of water and the lemon juice; stir to combine. Peel the apples and remove the stems. Using a melon baller, hollow out the apples, removing a core about 1 inch wide and 2½ inches deep. Set the apples aside in the bowl of lemon water.

3. In a medium-size saucepan, add the heavy cream, cinnamon sticks, vanilla bean, and lemon zest; stir to combine, and bring the mixture to a boil. Immediately remove the pan from the heat and allow the cream to steep for 1 hour.

4. Preheat the oven to 400°F. Line a baking pan with parchment paper.
5. In a medium-size saucepan, add the white rice, Madeira, and the remaining 1½ cups of water; bring to a boil. Reduce the heat to a simmer, cover, and cook until the rice is tender but firm, about 10 minutes. Strain and pat the rice dry in a piece of white linen (or use paper towels).
6. With a slotted spoon, remove the cinnamon sticks and vanilla bean from the cream. Bring the cream back to a boil.
7. In a medium-size stainless steel bowl, whisk together the eggs and sugar. Temper the cream into the egg mixture by adding ¼ cup at a time of the hot cream to the eggs, whisking all the while.
8. Bring a medium-size pot of water to a simmer. Prepare an ice bath in a bowl twice the size of the custard bowl.
9. Add the rice, figs, and raisins to the custard mixture, and stir to combine.
10. Place the rice custard mixture atop the water bath and cook, stirring constantly, until the mixture is thickened, about 8 minutes. Immediately set the custard in the ice bath. Stir occasionally until the mixture is cool.
11. Roll out the Puff Pastry to ¼-inch thickness and, using a paring knife, cut four 6-inch squares.
12. Prepare the Cinnamon Sugar: In a small bowl, add the sugar, cinnamon, and nutmeg; and stir to combine. Remove the apples from the lemon water and pat them dry. Lightly brush each apple, inside and out, with the melted butter, and dust lightly with some of the cinnamon sugar, inside and out.
13. Place 1 apple in the center of each puff pastry square. Generously fill each apple with the custard filling.
14. Lightly brush the exposed corners of the pastry with the egg wash.
15. Make 2-inch incisions at each pastry corner, cutting toward the center of the square. Bring alternating corners of the pastry to the top center of each apple, partially encasing the apples in pastry, and creating a star effect (see Illustrations #1–3).
16. Brush the puff pastry with egg wash, and dust generously with cinnamon sugar. Place the apples on the parchment-lined baking pan, transfer to the oven, and immediately reduce the temperature to 350°F. Bake for 20 minutes, or until golden. Serve hot.

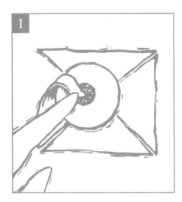
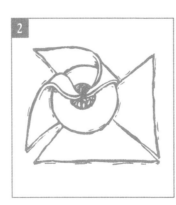
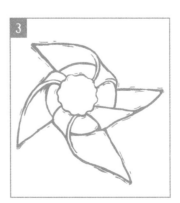

# Vol–au–Vent with Berries

This dessert was inspired by the fruit-filled Puff Pastry pies and tarts of the eighteenth century. In fact, *vol-au-vents* are said to have first been prepared by the esteemed gastronome and chef Marie Antoine Carême (1784–1833), who cooked for such renowned patrons as Talleyrand, Czar Alexander I, George IV, and Baron Rothschild (Herbst 492). If this attribution is to be believed, then it would appear that Carême himself elaborated on the late-eighteenth- and early-nineteenth-century English and French dishes that combined puff pastry with a variety of fillings.

*Vol-au-vents* are puff pastry shells traditionally filled with creamy, savory combinations of meat and/or vegetables and topped with puff pastry lids. They may be prepared as individual servings or in larger sizes suitable for a table of guests. In modern times, it has become popular to serve these shells for dessert as well, filled with fresh or cooked fruit and whipped cream or *crème anglaise*. Once the puff pastry is prepared, this dish comes together quickly and elegantly completes any menu.

Serves 6

> 3 pounds Puff Pastry (see page 188), or use store-bought sheets
> 3 large eggs, beaten with 1 tablespoon water and pinch of salt, for egg wash
> 1 pound semisweet chocolate, melted
>
> **Filling**
> 4 cups (1 quart) heavy cream
> ½ cup confectioners' sugar, plus extra for dusting
> 1 tablespoon vanilla extract
> 3 tablespoons orange liqueur (such as Triple Sec or Cointreau)
>
> 1 pint each raspberries, blackberries, blueberries, and strawberries—cut in half and stems removed
> 1½ cups *Crème Anglaise* (see page 122)
> Fresh mint sprigs, for garnish

1. Preheat the oven to 425°F. Line an 11 x 17-inch baking pan with parchment paper.
2. Roll out 1 sheet of Puff Pastry to a ⅛-inch thickness. Prick the pastry all over using a fork. Using a 4-inch biscuit cutter, cut the pastry into 6 rounds (Illustration #1). Alternatively, use a 4-inch diameter bowl and cut the pastry with a paring knife. Set these rounds aside; they will be the bases of your *vol-au-vents*.
3. Roll out another sheet of Puff Pastry to ½-inch thickness and, using the same 4-inch template, cut 6 more rounds. Take a 3-inch biscuit cutter, or an alternative template, and cut the center from these ½-inch-thick rounds to make rings (Illustration #2).
4. Brush the thinner ⅛-inch-thick bases with the egg wash. Set the Puff Pastry rings precisely atop the bases, making certain the edges are aligned (Illustration #3). Brush the *vol-au-vents* with the egg wash, and refrigerate for 30 minutes (Illustration #4).
5. Using a paring knife, make shallow incisions, ¼ inch apart, around the perimeter of each *vol-au-vent* (Illustration #5). Brush each base with egg wash again.
6. Place the pastries on the baking sheet. Transfer to the oven and bake for 20 minutes, or until golden. Remove from the oven, and set aside to cool.
7. Bring a medium-size pot of water to a simmer. In a small metal bowl, add the chocolate. Set the bowl over the simmering pot of water, and heat until the chocolate is melted, stirring occasionally. Remove the bowl of chocolate from the heat, and let cool briefly. When cool enough to touch, using a pastry brush, paint the inside of the cool *vol-au-vents* with the melted chocolate.

8. Prepare the Filling: In an electric mixer fitted with the whip attachment on medium-high speed, whip the cream and ½ cup confectioners' sugar to medium peaks. Add the vanilla extract and orange liqueur, and whip to stiff peaks.

9. Using a large spoon, fill each *vol-au-vent* with the whipped cream. Top with the berries, and serve with *Crème Anglaise*. Dust with confectioners' sugar, and garnish with a fresh mint sprig.

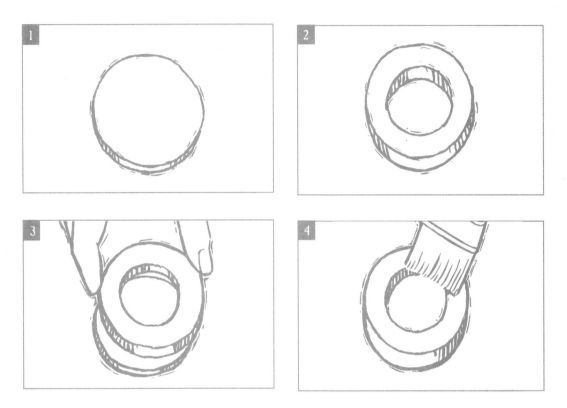

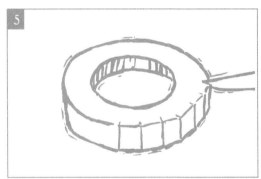

# Turnovers

Based on eighteenth-century fruit and/or cream-filled pies and tarts, turnovers are simply rounds of pastry spread with filling, folded in half (crimped at the edges), and baked. Stuffed with meat and vegetables as well as fruit, these pastries were originally prepared in Europe as complete meals that were consumed conveniently without flatware or plates. Today, turnovers are considered elegant, individual pastries that may be served in place of slices of pies or tarts. The following fillings—prepared with dried and fresh fruits, nuts, spices, and cheese—were inspired by eighteenth-century preserves as well as by pie and tart fillings.

## Dried Cherry and Apricot Turnovers

Serves 6

8 fresh apricots
3 cups dried cherries
4 tablespoons (½ stick) unsalted butter
1 tablespoon chopped fresh ginger
2 cups Orange Marmalade (see page 247)
¼ cup lavender honey, or regular honey
3 pounds Puff Pastry (see page 188), or use store-bought sheets
3 large eggs, beaten with 1 tablespoon water and pinch of salt, for egg wash
½ cup granulated sugar
2 tablespoons ground ginger

1. Preheat the oven to 350°F. Line a baking pan with parchment paper.
2. Slice the apricots in half, remove the pit, and cut into 1-inch cubes. Place the apricots aside in a medium-size bowl, and add the cherries.
3. In a medium-size skillet, melt the butter over medium heat. Add the ginger, and cook, stirring, for 30 seconds. Remove the skillet from the heat, and whisk in the Orange Marmalade and lavender honey. Pour this mixture over the apricots and cherries; stir to combine.
4. Lightly dust your countertop with flour. With a lightly floured rolling pin, roll out the Puff Pastry to a ¼-inch thickness. Trim the dough so that you have a 12 x 18-inch rectangle. Cut the sheet of pastry in half lengthwise; then cut each half into thirds.
5. Divide the filling evenly among each square and center it.
6. Lightly brush the egg wash on the pastry around the filling. Fold the top left corner of the pastry over to the bottom right corner of the pastry, making a triangle-shaped pastry. Seal the edges with a fork. Repeat the process until you have 6 turnovers.
7. Place the turnovers on the prepared baking pan. Make three ½-inch incisions on the top of each turnover. Brush the turnovers with the egg wash, and chill for 30 minutes.
8. Brush the turnovers with the egg wash again, and sprinkle with the granulated sugar and ground ginger.
9. Bake the turnovers for 20 minutes, or until golden. Serve hot.

# Apple–Golden Raisin Turnovers

**Serves 6**

4 apples (Gala or Granny Smith), peeled and cored
½ lemon, juiced
1 cup golden raisins
4 tablespoons (½ stick) unsalted butter
2 tablespoons honey
2 teaspoons vanilla extract
1 cup plus 2 tablespoons granulated sugar
¼ cup all-purpose flour
1 tablespoon ground cinnamon
⅛ teaspoon ground nutmeg
3 pounds Puff Pastry (see page 188), or use store-bought sheets
½ cup apple butter
3 large eggs, beaten with 1 tablespoon water and pinch of salt, for egg wash
½ cup light brown sugar
Pinch of ground cardamom

1. Preheat the oven to 350°F. Line a baking sheet with parchment paper.
2. Chop the apples into 1-inch cubes, and set them aside in a medium-size bowl. Add the lemon juice and raisins to the apples, and toss to combine.
3. In a small saucepan, melt the butter. Remove from the heat, and whisk in the honey and vanilla extract. Pour this mixture over the apples and raisins; toss to combine.
4. In a separate bowl, whisk together the sugar, flour, cinnamon, and nutmeg. Add this mixture to the apples, and stir to combine.
5. Lightly dust your countertop with flour. With a lightly floured rolling pin, roll out the Puff Pastry to a ¼-inch thickness. Trim the dough so that you have a 12 x 18-inch rectangle. Cut the sheet of pastry in half lengthwise; then cut each half into thirds.
6. Place 1 heaping tablespoon of apple butter in the center of each square. Divide the filling evenly among each square and center it.
7. Lightly brush the egg wash on the pastry around the filling. Fold the top left corner of the pastry over to the bottom right corner of the pastry, making a triangle-shaped pastry. Seal the edges with a fork. Repeat the process until you have 6 turnovers.
8. Place the turnovers on the prepared baking pan. Make three ½-inch incisions on the top of each turnover. Brush the turnovers with the egg wash, and chill for 30 minutes.
9. Brush the turnovers with the egg wash again, and sprinkle with the brown sugar and cardamom.
10. Bake the turnovers for 20 minutes, or until golden. Serve hot.

# Quince, Currant, and Dried Fig Turnovers

Serves 6

    4 quince
    1 cup dried figs, roughly chopped
    ½ cup dried currants
    1 lemon, juiced
    4 tablespoons (½ stick) unsalted butter
    1 cup plus 2 tablespoons granulated sugar
    ¼ cup all-purpose flour
    ½ teaspoon ground cardamom, plus extra for sprinkling
    Freshly grated nutmeg, to taste
    3 pounds Puff Pastry (see page 188), or use store-bought sheets
    ½ cup apple butter
    3 large eggs, beaten with 1 tablespoon water and pinch of salt, for egg wash
    Light brown sugar, for dusting

1. Preheat the oven to 350°F. Line a baking pan with parchment paper.
2. Chop the quince into 1-inch cubes, and transfer to a medium-size bowl. Add the figs, currants, raisins, and half the lemon juice; toss to combine.
3. In a small saucepan, melt the butter. Pour the melted butter over the quince mixture, and toss to combine.
4. In a separate bowl, whisk together the sugar, flour, cardamom, and nutmeg. Add this mixture to the quince mixture, and stir to combine.
5. Lightly dust your countertop with flour. With a lightly floured rolling pin, roll out the Puff Pastry to a ¼-inch thickness. Trim the dough so that you have a 12 x 18-inch rectangle. Cut the sheet of pastry in half lengthwise; then cut each half into thirds.
6. Place 1 heaping tablespoon of the apple butter in the center of each square. Divide the filling evenly among each square and center it.
7. Lightly brush the egg wash on the pastry around the filling. Fold the top left corner of the pastry over to the bottom right corner of the pastry, making a triangle-shaped pastry. Seal the edges with a fork. Repeat the process until you have 6 turnovers.
8. Place the turnovers on the prepared baking pan. Make three ½-inch incisions on the top of each turnover. Brush the turnovers with the egg wash, and chill for 30 minutes.
9. Brush the turnovers with the egg wash again, and sprinkle with the brown sugar and cardamom.
10. Bake the turnovers for 20 minutes, or until golden. Serve hot.

# Mixed Berry and Cream Cheese Turnovers

Serves 6

### Cream Cheese Dough
6 ounces (1½ sticks) cold unsalted butter, cut into bits
8 ounces cold cream cheese
½ teaspoon salt
2½ cups all-purpose flour

### Filling
2 pints blueberries
1 cup granulated sugar
1 lemon, zest grated and juiced
3 tablespoons cornstarch
¼ cup water
½ pint strawberries, hulled and cut in half
½ pint raspberries
½ pint blackberries

3 large eggs, beaten with 1 tablespoon water and pinch of salt, for egg wash
Light brown sugar, for dusting
Ground ginger, for dusting

1. Prepare the Cream Cheese Dough: In an electric mixer fitted with the paddle attachment, on medium speed, cream together the butter and cream cheese. Add the salt, and beat to combine. Add the flour, and mix only until the dough comes together. Wrap the dough in plastic wrap, and refrigerate for later use.
2. Preheat the oven to 350°F. Line a baking pan with parchment paper.
3. Prepare the Filling: In a medium-size saucepan over medium heat, add the blueberries with ¾ cup of the sugar, the lemon zest, and the lemon juice. Cook, stirring occasionally, until the blueberries dissolve and the mixture begins to thicken, about 5 minutes.
4. Meanwhile, in a small bowl, whisk together the cornstarch and water. When the blueberry sauce boils, add the cornstarch mixture, stirring vigorously to combine. When the sauce thickens, cook for 1 minute more, stirring constantly. Pour the blueberry mixture into a bowl, and set the bowl in an ice bath to cool to room temperature.
5. Once the mixture has cooled, fold in the strawberries, raspberries, and blackberries.
6. Lightly dust your countertop with flour. With a lightly floured rolling pin, roll out the Cream Cheese Dough to a ¼-inch thickness. Trim the dough so that you have a 12 x 18-inch rectangle. Cut the sheet of pastry in half lengthwise; then cut each half into thirds.
7. Divide the Filling evenly among each square and center it.
8. Lightly brush the egg wash on the pastry around the Filling. Fold the top left corner of the pastry over to the bottom right corner of the pastry, making a triangle-shaped pastry. Seal the edges with a fork. Repeat the process until you have 6 turnovers.
9. Place the turnovers on the prepared baking pan. Make three ½-inch incisions on the tops of each turnover. Brush the turnovers with the egg wash, and chill for 30 minutes.
10. Brush the turnovers with the egg wash again, and sprinkle with the brown sugar and ginger.
11. Bake the turnovers for 20 minutes, or until golden. Serve hot.

# Strudel

Strudel arrived in Philadelphia with the Germans who settled in colonial America. As the following recipes reveal, the delicate dough may be filled with a variety of fruits, nuts, and creams. Like many other desserts of its type, strudel reflects the mergence of European and American cultures. The golden crust of this pastry is testament to the artistry of German and northern European baking traditions. The sweet fillings, howeer—prepared with such items as apples, cranberries, cherries, raspberries, peaches, apricots, gooseberries, pears, raisins, citrus, and spices—pay tribute to the rich variety of ingredients available in late-eighteenth-century Philadelphia.

**Serves 10 to 12**

### Strudel Dough
4 tablespoons (½ stick) unsalted butter, melted and cooled to
    room temperature
3 large egg yolks
2 tablespoons white vinegar
½ teaspoon salt
½ cup water
1¼ cups high-gluten flour (see Chef's Note)
Nonstick cooking spray

½ pound (2 sticks) unsalted butter, melted
4 cups plain, unflavored bread crumbs
Strudel filling of your choice (see pages 204–206)
3 large eggs, beaten with 1 tablespoon water and pinch of salt, for
    egg wash
Confectioners' sugar, for dusting
Ice cream, for serving

*If you can't find high-gluten flour in your area supermarkets, King Arthur Flour makes a product called Sir Lancelot Hi-Gluten Flour (see Sources, page 252).*

1. Prepare the Strudel Dough. In the bowl of an electric mixer fitted with the dough hook attachment, add the butter, egg yolks, vinegar, and salt. Mix on medium speed to combine.
2. Add the flour to the mixer bowl, and mix on low speed until the ingredients come together. Increase the mixer speed to medium, and mix until the dough pulls away from and slaps against the sides of the bowl, about 8 minutes. When the dough is fully and properly developed, it will stretch 3 to 4 inches above the bowl when pulled, without breaking.
3. Coat a large bowl with cooking spray. Transfer the dough to the coated bowl. Spray the dough lightly with cooking spray, and place a piece of plastic wrap directly atop the dough. Make certain no part of the dough is exposed to the air. Allow the dough to relax in a warm environment for at least 1 hour.
4. Meanwhile, prepare the filling of your choice.
5. Preheat the oven to 425°F. Line a baking pan with parchment paper.
6. You'll need a 3 x 4-foot working surface to prepare the Strudel Dough. Cover the entire surface with a large, clean linen. Make certain that there are no impurities on the table or linen. Lightly dust the linen with flour. Unwrap and place the strudel dough on the center of the linen-covered surface. Dust the dough with flour. Roll the strudel dough out so that it covers three quarters of the surface. The dough will measure 3 feet 4 inches by 3 feet 2 inches.

7. Lightly flour the back of your hands. Place your hands under the dough and, working from the center outward, stretch the dough to the length of the table. Stretch the dough until it is transparent and overhangs the table by about 2 inches.

8. Working lengthwise, brush two thirds of the dough with melted cool butter. Cover the remaining third of the dough with breadcrumbs (Illustration #1).

9. Place the filling atop the crumbs in an even, concise strip (Illustration #2), about 3 inches wide and 2 inches high. Lift the overhanging dough and cover the filling (Illustration #3).

10. Begin to roll the dough by lifting the linen and allowing the dough to fall over itself (Illustration #4). Continue lifting and folding the dough until no excess remains and you have a long tube of dough. Fold the ends under to seal (Illustration #5).

11. Transfer the strudel to the prepared baking pan. Brush the strudel with the egg wash, and prick it all over with a fork (Illustration #6). Bake for 20 minutes, or until golden.

12. Allow the strudel to cool before slicing. Dust with confectioners' sugar and serve warm, with ice cream.

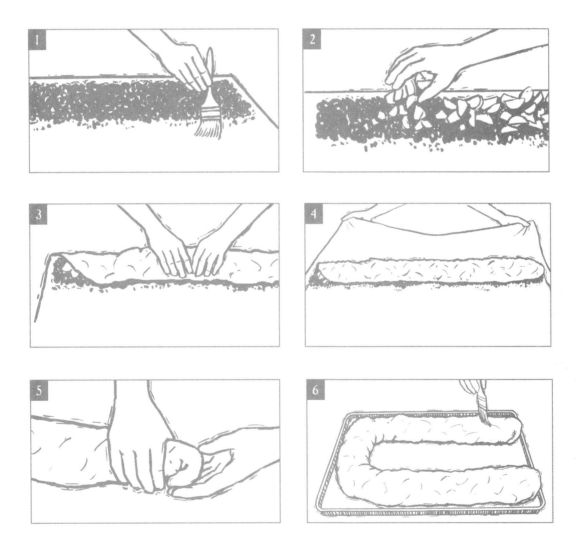

# Apple–Cranberry Strudel Filling

5 apples (Gala or Granny Smith), peeled and cored
1 cup fresh cranberries
½ cup golden raisins
½ cup plus 2 tablespoons granulated sugar
3 tablespoons cake flour
2 teaspoons ground cinnamon
Pinch of ground nutmeg

1. Cut the apples into 2-inch cubes. In a medium-size bowl, add the apples, cranberries, and raisins, and toss to combine.
2. In a separate bowl, add the sugar, flour, cinnamon, and nutmeg. Add the sugar mixture to the fruit mixture, and toss to combine. Set the mixture aside at room temperature, or store covered in the refrigerator.

# Cherry–Cheese Strudel Filling

2 cups sun-dried cherries
½ cup golden raisins
2 cups water
½ cup kirschwasser (cherry-flavored liqueur)
1 vanilla bean, or 2 teaspoons vanilla extract
1½ cups cream cheese
½ cup confectioners' sugar
2 tablespoons all-purpose flour
3 large egg yolks
1 cup pistachios, shelled

1. In a small bowl or container, add the cherries, raisins, water, and kirschwasser, and stir to combine. Let soak overnight. Strain the cherries and raisins.
2. Using a paring knife, slice the vanilla bean in half lengthwise and, using the back of the knife, scrape the seeds from the pod. Discard the pod.
3. In the bowl of an electric mixer fitted with the paddle attachment on medium speed, beat the cream cheese, confectioners' sugar, and vanilla seeds (or vanilla extract) until combined, scraping down the sides of the bowl often.
4. Add the flour, and mix to combine. With the mixer on low speed, add the yolks one at a time, and mix until incorporated.
5. With a rubber spatula or wooden spoon, fold in the pistachios, raisins, and cherries. Set the mixture aside at room temperature, or store covered in the refrigerator.

# Peach–Raspberry Strudel Filling

5 peaches
1 pint raspberries
½ cup golden raisins
½ cup plus 2 tablespoons granulated sugar
3 tablespoons all-purpose flour
1 tablespoon ground ginger
Pinch of ground nutmeg

1. Cut the peaches in half and remove the pit. Cut the peaches into 2-inch cubes. In a medium-size bowl, add the peaches, along with the raspberries and raisins, and toss to combine.
2. In a separate bowl, stir together the sugar, flour, ginger, and nutmeg. Add the dry ingredients to the fruit, and toss to combine. Set the mixture aside at room temperature, or store covered in the refrigerator.

# Apricot–Gooseberry Strudel Filling

10 apricots
1 pint gooseberries, husked
1 vanilla bean, or 2 teaspoons vanilla extract
3 tablespoons all-purpose flour
1 cup plus 1 tablespoon light brown sugar
1 orange, zest grated
½ teaspoon ground cardamom

1. Cut the apricots in half and remove the pit. Cut the apricots into 2-inch cubes.
2. Remove the gooseberries from their papery husks, and, using a paring knife, slice them in half. In a medium-size bowl, add the apricots and gooseberries, and toss to combine.
3. Using a paring knife, slice the vanilla bean in half lengthwise and, using the back of the knife, scrape the seeds from the pod. Discard the pod.
4. In another bowl, stir together the flour, brown sugar, orange zest, cardamom, and vanilla seeds (or vanilla extract). Add the dry ingredients to the fruit, and toss to combine. Set the mixture aside at room temperature, or store covered in the refrigerator.

# Pear, Pecan, and Currant Strudel Filling

6 Bartlett pears, peeled and cored
2 cups dried currants
2 tablespoons anise-flavored liqueur (such as Pernod or Sambuca)
1 tablespoon vanilla extract
1 cup granulated sugar
3 tablespoons all-purpose flour
1 tablespoon freshly ground star anise (ground in a coffee grinder)

1.  Cut the pears into 1½-inch cubes. In a medium-size bowl, add the pears, currants, liqueur, and vanilla extract, and toss to combine.

2.  In a separate bowl, add the sugar, flour, and anise; stir to combine. Add the dry ingredients to the fruit, and toss to combine. Set the mixture aside at room temperature, or store covered in the refrigerator.

# German Pancakes with Apples

This dish marries the traditions of two preparations: pancakes and what were commonly called "German fritters" (Farley 215). American and European cooks of the eighteenth century commonly prepared pancakes of all kinds based on a variety of grains and flavorings. German fritters seem to have generally been prepared with a light batter or simply flour, as well as apples cooked in liquor (often brandy), sugar, butter or lard, and spices. Both of these dishes have significant roots in northern European cooking traditions and were popular in Philadelphia due to the city's large German population. Flavored with nutmeg, cinnamon, apples, and rum, these pancakes pay tribute to the influences of German foodways on English cooking in Philadelphia.

Makes 1 dozen pancakes

**Pancakes**
1⅓ cups all-purpose flour
2 tablespoons granulated sugar
1 teaspoon baking powder
½ teaspoon salt
Ground nutmeg, to taste
1 cup whole milk
6 large eggs
6 large egg yolks
3 tablespoons light rum

**Filling**
Nonstick cooking spray
6 ounces (1½ sticks) unsalted butter, melted
4 apples, peeled, cored, and cut into ½-inch cubes
2 cups walnuts
1 cup granulated sugar
Ground cinnamon, to taste
Ground nutmeg, to taste

Maple Whipped Cream (see page 121), for serving

1. Prepare the Pancakes: In a medium-size bowl, add the flour, sugar, baking powder, salt, and nutmeg; stir to combine. Whisk in the milk.
2. To the milk-flour mixture, gradually add the eggs and yolks, whisking each in before adding the next cluster. Whisk in the rum. Chill the batter for at least 1 hour or overnight.
3. Prepare the Filling and Pancakes: Warm a 6-inch omelet pan or crêpe pan over high heat. Spray the pan with cooking spray, and add 2 tablespoons of the melted butter. Add a handful of apples and walnuts, and sprinkle with a tablespoon of the sugar and some cinnamon and nutmeg. Cook, stirring, until the apples are tender but still firm, about 1 minute. Using a 3-ounce ladle, pour the pancake batter into the center of the hot pan. Lift the pan from the heat and tilt it, spreading the batter evenly across the pan. Increase the heat to medium-high heat, and cook the pancake until bubbles begin to form and the pancake is lightly browned, about 45 seconds. Flip the pancake and cook 45 seconds more, until the opposite side is golden. Transfer the pancake to a plate.
4. Continue cooking the pancakes, starting with Step 3, until the batter is finished.
5. Serve with Maple Whipped Cream and cinnamon.

# Orange Curd–Filled Meringue Cup with Berries

This dessert merges two sweet preparations common to eighteenth-century American pâtisserie. Orange curd was most often referred to in the period as "orange pudding" or "orange cream"—recipes that frequently appeared in eighteenth-century cookbooks and called for frugally using the entire fruit (rind, pulp, and juice). Meringue, too, a term so commonly used today, appears mostly to have been used in French cookery and published in French books. In English and American texts, meringue is usually referred to in macaroon recipes not as a distinctive preparation but, rather, as egg whites and sugar "beat to a froth" (Hooker 73) or "beat . . . till they stand alone" (Leslie, *Seventy-Five Receipts, For Pastries, Cakes, and Sweetmeats* 55).

It seems that meringue desserts (composed primarily of egg whites and sugar without nuts or flour) did not appear in American cookery books until the early nineteenth century. Eliza Leslie included one such meringue recipe, entitled "Kisses," in her 1828 book *Seventy-Five Receipts, for Pastry, Cakes, and Sweetmeats* (58), and in her 1848 publication *Directions for Cookery, in Its Various Branches* (354). Prepared with egg whites, confectioners' sugar, and lemon juice or "essence" (extract), these meringues would have been virtually identical to City Tavern's version. Like many instructive cookery book authors of the early nineteenth century, Eliza Leslie intended to teach her readers efficient cooking methods. It is thus with this in mind that she added to her "Kisses" recipe of 1848 this caveat: "To manage them properly, requires so much practice and dexterity, that it is best, when practicable, to procure your kisses from a confectioner's shop" (Leslie, *Directions for Cookery* 355).

Serves 8

### Meringue Cups
¾ cup granulated sugar
¼ cup water
4 large egg whites
Dash of freshly squeezed lemon juice
1 orange, zest grated
1 cup confectioners' sugar

### Berries
1 pint each blueberries, raspberries, blackberries, and strawberries
½ cup sugar
3 tablespoons fresh lavender leaves, or 2 teaspoons dried
1 cup orange liqueur (such as Triple Sec or Cointreau)

### Orange Curd
6 large eggs
6 large egg yolks
1 cup plus 1 tablespoon granulated sugar
4 oranges, zest grated
¾ cup freshly squeezed orange juice
¼ cup plus 2 tablespoons freshly squeezed lemon juice

Confectioners' sugar, for dusting
Fresh berries, for garnishing
Fresh mint sprigs, for garnishing

1. Preheat the oven to 150°F. Line a baking pan with parchment paper. Place eight 3-inch ramekins on the tray. Wrap the outside of the ramekins tightly in aluminum foil and spray the foil with cooking spray (Illustration #1).
2. Prepare the Meringue Cups: In a small saucepan, stir the sugar and water together. Wash the sides of the saucepan with cool water and a pastry brush, rinsing away all granules of sugar. Bring the sugar and water to a boil, and cook until the mixture reaches a temperature of 250°F on a candy thermometer.
3. Meanwhile, in the bowl of an electric mixer fitted with the whip attachment on high speed, whip the egg whites to soft peaks.
4. In a thin steady stream, slowly pour the hot sugar syrup into the egg whites, constantly whipping on medium speed. Try not to hit the sides of the bowl or the whip with the hot sugar syrup. Once all the syrup has been added, beat until cool. Fold the orange zest and confectioners' sugar into the meringue.
5. Transfer the meringue to a pastry bag with a #16 straight tip. Hold the pastry bag 1 inch above the bottom of a ramekin at a 90-degree angle. Applying light and even pressure to the bag, pipe the meringue around the base of the ramekin with a slow and steady circular motion. Pipe a second layer atop the first. Continue until you reach the top of the ramekin (Illustration #2).
6. Transfer the baking pan to the preheated oven to dry the meringues for about 8 hours, or overnight, until firm.
7. Prepare the Berries: Place all of the berries in a medium-size bowl. Cover with the sugar and gently toss to combine. Add the lavender and gently toss to combine. Add the liqueur, toss to combine, and refrigerate overnight.
8. Prepare the Orange Curd: Bring a medium-size pot of water to a simmer. Prepare an ice bath in a large bowl.
9. In a medium-size metal bowl, add the eggs, yolks, and sugar; whisk to combine. Whisk in the orange zest, orange juice, and lemon juice.
10. Place the metal bowl over the simmering water, and whisk constantly until thick, about 10 minutes. Immediately set the bowl of curd in the ice bath, and whisk it until it has cooled.
11. Final assembly: Carefully unmold the Meringue Cups from the foiled rings.
12. Place one cup in the center of each 6-inch serving plate. Fill each cup with curd, and dust generously with powdered sugar. Spoon the berry sauce around the cup. Garnish each cup with fresh berries and a sprig of mint.

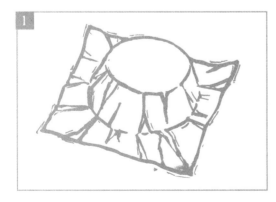

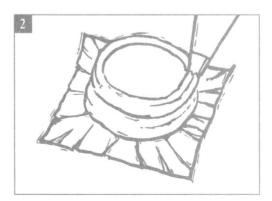

# German Puffs

These fritters were clearly inspired by the numerous German pastries prepared in America and abroad during the mid- to late eighteenth century, if not earlier. Period recipes reveal that these delicate, rich, golden "puffs" were prepared and served in a variety of ways. Although flour and eggs were always mandatory, the liquid could be milk or water. Butter, too, was optional, as were spices. In addition, some recipes called for frying the puffs, while others recommended baking them. And further, while still warm, these pastries were either sprinkled with sugar or served plain.

Even William Verral, self-proclaimed Francophile, published a recipe for these pastries in his *Complete System of Cookery*. He called them "Puffed fritters," however, and included a French title, "*Beignets soufflez.*" In addition, he gave readers the option of serving them not only plain or with sugar, but with preserved fruits as well. "[C]ut a little hole in each but not off," he instructed, "croud [*sic*] in a little jelly or conserve, and dish them up with sugar. These fritters are often sent to table without any thing [*sic*] withinside [*sic*]. Any sort of preserved fruits, raspberries, or quinces, &c" (116).

Makes 3 dozen fritters

### Fritter Batter
12 cups melted lard or vegetable oil
4 large egg yolks, at room temperature
4 tablespoons (½ stick) unsalted butter, melted
⅛ teaspoon ground nutmeg
¾ cup all-purpose flour
½ teaspoon salt
⅛ teaspoon baking powder
¾ cup rosé wine
¾ cup seltzer water
4 large egg whites
⅛ teaspoon cream of tartar
3 tablespoons granulated sugar

### Fruit Options (choose one of the following)
6 apples or pears, peeled, cored, and cut into ½-inch slices
6 peaches, peeled, cored, and cut into ¾-inch slices
3 pints strawberries, stems removed
6 bananas, peeled and cut on the bias into 2-inch pieces

1. In a medium-size pot, heat the melted lard or vegetable oil over medium heat to 375°F.
2. In a small bowl, whisk together the eggs yolks, butter, and nutmeg.
3. In a separate medium-size bowl, whisk together the flour, salt, and baking powder. Add the egg-butter mixture to the flour and, using a wooden spoon, stir to combine. Add the rosé wine and seltzer, and stir to combine. Let the mixture stand at room temperature for at least 30 minutes.
4. Line a few dinner plates with paper towels.
5. In the bowl of an electric mixer fitted with the whip attachment on medium speed, beat the egg whites and cream of tartar until foam forms. Add the sugar and whip to stiff peaks.

6. Add ½ cup of the batter to the whites, and stir gently to combine. Fold the meringue back into the batter.

7. Using a skewer or fork, dredge the fruit of your choice in the batter. Shake the fruit to remove the excess.

8. Carefully place the fruit in the oil, holding it close to the oil before dropping it in, 5 pieces at a time. Fry the fruit until it floats to the surface and is light golden brown, 2 to 3 minutes. Remove the fruit from the oil with a slotted spoon, and place it on the plates lined with paper towels. Serve hot.

Hannah Glasse published one of the richer versions of this recipe in _The Art of Cookery Made Plain and Easy_. She instructed readers to make a dough out of cream, butter, eggs, and spices that was then to be baked in molds. Glasse also recommended sprinkling the warm puffs with "powder-sugar" (fine granulated sugar):

To make German Puffs.

Take two spoonfuls of fine flour, two eggs beat well, half a pint of cream or milk, two ounces of melted butter, stir it all well together, and add a little salt or nutmeg, put them in tea-cups or little deep tin moulds, half full, and bake them a quarter of an hour in a quick oven; but let it be hot enough to colour them at top and bottom; turn them into a dish, and strew powder-sugar over them (259).

# Ice Cream & Sorbet

Ice cream and sorbet, so common today as to be almost ordinary, were among the most celebrated of eighteenth-century confections. By the late 1700s, frozen creams and flavored ices had already been enjoyed for centuries, their beginnings dating back to the ancient world. It was in England and France, however, that these desserts gained their popularity, as the aristocracy enjoyed them served in elegant glasses or elaborate molds.

Perhaps the panache associated with ice cream and sorbet (prepared with fruit or liquor and without milk) during the period can be partially attributed to the arduousness of their preparations. Cooks employed several methods, all of which were time-consuming. Some recipes advocated placing the mixture to be frozen in a tin set in a larger container of ice and salt. It was to be stirred occasionally until uniformly frozen. Then, if desired, the ice cream or sorbet was placed into a mold and set again in the ice and salt until firm, which, according to period recipes, required about four hours. For those who owned them, *sorbetières*, or ice pails, offered another method of preparing the dessert. The concept of freezing the mixture in salt and ice remained the same but, rather than using generic kitchen tins, this tool—a covered pail that was placed in a larger pail—was designed especially for preparing frozen desserts. George Washington and Thomas Jefferson both owned *sorbetières* and were known to frequently serve ice cream and flavored ices. It should be noted that the term *sorbetière* also refers to a decorative container, also called a *glacier*, from which ice cream and sorbet were served. Made of costly European and Chinese export porcelain, they were imported into Philadelphia and appeared on only the most well-to-do of the city's dining tables.

By the mid-eighteenth century, confectioners' shops in England and France were regularly serving ice cream and flavored ices. Colonists continued to satisfy their desire for the dessert in Philadelphia, and by the third quarter of the eighteenth century, the city could boast not only of the number of establishments that offered ice cream but of the particularly rich product they sold as well. Frozen desserts were available in specialty shops, like that of Victor Collet on North Front Street, who sold *glaces* (ice creams) and *fromages glacés* (iced cheeses), as well as in larger confectioners' shops (Weaver 26). In late June 1791, a notice appeared in the *Pennsylvania Gazette* announcing the details of that year's July 4th celebration. Among the entertainments to be featured at Grays Gardens were the confections of Mr. de la Croix, who, in addition to "fine cakes and maccaroons [*sic*], with different kinds of sweetmeats," was to serve "iced creams of a great variety" (June 29, 1791).

The ice cream and sorbet recipes that follow feature ingredients that were available and desired in eighteenth-century Philadelphia. As with other desserts, those calling for chocolate, citrus, vanilla, or spices are likely to have been more costly than others flavored with less exotic ingredients. In general, however, these frozen treats were affordable to most Philadelphians. Unlike in European cities, where ice was more difficult and expensive to obtain, it was available in great quantities in late-eighteenth-century America, resulting in the affordability of ice cream and sorbet throughout the year (Mariani 163).

Describing Martha Washington's parties at Richmond Hill, New York, in July 1790, Abigail Adams wrote to her elder sister, Mary Cranch, that "She gives Tea, Coffe [*sic*], Cake, Lemonade & Ice Creams in summer" (Adams 55).

# Chocolate Ice Cream

As are all of City Tavern's ice creams, this version is a variation of the basic French recipe so admired by Thomas Jefferson. The addition of chocolate pays tribute to the popularity of the confection in eighteenth-century Philadelphia.

Makes 1 quart

> 3 cups whole milk
> 6 tablespoons granulated sugar
> 9 large egg yolks
> ¾ heaping cup finely chopped semisweet chocolate, melted

1. Prepare an ice bath in a large bowl.
2. In a medium-size saucepan, add the milk and sugar; stir to combine, and bring the mixture to a boil.
3. Meanwhile, in a medium-size bowl, whisk the egg yolks.
4. Temper the yolks by adding ¼ cup at a time of the hot liquid to the yolks, whisking all the while. When all of the hot milk has been added, return the custard to the saucepan, and cook, stirring constantly, over low heat until the mixture thickens and reaches a temperature of 185°F on a candy thermometer. Immediately stir in the melted chocolate, and whisk until completely incorporated.
5. Strain the mixture back into the medium-size bowl, and set the bowl in the ice bath. Once the mixture has cooled, place the mixture in the refrigerator for at least 1 hour, or overnight.
6. Add the cream to your ice cream machine, and churn and freeze according to your machine's instructions.

Although Philadelphia was recognized for its rich ice cream prepared simply with milk or cream, sugar, and flavorings, French-style ice cream, introduced into the country by Thomas Jefferson, quickly gained popularity. Rich and flavorful due to the addition of egg yolks, it was undoubtedly offered by the city's numerous confectioners, much to the pleasure of their patrons. Philadelphian Jane Janvier, who prepared her own French-style ice cream, felt strongly that it was more flavorful than the traditional Philadelphia variety, writing, "It is very poor without any eggs" (Belden 154).

# French Vanilla Ice Cream

Throughout most of the eighteenth century, ice cream made in Philadelphia and elsewhere in the colonies was prepared with various combinations of sugar, milk and/or cream, and flavorings. Thomas Jefferson was to change this. During his stay in Paris in the mid-1780s, Jefferson appears to have been introduced to ice cream prepared with egg yolks, and it is this rich, silky dessert, which was pale yellow due to the yolks, that Americans came to know as French Vanilla Ice Cream. The following recipe, perfumed with vanilla and sweetened not only with sugar but with honey, is a flavorful variation of Jefferson's own recipe.

**Makes 1 quart**

> 1 vanilla bean
> 2 cups whole milk
> ½ cup granulated sugar
> 1 tablespoon honey
> 6 large egg yolks

1. Prepare an ice bath in a large bowl.
2. Using a paring knife, slice the vanilla bean in half lengthwise, and scrape the seeds from the pod with the back of the knife.
3. In a medium-size saucepan, add the vanilla seeds, pod, milk, and sugar; stir to combine, and bring the mixture to a boil. Remove the vanilla bean pod with a slotted kitchen spoon.
4. Meanwhile, in a medium-size bowl, whisk together the honey and egg yolks.
5. Temper the egg yolk mixture by adding ¼ cup at a time of the hot liquid to the yolks, whisking all the while. When all of the hot milk has been added, return the custard to the saucepan, and cook, stirring constantly, over low heat until the mixture thickens and reaches a temperature of 185°F on a candy thermometer.
6. Strain the mixture back into the medium-size bowl, and set the bowl in the ice bath. Once the mixture has cooled, place the mixture in the refrigerator for at least 1 hour, or overnight.
7. Add the cream to your ice cream machine, and churn and freeze according to your machine's instructions.

### Variation: Cinnamon Ice Cream
Add 2 cinnamon sticks in step #3, along with the vanilla seeds and pod.

The following is Jefferson's recipe for ice cream, found in the Jefferson Papers collection at the Library of Congress:

2 bottles of good cream.
6 yolks of eggs.
½ lb. sugar
mix the yolks & sugar
put the cream on a fire in a casserole, first putting in a stick of Vanilla.
when near boiling take it off & pour it gently into the mixture of eggs and sugar.
stir it well.
put it on the fire again stirring it thoroughly with a spoon to prevent it's [sic] sticking to the casserole.
when near boiling take it off and strain it thro' a towel.
put it in the Sabottiere
then set it in ice an hour before it is to be served.
put into the ice a handful of salt.
put salt on the coverlid [sic] of the Sabotiere [sic] & cover the whole with ice.
leave it still half a quarter of an hour.
then turn the Sabottiere in the ice 10 minutes
open it to loosen with a spatula the ice from the inner sides of the Sabotiere [sic].
shut it & replace it in the ice
open it from time to time to detach the ice from the sides
when well taken (prise) stir it well with the Spatula.
put it in moulds, jostling it well down on the knee.
then put the mould into the same bucket of ice.
leave it there to the moment of serving it.
to withdraw it, immerse the mould in warm water, turning it well till it will come out & turn it into a plate.

# Strawberry–Anise Ice Cream

Ripe strawberries that grew abundantly in eighteenth-century Philadelphia gardens might well have been used to flavor ice cream. Such a fruit-filled dessert would have been fairly affordable to prepare. The addition of lemon and anise—two costly, imported ingredients during the period—would have transformed a flavorful but simple strawberry ice cream into a special dessert indeed.

**Makes 1 quart**

> 1 vanilla bean
> 2 cups whole milk
> ½ cup granulated sugar
> 6 whole star anise
> 2 teaspoons grated lemon zest
> 6 large egg yolks
> 2 tablespoons honey
> ½ cup strawberry purée, or substitute frozen strawberries, thawed and puréed
> 1 tablespoon anise-flavored liqueur (such as Pernod or sambuca)
> ½ cup chopped strawberries

1. Prepare an ice bath in a large bowl.
2. Using a paring knife, slice the vanilla bean in half lengthwise, and scrape the seeds from the pod with the back of the knife.
3. In a medium-size saucepan, add the vanilla seeds, pod, milk, sugar, star anise, and lemon zest; stir to combine, and bring the mixture to a boil. Remove the vanilla bean pod with a slotted kitchen spoon.
4. Meanwhile, in a medium-size bowl, whisk together the honey and egg yolks. Temper the egg yolk mixture by adding ¼ cup at a time of the hot liquid to the yolk mixture, whisking all the while. When all of the hot milk has been added, return the custard to the saucepan, and cook, stirring constantly, over low heat until the mixture thickens and reaches a temperature of 185°F on a candy thermometer.
5. Strain the mixture back into the medium-size bowl, and set the bowl in the ice bath. Whisk in the strawberry purée and liqueur. Once the mixture has cooled, place the mixture in the refrigerator for at least 1 hour, or overnight.
6. Add the cream to your ice cream machine, and churn according to your machine's instructions. Once the ice cream has churned and is still soft, fold in the strawberries. Freeze according to your machine's instructions.

# Apricot–Orange Ice Cream

This ice cream gives a respectful and thankful nod to the eighteenth-century palate, which so appreciated vibrant flavors. Orange zest, liqueur, golden raisins, vanilla, and apricots—all imported and costly items in Philadelphia during the period—are combined to create a colorful and highly perfumed dessert that is as elegant and complex as apricot-colored silk damask.

**Makes 1 quart**

> 2 cups whole milk
> ½ cup granulated sugar
> 1 orange, zest grated
> 6 large egg yolks
> 2 tablespoons honey
> 1 tablespoon vanilla extract
> ¾ cup strained apricot purée, or substitute frozen apricots, thawed, puréed, and strained
> 2 tablespoons orange cognac
> 1 cup golden raisins, soaked in 1 cup orange liqueur overnight
> ½ cup chopped fresh apricots

1. Prepare an ice bath in a large bowl.
2. In a medium-size saucepan, add the milk, half-and-half, sugar, and orange zest; stir to combine, and bring the mixture to a boil. Remove the vanilla bean pod.
3. Meanwhile, in a medium-size bowl, whisk together the egg yolks, honey, and vanilla extract.
4. Temper the egg yolk mixture by adding ¼ cup at a time of the hot liquid to the yolks, whisking all the while. When all of the hot milk has been added, return the custard to the saucepan, and cook, stirring constantly, over low heat until the mixture thickens and reaches a temperature of 185°F on a candy thermometer. Whisk in the apricot purée and the orange cognac.
5. Strain the mixture back into the medium-size bowl, and set the bowl in the ice bath. Once the mixture has cooled, place the mixture in the refrigerator for at least 1 hour, or overnight.
6. Add the cream to your ice cream machine, and churn according to your machine's instructions. Once the ice cream has churned and is still soft, fold in the raisins and apricots. Freeze according to your machine's instructions.

Elizabeth Raffald and Hannah Glasse published similar recipes for apricot ice-cream. After sieving a mixture of hot cream, sugar, and mashed apricots, Glasse instructed readers to:

> put it in a tin with a close cover, and set it in a tub of ice broke small, with four handfuls of salt mixed among the ice. When you see your cream grows thick round the edges of your tin, stir it well, and put it in again till it is quite thick; when the cream is all froze up, take it out of the tin, and put it into the mould you intend to turn it out of; put on the lid and have another tub of salt and ice ready as before; put the mould in the middle, and lay the ice under and over it; let it stand four hours, and never turn it out till the moment you want it, then dip the mould in cold spring water, and turn it into a plate" (231–232).

# Raspberry Sorbet

Eighteenth-century cooks looked for creative ways to use the abundance of fruit picked from summer gardens. The most beautiful raspberries were most likely preserved or eaten fresh and whole, while bruised berries were mashed and used for jams and, perhaps, frozen desserts. This sorbet's vibrant flavor relies on the freshest of ripe berries or the best quality purée available.

**Makes 1 quart**

> 1 cup granulated sugar
> ¾ cup water
> 1 vanilla bean
> 1 lemon, zest grated and juiced
> 2 cups raspberry purée, or substitute frozen raspberries, thawed and puréed

1. In a medium-size saucepan, add the sugar, water, and lemon juice; stir to combine. Wash down the sides of the pot with cool water and a pastry brush, making certain no granules of sugar remain.
2. Using a paring knife, slice the vanilla bean in half lengthwise, and scrape the seeds from the pod with the back of the knife. Add the vanilla seeds and pod to the pan, and bring the syrup to a boil.
3. Remove the pan from the heat, add the raspberry purée, and stir to combine. Transfer the sorbet base to a bowl, and chill in the refrigerator for at least 2 hours.
4. Remove the vanilla pod. Add the sorbet base to your ice cream machine, and churn according to your machine's instructions. Using a rubber spatula, fold in the lemon zest. Freeze according to your machine's instructions.

# Mango–Papaya Sorbet

This recipe was influenced by eighteenth-century Philadelphians' affinity for the exotic fruits and spices that were arriving daily just blocks away from City Tavern at the city's port. Documents reveal that even though many tropical fruits, more commonly available in today's markets, were never shipped into Philadelphia, residents were familiar with them through either travel or European cookery books. This sorbet certainly would have pleased eighteenth-century Philadelphians, who had developed a fondness for many vibrantly flavored, imported ingredients.

**Makes 1 quart**

¾ cup granulated sugar
1 cup orange juice
¼ cup honey
1 tablespoon chopped fresh ginger
1 vanilla bean
2 cups mango purée, or substitute frozen mango, thawed and puréed
1 papaya
¼ cup chopped Candied Ginger (see page 235)

1. In a medium-size saucepan, add the sugar, orange juice, honey, and fresh ginger; stir to combine. Wash down the sides of the pot with cool water and a pastry brush, making certain no granules of sugar remain.
2. Using a paring knife, slice the vanilla bean in half lengthwise, and scrape the seeds from the pod with the back of the knife. Add the vanilla seeds and pod to the pan, and bring the syrup to a boil.
3. Remove the pan from the heat, and strain over a large mixing bowl. Add the mango purée, and stir to combine. Transfer the sorbet base to a bowl, and chill in the refrigerator for at least 2 hours.
4. Remove the vanilla pod. Add the sorbet base to your ice cream machine, and churn according to your machine's instructions.
5. Meanwhile, peel the papaya with a vegetable peeler and slice it in half. Cut it open lengthwise, and remove the seeds from the center with a spoon. Rinse the papaya in cold water. Finely chop the papaya using a chef's knife. You'll need about 1 cup of fresh fruit.
6. Once the sorbet has finished churning, add the chopped fresh papaya and Candied Ginger. Freeze according to your machine's instructions.

# Lemon Sorbet

The elegance of lemon sorbet was undoubtedly as much admired in eighteenth-century Philadelphia as it is today. The addition of vanilla lends this version a pleasant depth of flavor.

**Makes 1 quart**

> 1½ cups granulated sugar
> ¾ cup water
> 1 vanilla bean
> 1 lemon
> 2¼ cups strained citron purée (see Chef's Note)
> ¼ cup chopped Candied Lemon Peel (see page 234)

1. In a medium-size saucepan, add the sugar and water; stir to combine. Wash down the sides of the pot with cool water and a pastry brush, making certain no granules of sugar remain.
2. Using a paring knife, slice the vanilla bean in half lengthwise, and scrape the seeds from the pod with the back of the knife. Add the vanilla seeds and pod to the saucepan.
3. Slice the lemon in half and place it in the pot. Bring the syrup mixture to a boil.
4. Remove the pan from the heat, and strain over a large mixing bowl. Add the citron purée, and stir to combine. Transfer the sorbet base to a bowl, and chill in the refrigerator for at least 2 hours.
5. Remove the vanilla pod. Add the sorbet base to your ice cream machine, and churn according to your machine's instructions.
6. Once the sorbet has finished churning, fold in the Candied Lemon Peel. Freeze according to your machine's instructions.

*Citron purée is available in some specialty food markets, such as Caviar Assouline (see Sources, page 252).*

# Plum Sorbet

The natural sweet and tart flavor of plums makes the fruit a perfect choice for sorbet. Plums of many varieties were enjoyed in the colonies, each admired for its unique character. The flavor of this sorbet will vary depending upon the type of plum used.

**Makes 1 quart**

> 1 cup granulated sugar
> 1 cup water
> 1 vanilla bean
> 1 tablespoon honey
> 2 cups plum purée (see Chef's Note), or substitute about 12 medium-size plums, pitted, puréed, and strained through a fine sieve

1. In a medium-size saucepan, add the sugar and water, and stir to combine. Wash down the sides of the pot with cool water and a pastry brush, making certain no granules of sugar remain.

2. Using a paring knife, slice the vanilla bean in half lengthwise, and scrape the seeds from the pod with the back of the knife. Add the vanilla seeds, pod, and honey to the pan, and bring the syrup to a boil.

3. Remove the pan from the heat, and strain over a large mixing bowl. Add the plum purée, and stir to combine. Transfer the sorbet base to a bowl, and chill in the refrigerator for at least 2 hours.

4. Remove the vanilla pod. Add the sorbet base to your ice cream machine, and churn according to your machine's instructions. Freeze according to your machine's instructions.

*Plum purée is available in some specialty food markets, such as Caviar Assouline (see Sources, page 252).*

# Sweetmeats

The term "sweetmeats" can be quite confusing to present-day students of food history. In some contexts, the term is limited to fruit cooked and preserved in sugar, while in others it expands to include not only these dishes but a variety of baked goods as well. Like many terms, this one, too, has changed over time. Throughout the eighteenth century, "sweetmeats" referred broadly to cakes, biscuits, cookies, and candied items such as fruit, seeds, flowers, and nuts (also known as "comfits"), as well as a variety of dishes based on large quantities of sugar and fruit, including jellies, marmalades, jams, and preserved fruit (also known as "sucket"). Martha Washington, for example, listed over two hundred sweetmeat recipes in her cookery book. By the nineteenth century, however, the term was limited primarily to fruit cooked and preserved in sugar. In contrast to Washington's manuscript, Eliza Leslie's 1828 edition of *Seventy-Five Receipts, for Pastry, Cakes, and Sweetmeats* includes only sixteen sweetmeats, all of which are preserves, jams, or jellies.

It is, of course, the broad definition of sweetmeats that is apropos to the history of City Tavern and the special, sweet dishes that were available in eighteenth-century Philadelphia. So broad is this term, however, that it could refer to nearly all of the recipes in this book. This chapter, therefore, focuses on those sweetmeats that functioned as colorful additions to the cakes, pies, and pastries that appeared on the eighteenth-century dining table. Today they are known as petits fours or *mignardises* and include such items as nut pastes, chocolates, jellies, and candied fruits and nuts.

Preserves and marmalades were some of the most desired and costly sweetmeats of the period. It should be noted, however, that in the eighteenth and early nineteenth centuries, the term "preserves" referred to the finest whole fruit cooked and stored in sugar syrup. Today preserves have become nearly synonymous with jam and marmalade, which traditionally have been prepared with sugar and ripe, but not necessarily pristine, mashed fruit.

Over the years, the panache associated with sweetmeats has waned. Items such as candied nuts, chocolate bars, and jam have become so readily available as to be ordinary and even lackluster. Eighteenth-century sweetmeats, however, were some of the most celebrated and elegant items one encountered at the dining table. This was due in part to the cost of the ingredients, especially sugar, and even more to the labor-intensive preparations. The following recipes are just some of those that might have been enjoyed in wealthy Philadelphia homes as well as in elegant public eateries like City Tavern.

Young Philadelphian Nancy Shippen often mentioned sweetmeat preparation in her journal. In 1783 she noted: "I passed a most agreeable even'ing—though a large company—which is seldom the case—a most admirable supper—excellent wine an elegant desert of preserv'd fruits & every body in spirits & good humor.—It is now late & I am sleepy" (Armes 141).

In late summer 1784 she wrote: "I spent the day at home very busy making sweet-meets for the winter" (Armes 204).

And again on Monday, September 13, 1784, she commented: "This day employ'd as usual in domestic affairs, preserving peaches &c" (Armes 212).

# Marzipan

By the late eighteenth century, the European tradition of preparing marzipan was already more than three hundred years old. First appearing in fifteenth-century English texts as "march payne" and later as "marchpane," this sweetmeat was so influenced by Germany and Austria that it adopted the northern European spelling and pronunciation, marzipan (Hess 322).

Prepared with almonds, sugar, and rose or orange water, marzipan was one of the most costly confections available in Europe. Although it had been highly prized in England for centuries, the paucity of recipes in American cookery books suggests that its popularity waned in the colonies and that, for those who did desire it, marzipan was mostly available in confectioners' shops (Hess 324).

Two significant texts did include "March-pane" or "Marchpane" recipes, however: Eliza Smith's *The Compleat Housewife* and Martha Washington's cookbook. Washington listed no less than five recipes. Like Smith, she called for shaping the marzipan and then icing and baking it. These last two steps—essentially sugaring and drying—are usually omitted in modern versions and most likely helped to preserve the sweetmeat.

Marzipan was primarily a confection of the wealthy. Not only were the ingredients expensive, but the colorful, fanciful shapes detailed in these recipes reveal that they were also primarily "conceits"—whimsical, elegant sweetmeats that were meant as much to please the eye as the palate. Shining with gold leaf, sparkling with sugar, and decorated with dried fruit (Hess 327), marzipan was probably most enjoyed at dining tables filled with exotic foodstuffs, elaborate sugar figures, and fine wines.

**Makes 1½ pounds, or about 20 pieces**

> 1⅓ cups Almond Paste (see page 40), or 14 ounces store-bought almond paste
> 5 tablespoons corn syrup
> 2 cups confectioners' sugar
> 3 tablespoons flavored liqueur of your choice (for example, use applejack brandy to make marzipan apples)
> ¼ cup warm water
> 3 drops food coloring of your choice (for example, red for making marzipan apples)

1. In the bowl of an electric mixer fitted with the paddle attachment on medium speed, beat together the Almond Paste and corn syrup.
2. Sift the confectioners' sugar. With the mixer running on low speed, add the sugar in three intervals, incorporating each addition before adding the next. Mix the marzipan until it is smooth. It will be stiff but malleable—the consistency of Silly Putty. Remove the marzipan from the bowl and knead in the liqueur by hand, 1 tablespoon at a time.
3. You may shape the marzipan into whatever shape you desire, such as apples, and let them dry on a plate for 1 hour. Stir together the water and food coloring, and paint the sides of the marzipan with a small pastry brush. To store, place the marzipan in a plastic storage container, lay plastic wrap directly on top of the marzipan, and cover with a tight-fitting lid.

# Stuffed Dates

This sweetmeat was inspired by the numerous dried fruits prepared in eighteenth-century home kitchens and that were available in shops. Sweet, dried dates, delicious and exotic on their own, become even more special when enhanced by the almond flavor of marzipan. Such elegant sweetmeats would have been served on dinner tables and as part of festive dessert displays during tea parties in eighteenth-century Philadelphia.

**Makes 18 pieces**

18 Medjool dates
1½ pounds Marzipan (see page 223; use kirschwasser liqueur)

1. Slice each date in half lengthwise.
2. Roll the Marzipan into one long ½-inch log. Cut the log into 2-inch portions, or to the length of each date.
3. Fill each date with marzipan segments, and serve. Prepare the stuffed dates no more than 2 to 3 hours before serving, and keep at room temperature.

# Chocolate Truffles

Although the enthusiasm for some sweet dishes has waxed and waned over the centuries, the desire for chocolate has only strengthened since the eighteenth century. In American homes and confectioners' shops of the mid- to late 1700s, chocolate was most often served as a hot, creamy beverage, sometimes flavored with spices in the South American fashion. It appears, however, that many forms of chocolate were available in the cosmopolitan center that was late-eighteenth-century Philadelphia. Confectioners and chocolatiers opened shops throughout the city, meeting the demands of a stylish public that had grown so fond of this ancient sweet. Surely, chocolate truffles similar to the following version satisfied the cravings of numerous Philadelphians.

**Makes 2 dozen truffles**

> 24 ounces bittersweet (not unsweetened) chocolate, chopped
> 4 tablespoons (½ stick) unsalted butter, cut into pieces
> ¼ cup heavy cream
> 1 tablespoon instant espresso powder, dissolved in 1 tablespoon boiling water
> 2 tablespoons sambuca or other flavored liqueur
> 1 cup unsweetened cocoa powder, for coating

1. In a double boiler or in a metal bowl set over a saucepan of barely simmering water, melt 12 ounces of the chocolate and the butter with the cream and espresso, stirring until smooth.
2. Remove the top of the double boiler or the bowl from the heat, and stir in the liqueur.
3. Cool the mixture, and chill, covered, for at least 3 hours, or until firm.
4. To temper the remaining 12 ounces of chocolate, place 8 ounces of the chocolate in a metal bowl set over a pan of barely simmering water. Melt the chocolate slowly, stirring often. Heat the melted chocolate, stirring slowly and constantly, until it reaches a temperature of 115°F on a candy thermometer.
5. Remove the bowl from the heat, and add the remaining 4 ounces of chocolate, stirring constantly, until the chocolate has melted and it cools to 80°F. Return the bowl of chocolate to the pan of simmering water, and heat until it reaches a temperature of 89°F. Remove from the heat.
6. Remove the chilled chocolate mixture from the refrigerator. With a small ice cream scoop or tablespoon, scoop out walnut-sized portions. Roll each portion into a round ball.
7. Place the cocoa powder on a large plate.
8. Pour about 1 tablespoon of the cooled melted chocolate in your hand. Take one of the walnut-sized portions of chilled chocolate and roll it in your hand to thoroughly coat it in the melted chocolate.
9. Drop the truffles in the cocoa powder and coat, shaking off any excess. Set on a parchment-lined baking pan and let stand in a cool place. Repeat the process until all of the chilled chocolate has been used. (You may have some tempered chocolate left over. It can be stored in the refrigerator, tightly covered, for up to 2 weeks. You can drizzle it on serving plates for another dessert or use it as a topping for ice cream.)
10. Store the truffles in an airtight container in the refrigerator for up to 2 weeks.

# Pâte de Fruits

Jellies were enormously popular in the eighteenth century. Not to be confused with the jarred jellies of today that are most often spread on toast, these period desserts were essentially gelatins flavored with cooked and strained fruit juice. Usually set in elegant molds or in clear glasses, these translucent, colorful jellies sparkled among the many dishes that graced eighteenth-century dining tables.

Pâte de fruits, bite-sized pieces of intensely flavored jellies, are related to the eighteenth-century gelatin desserts that were sometimes cut into shapes. In her recipe for apple "Jeley," Martha Washington instructed, "[C]ut them [the jellies] round & put them up in boxes." In her recipe for "Jelly of White Currans [*sic*]," she wrote, "[L]et them stand two or three dayes [*sic*] in ye stove & paper them up" (Hess 358–359). Literally translated as "fruit pastes," pâte de fruits are traditional French confections, the likes of which very well might have been known in eighteenth-century Philadelphia. Colorful, translucent, and glittering under coatings of sugar, they are elegant additions to any contemporary dessert table.

# Raspberry Pâte de Fruits

**Makes about 20 pieces**

Nonstick cooking spray
4 pints raspberries
3½ cups granulated sugar
½ cup pectin powder (available in the jelly section of better supermarkets)
¾ cup water
1 tablespoon freshly squeezed lemon juice
¾ cup finely chopped Candied Lemon Peel (see page 234)

1. Line an 11 x 17-inch baking pan with plastic wrap, and coat it with cooking spray.
2. Place the berries in a strainer and rinse well with cold water. Pat the berries dry with a paper towel.
3. In a medium-size saucepan over medium heat, cook the raspberries, stirring constantly with a wooden spoon, until the mixture is thick and has reduced by half, 8 to 10 minutes. You should have about 2 cups of raspberry reduction. Remove from the heat.
4. In a small bowl, stir together ½ cup of the sugar and the pectin, and sprinkle the mixture evenly over the raspberry reduction. Let sit for about 10 minutes.
5. Prepare an ice bath in a large stainless steel bowl. Choose a stainless steel pot large enough to hold three times the amount of ingredients being used. Add the remaining 3 cups of sugar, the water, and the lemon juice; stir to combine. Wash down the sides of the pot with cool water and a pastry brush, making certain no sugar crystals remain.
6. Bring the sugar syrup to a boil over high heat, washing down the sides of the pot often. Cook until the syrup reaches a temperature of 285°F on a candy thermometer.
7. Remove from the heat and *carefully* add the berry reduction to the sugar syrup. The mixture will spatter, so add it slowly, close to the syrup, stirring constantly. Once the berry reduction has been added, continue to cook the mixture, stirring, until all of the sugar and pectin has been dissolved and the mixture is thickened, 3 to 4 minutes. Do not let the mixture come to a rapid boil.
8. Transfer the mixture to a stainless steel bowl and set the bowl in the ice bath. Chill the mixture, stirring constantly, until it reaches room temperature. Stir in the Candied Lemon Peel.
9. Pour the raspberry mixture onto the prepared baking pan, spray the top with cooking spray, and cover with plastic wrap. Chill overnight in the refrigerator. Remove the top layer of plastic wrap. Choose a small cookie cutter of desired shape, and cut portions.

**Variation:**
Roll some of the portions in granulated sugar for a decorative touch.

# Apple Spice Pâte de Fruits

**Makes about 20 pieces**

> Nonstick cooking spray
> 12 apples (Gala or Granny Smith), peeled, cored, and cut into ½-inch wedges
> 2½ cups plus 5 tablespoons granulated sugar
> 5 tablespoons pectin powder (available in the jelly section of better supermarkets)
> ¼ cup water
> 1 tablespoon freshly squeezed lemon juice
> 2 tablespoons honey
> 1 tablespoon ground cinnamon
> 1 teaspoon ground ginger
> 1 teaspoon ground allspice
> ½ cup finely chopped Candied Ginger (see page 235)

1. Line an 11 x 17-inch baking pan with plastic wrap, and coat it with cooking spray.

2. In a large pot over medium heat, cook the apples, stirring constantly with a wooden spoon, until they begin break down, 8 to 10 minutes. Turn the heat up to high, and cook off all of the resulting liquid, stirring vigorously all the while. Cook the mixture until it is thickened, about 3 minutes more.

3. Remove the pot from the heat, and let it stand at room temperature for 5 minutes. In a small bowl, stir together 5 tablespoons of the sugar and the pectin. Sprinkle the pectin mixture evenly over the apple reduction, and let it stand for 10 minutes.

4. Prepare an ice bath in a large stainless steel bowl. Choose a saucepan large enough to hold three times the amount of ingredients being used. Add the remaining 2½ cups sugar, the water, lemon juice, and the honey; stir the ingredients together. Wash down the sides of the pot with cool water and a pastry brush, making certain no sugar crystals remain.

5. Bring the sugar syrup to a boil over high heat, washing down the sides of the pot often. Cook until the syrup reaches a temperature of 285°F on a candy thermometer.

6. Remove from the heat and *carefully* add the apple reduction to the sugar syrup. The mixture will spatter, so add it slowly, close to the syrup, stirring constantly. Once all of the apple reduction has been added, continue to cook the mixture, stirring, until all of the sugar and pectin has been dissolved and the mixture is thickened, 3 to 4 minutes. Do not let the mixture come to a rapid boil. Stir in the ginger, cinnamon, allspice, and Candied Ginger.

7. Transfer the mixture to a stainless steel bowl, and set the bowl in the ice bath. Chill the mixture, stirring constantly, until it reaches room temperature.

8. Pour the apple mixture onto the prepared tray, spray the top with cooking spray, and cover with plastic wrap. Chill overnight in the refrigerator. Remove the top layer of plastic wrap. Choose a small cookie cutter of desired shape, and cut portions.

9. Dip the tops of the portions in granulated sugar, and sprinkle lightly with cinnamon.

# Grape Pâte de Fruits

**Makes about 20 pieces**

Nonstick cooking spray
12 cups red or green seedless grapes (about 3 bunches)
2 cups apple cider
3 cups plus 6 tablespoons granulated sugar
6 tablespoons pectin powder (available in the jelly section of better supermarkets)
¾ cup water
1 tablespoon freshly squeezed lemon juice
1 tablespoon honey

1. Line an 11 x 17-inch baking pan with plastic wrap, and coat it with cooking spray.
2. In a large pot over high heat, add the grapes and apple cider. Bring the mixture to a boil and cook, stirring occasionally, until the grapes begin to break down and lose their form, 3 to 5 minutes. Reduce the heat to medium, and cook, stirring occasionally, until all of the resulting liquid is cooked off, and the mixture is thickened and has reduced by two thirds, 8 to 10 minutes.
3. Remove the pot from the heat, and let it stand at room temperature for 5 minutes. In a small bowl, stir together 6 tablespoons of the sugar and the pectin. Sprinkle the pectin mixture evenly over the grape reduction, and let it stand for 10 minutes.
4. Prepare an ice bath in a large stainless steel bowl. Choose a saucepan large enough to hold three times the amount of ingredients being used. Add the remaining 3 cups sugar, the water, the lemon juice, and the honey; with a wooden spoon, stir the ingredients together. Wash down the sides of the pot with cool water and a pastry brush, making certain no sugar crystals remain.
5. Bring the sugar syrup to a boil over high heat, washing down the sides of the pot often. Cook until the syrup reaches a temperature of 285°F on a candy thermometer.
6. Remove from the heat and *carefully* add the grape reduction to the sugar syrup. The mixture will spatter, so add it slowly, close to the syrup, stirring constantly. Once all the grapes have been added, continue to cook the mixture, stirring, until all of the sugar and pectin has been dissolved and the mixture is thickened, 3 to 4 minutes. Do not let the mixture come to a rapid boil.
7. Transfer the mixture to a stainless steel bowl, and place the bowl in the ice bath. Chill the mixture, stirring constantly, until it reaches room temperature.
8. Pour the grape mixture onto the prepared pan, spray the top with cooking spray, and cover with plastic wrap. Chill overnight in the refrigerator. Remove the top layer of plastic wrap. Choose a small cookie cutter of desired shape, and cut portions.
9. Dip the portions in granulated sugar.

# Rum Balls

These small but rich confections bring together some of the most prized flavors in eighteenth-century Philadelphia: chocolate, rum, almonds, and sugar. Given the cost of these ingredients in the period, these rum balls certainly would have been costly. Yet, as with many sweetmeats, they take advantage of items that would have been stocked in eighteenth-century confectioners' shops and probably some wealthy households. Additionally, in keeping with the frugality of the period, chocolate cake that might have been a few days old was (and still is) easily converted into cake crumbs and used in this sort of recipe.

**Makes 20 pieces**

> 3 cups sliced almonds
> ½ cup confectioners' sugar
> 10 cups chocolate cake crumbs
> 2 cups Simple Syrup (see Chef's Note, page 54)
> ½ cup dark rum
> 2 pounds chopped semisweet chocolate

1. Preheat the oven to 375°F.
2. Spread the almonds on a baking pan, and toast for 8 minutes, or until golden. Remove from the oven, and allow to cool.
3. In a food processor, grind the cool, toasted almonds with the confectioners' sugar until finely ground.
4. In a large bowl, toss together the cake crumbs and almond mixture. Add the Simple Syrup and rum, and mix the ingredients with your hands until they clump together.
5. Shape the mixture into 1½-inch balls, and arrange the rum balls, spaced 1 inch apart, on a wire screen set atop a baking pan.
6. To temper the chocolate, place 1½ pounds of the chopped chocolate in a stainless steel bowl, and set over a pan of simmering water. Melt the chocolate slowly, stirring often. Heat the chocolate, stirring slowly and constantly, until it reaches a temperature of 115°F on a candy thermometer.
7. Remove the bowl from the heat, and add the remaining 1 cup chopped chocolate. Stir the chocolate slowly and constantly until the added chocolate has melted and the mixture cools to 80°F. Return the bowl of chocolate to the pan of simmering water, and heat until it reaches a temperature of 89°F.
8. Pour the chocolate over the rum balls in one steady sweeping motion. Try to coat each ball completely and evenly.
9. Once all the rum balls have been coated, tap the tray gently against the table a few times to settle the chocolate. Allow the rum balls to cool at room temperature until set. Store in an airtight container in the refrigerator for up to 1 week.

# Candied Almonds

This recipe was inspired by the many candied fruits, flowers, and even spices that were prepared in eighteenth-century homes and confectioners' shops. Today, candied nuts of many varieties are readily available and quite common. In Philadelphia during the mid- to late 1700s, however, sugar and almonds were costly and enjoyed sparingly.

These sweet, crunchy almonds are delicious enjoyed on their own as a traditional sweetmeat or as a topping for ice cream.

**Serves 6 to 10**

> 4 cups whole almonds
> Nonstick cooking spray
> Vegetable oil
> 2½ cups granulated sugar
> ¼ cup water
> 1 lemon, juiced
> 1 cup honey

1. Preheat the oven to 375°F.
2. Spread the almonds on a baking pan, and toast the almonds for 8 minutes, or until golden. Remove from the oven, and allow to cool.
3. Coat a baking pan with cooking spray. Lightly brush a wire rack with vegetable oil, and set it atop the tray.
4. In a large saucepan, stir together the sugar, water, and lemon juice. Using cool water and a pastry brush, wash down the sides of the pot, making certain no sugar crystals remain. Bring the mixture to a boil; then remove it from the heat.
5. With a wooden spoon, stir in the honey. Return the saucepan to the heat, bring the mixture to a boil, and cook until it reaches 320°F on a candy thermometer. Again, wash down the sides of the pot, making certain no sugar crystals remain.
6. Remove from the heat. With a wooden spoon, carefully stir in the almonds. Immediately pour the almonds over the prepared wire rack and baking pan. Let cool completely. Store the almonds in an airtight container at room temperature in low humidity for up to 1 week.

# Coconut Drops

These rich sweetmeats were inspired by the various coconut desserts prepared with the exotic fruit in the eighteenth century. Coconuts were imported up and down the eastern coast from New England to the South, and by the nineteenth century, as coconuts became increasingly available and affordable, the fruit was incorporated into numerous dishes. These drops, in fact resemble both the "Cocoa Nut Puffs" Harriott Pinckney Horry included in her recipe book of 1770, as well as the "Cocoa-Nut Jumbles" that Eliza Leslie published in her 1848 edition of *Directions for Cookery, in Its Various Branches* (Hooker 71; Leslie 353).

**Makes 12 to 16 drops**

> 2 coconuts
> One 14-ounce can sweetened condensed milk
> 1 tablespoon ground allspice
> 1 tablespoon vanilla extract
> Ground nutmeg, to taste
> 3 large egg whites
> 6 tablespoons granulated sugar
> Pinch of cream of tartar

1. Preheat the oven to 350°F.
2. Using a hammer and a Phillips head screwdriver, puncture 3 holes in the eyes located at the base of the coconut, and strain out the coconut juice.
3. Wrap the coconut in a towel and smack it with the hammer. Use the screwdriver to carefully remove the flesh from the shell, keeping the flesh in as large chunks as possible. Using a vegetable peeler, shave long thin strips of coconut. You will need 6 cups of strips.
4. Transfer the coconut to a baking pan and toast in the oven until golden, 7 to 10 minutes. Remove from the oven.
5. Reduce the oven temperature to 375°F. Line a baking pan with parchment paper.
6. In a large mixing bowl, stir together the toasted coconut, condensed milk, allspice, vanilla extract, and nutmeg.
7. In the bowl of an electric mixer fitted with the whip attachment on high speed, beat the egg whites, sugar, and cream of tartar to stiff peaks. Fold the whites mixture into the coconut mixture.
8. Drop the mixture by heaping tablespoons onto the prepared baking pan, and bake for 15 minutes, or until golden. Cool completely, and store covered at room temperature in low humidity, for up to 3 days.

# Glazed Chestnuts

Just like fruit, nuts were commonly preserved in the eighteenth century. Home cooks and confectioners cooked whole, shelled nuts in sugar syrup and, as with whole, unblemished fruit, they were stored in jars and served on the dining or sweetmeat table or added to other dessert preparations. Among the nuts most frequently preserved during the period were walnuts and chestnuts, which were abundant and readily available.

**Makes 18 pieces**

> 18 fresh chestnuts (about ½ pound)
> 2 cups granulated sugar
> 1¼ cups water
> 1 cup honey
> 1 teaspoon cream of tartar
> ¼ cup light rum
> One-pound box confectioners' sugar

1.  Bring a medium-size saucepan of water to a boil. Prepare an ice bath in a large stainless steel bowl.
2.  Using a paringl knife, slice an X in the skin of each chestnut. Add 5 chestnuts at a time to the pot of boiling water, and cook for 1 minute. Using a slotted spoon, remove the nuts from the pot, and set them atop a dry kitchen towel. Carefully remove the skins with a paring knife while they're still hot. Let them cool.
3.  In a medium-size saucepan with a wooden spoon, stir together the sugar, 1 cup of the water, the honey, and the cream of tartar. Wash down the sides of the pot with cool water and a pastry brush, making certain no sugar crystals remain. Bring the mixture to a boil; then remove the pot from the stove.
4.  Add the chestnuts to the syrup, return the pan to medium heat, and cook until the mixture reaches a temperature of 260°F on a candy thermometer, 5 to 10 minutes. Set the pot in the ice bath, and allow to cool to room temperature.
5.  Transfer the mixture to a plastic container. With a wooden spoon, stir in the rum. Cover and refrigerate the chestnuts in the syrup for 2 days in order to allow them to absorb the syrup.
6.  Strain the chestnuts and set them atop a wire rack to dry at room temperature for half an hour.
7.  Meanwhile, in a small bowl, stir together the confectioners' sugar and the remaining ¼ cup of water until a paste the consistency of yogurt is formed. Pour the glaze over the chestnuts, to coat each evenly and completely. Serve immediately, or store covered in the refrigerator for up to 3 to 4 days.

# Candied Citrus

In stylish eighteenth-century cities like Philadelphia, candied lemons and oranges were arguably among the most elegant and desired of sweetmeats. Nearly every cookery book included recipes for them. Confectioners' shops, too, regularly offered these candied jewels to patrons who maintained a great fondness for the costly, imported citrus fruits, which became even more expensive once cooked in sugar. In fact, the great number of recipes for candied lemons and oranges are in keeping with the number of advertisements that mentioned these items. Most were similar to those of Philadelphia confectioner Patrick Wright, who commonly listed "orange and lemon chips" (another oft-used term for the same during the period) among his jams, marmalades, and cakes (*Pennsylvania Gazette*, August 9, 1775).

Today's methods for candying citrus differ little from those of the eighteenth century. The whole fruit or the peel alone was briefly boiled in water and strained numerous times before being cooked in a series of sugar syrups. This was primarily important for oranges, for those most available were commonly the imported Seville variety from Spain and more bitter than other types. Even today, regardless of the type of citrus used, successive boiling is recommended to dissipate the bitter oils before candying.

The eighteenth-century candying process does differ slightly from today's techniques, however. Whereas period recipes instruct the syrup-cooked pieces of fruit to be simply left to dry, most contemporary confectioners suggest tossing them in granulated sugar after the drying process. This keeps the pieces from sticking together and cloaks them in a glistening sugar coating.

Makes 4 cups

> 8 oranges or 12 lemons
> 6 cups granulated sugar
> 4 cups water
> 4 cups granulated sugar, for coating

1. Using a paring knife, carefully remove the rind from the oranges or lemons in 2-inch strips. Try to leave as little pith on the peel as possible. Scrape any remaining pith from the peel with the back of the paring knife.
2. Place the oranges or lemons in a medium-size saucepan, and cover with cold water. Place the pan over high heat, and bring the mixture to a boil. Strain and rinse the peel under running water. Repeat the boiling, straining, and rinsing process three more times to remove the bitterness from the peel.
3. In a medium-size pot, add the orange or lemon peel, 6 cups of sugar, and water; stir to combine. Using cool water and a pastry brush, wash down the sides of the pot, making certain no crystals of sugar remain. Bring the mixture to a boil, and cook the syrup until it reaches a temperature of 260°F on a candy thermometer, about 10 minutes. Remove from the heat, and allow it to cool to room temperature. Cover the pot with plastic wrap, and let the oranges or lemons steep overnight at room temperature.
4. Strain the oranges or lemons from the syrup and arrange them atop a wire rack. Cover generously with 2 cups of the sugar. Turn the peels over, and repeat the process with the remaining 2 cups of sugar.
5. Let the sugar-coated peel sit out for 8 hours. Store in an airtight container for up to 3 weeks at room temperature.

# Candied Ginger

By the eighteenth century, Europeans had been enjoying ginger, usually imported from the East Indies, for about four hundred years (Hess 283). Cooks incorporated the spice into savory and sweet dishes; perhaps candying ginger became a popular method not only of preserving the perishable root but also of taming its fiery flavor.

Ginger can certainly be candied like orange or lemon rinds (by successively boiling it in water and sugar syrup), but Martha Washington wrote a recipe that appears to more closely resemble the *dragée* method of candying nuts—a process that coats them with hard sugar. Washington instructed the ginger to be soaked in water overnight. She then explained that sugar was to be boiled and cooled, and the ginger added to it, stirring until the lot was "hard to ye pan." The ginger was then removed, dried, and placed again in a hot pan, where, as it cooled, one was to "stir it about roundly, and it will be A rock Candy in A very short space" (Hess 283).

The following recipe marries both techniques, resulting in a sweetmeat that is translucent, tender, and coated with sugar.

Makes 4 cups

> 1 pound fresh ginger, peeled
> 6 cups granulated sugar
> 4 cups water
> 4 cups granulated sugar, for coating

1. Place the ginger in a medium-size saucepan, and add enough cold water to cover completely. Place the pan over high heat, and bring the mixture to a boil. Immediately remove from the heat, strain, and rinse the ginger under cool running water. Allow the ginger to cool to room temperature.

2. Using a mandoline, or carefully with a chef's knife, slice the cooled ginger into ¼-inch-thick slices. Place the slices in a pot, and cover with cold water. Bring to a boil. Strain and rinse the sliced ginger under cool running water. Repeat the boiling, straining, and rinsing process four more times to remove the bitterness from the ginger.

3. In a medium-size pot, add the sliced ginger, 6 cups of sugar, and the water; stir to combine. Using cool water and a pastry brush, wash down the sides of the pot, making certain no sugar crystals remain. Bring the mixture to a boil, and cook until the syrup reaches a temperature of 260°F on a candy thermometer, about 10 minutes. Remove the pot from the heat and allow it to cool to room temperature. Cover the pot with plastic wrap, and let the oranges steep overnight at room temperature.

4. Strain the slices from the syrup and arrange them atop a wire rack. Cover generously with 2 cups of the sugar. Turn the ginger slices over, and repeat the process with the remaining 2 cups of sugar.

5. Let the sugar-coated ginger sit out for 8 hours. Store in an airtight container for up to 3 weeks at room temperature.

# Candied Apricots

Apricots, cultivated with difficulty in the northern states but with greater success in the South, where George Washington and Thomas Jefferson enjoyed fertile crops, were much appreciated up and down the East Coast of eighteenth-century America (Leighton 228–229). Delicate and fragrant when fresh and perfectly ripe, this fruit transforms into a translucent jewel when candied.

Serves 10 to 12

> 10 apricots
> 4 cups granulated sugar
> 2 cups water
> ½ cup orange juice
> 2 tablespoons rose honey, or substitute regular honey
> 1 teaspoon cream of tartar
> 1 cinnamon stick
> 1 lemon
> ¼ cup orange liqueur (such as Cointreau or Triple Sec)

1. Fill a large stainless steel bowl with ice water. Bring a medium-size pot of water to a boil.
2. Using a paring knife, score the bottoms and tops of each apricot with an "X." Drop 5 apricots at a time into the boiling water and cook for 30 seconds. Remove the apricots from the pot and immediately submerge them in the ice water. Quickly peel the skin from the fruit. If the skin isn't easily peeled, return them to the pot for another 30 seconds. Save the ice bath for later use.
3. In a medium-size pot, add the 4 cups of sugar, water, orange juice, and honey; stir to combine. With cool water and a pastry brush, wash down the sides of the pot, making certain no crystals of sugar remain. Bring the sugar mixture to a boil. Remove the pot from the heat.
4. Add the apricots, cream of tartar, and cinnamon stick to the pot. Return the mixture to medium-high heat, and cook until it reaches a temperature of 260°F on a candy thermometer, about 10 minutes. Remove the pot from the heat, set it in the ice bath, and allow the apricots in syrup to cool to room temperature.
5. Transfer the mixture to a plastic container. Slice the lemon in half, squeeze the juice over the apricots, and stir to mix. With a wooden spoon, stir in the liqueur. Cover and refrigerate the apricots in the syrup for 2 days in order to allow them to absorb the syrup.
6. Serve, or store in an airtight container at room temperature for up to 2 weeks.

Martha Washington included a unique recipe for candied apricots in her cookery book. She incorporated "green wheat" into the boiling sugar and fruit, which dyed the apricots a vibrant green, a color much admired during the period:

> To Candy Green Apricock [*sic*] Chipps
>
> Take your Apricocks, pare them and cut them into chipps, and put them into running water with A good handfull [*sic*] of green wheat, before it be eard [*sic*]. then boyle them a little, after take them from the fire, and put them in a silver or earthen dish with a pritty [*sic*] quantety [*sic*] of good white sugar finely beat[en]. then set them over the fire till they be dry, and they will look clear and green. then lay them on glas[ses & put] them in a stove A while, & then box ym (Hess 287).

# Poached Fruit

The best way to enjoy fruit is fresh and perfectly ripe. Poached fruit is certainly different from fresh, but it is perhaps the closest one comes to eating it directly off the vine or tree. The finest poached fruit is prepared with fruit that is at its peak or very nearly so. Simmering the fruit in a combination of water, wine, sugar, and spices does certainly render it tender and flavorful, but the delicate flavor and texture of the product depend on high-quality produce. Furthermore, although blemished or bruised fruit is suitable for jams and jellies, such as whole fruit preserves, poached fruit is often served whole or sliced in such a manner as to maintain the integrity of the fruit's original shape.

Fruits suitable for poaching, such as stone fruits and pears, grew so abundantly in and around eighteenth-century Philadelphia that, for those without fruit trees, they were typically affordable. It should be noted, however, that the other ingredients necessary for poaching fruit—sugar, spices, wine—were indeed costly, making this dish a special one. In addition, unlike preserves, poached fruit is perishable, adding yet again to its high cost during the period.

Nonetheless, when prepared in eighteenth-century homes or at fashionable establishments like City Tavern, colorful, flavorful poached fruit dishes enhanced the elegance of dining and dessert tables.

## Poached Apples

Makes 4 apples; serves 4

> 4 underripe Gala apples, peeled, cored, and pricked with a fork
> 1 lemon
> 2 cups apple cider
> 3 cups Madeira wine
> ¾ cup granulated sugar
> 1 tablespoon allspice
> 3 cinnamon sticks
> 1 tablespoon whole black peppercorns

1. Place the peeled apples in a bowl. Squeeze the juice from the lemon over them to prevent browning, and set the bowl aside. Reserve the lemon rind.
2. In a large stainless steel or enameled saucepan, add the apple cider, wine, sugar, allspice, cinnamon sticks, peppercorns, and reserved lemon rind; bring to a boil, stirring occasionally. Reduce the heat to a simmer.
3. Add the apples to the pan. To make sure that the apples are evenly submerged in the liquid, weight them down with a heat-safe dinner plate. Simmer, covered, until the apples are fork tender, about 20 minutes.
4. Meanwhile, fill a large bowl with ice water.
5. With a slotted spoon, carefully remove the apples from the pot and immediately transfer them to the ice water. Return the cooled fruit to the poaching liquid, and store, covered and refrigerated, for up to 3 days.

# Poached Plums

Makes 4 plums; serves 4

4 underripe plums
1 lemon
1 tablespoon orange flower water
2 cups orange juice
1 cup sweet dessert white wine (such as a Riesling)
1 cup granulated sugar
4 ounces fresh ginger, roughly chopped

1. Fill a large bowl with ice water.
2. Using a paring knife, cut an "X" into the bottom, just through the skin, of each plum.
3. In a large saucepan, bring 2 quarts of water to a boil. Carefully place the plums in the boiling water. Cook the plums for 10 seconds; then remove them with a slotted spoon and transfer to the bowl of ice water.
4. After the plums have cooled, remove them from the ice water, and peel and discard the skins. Save the bowl of ice water for later use. Place the plums in a mixing bowl, and squeeze the lemon juice over them so they will not discolor.
5. In a large stainless steel or enameled saucepan, add the flower water, orange juice, wine, sugar, and ginger; stir to combine, and bring to a boil, stirring occasionally. Reduce the heat to a simmer.
6. Add the plums to the pan. To make sure that the plums are evenly submerged in the liquid, weight them down with a heat-safe dinner plate. Simmer, covered, until the plums are fork tender, 8 to 10 minutes.
7. With a slotted spoon, carefully remove the plums from the pan and immediately transfer them to the ice water. Return the cooled fruit to the cooled poaching liquid, and store, covered and refrigerated, for up to 3 days.

# Poached Pears with Chocolate Sauce

Poached fruit, as this version of poached pears reveals, is generally lighter in flavor and consistency than its baked or stewed counterparts, which become caramelized and softer during longer cooking. In addition, the use of Dutch cocoa powder creates an accompanying chocolate sauce that is mild and smooth—a perfect complement to the spiced, red wine-infused pears.

**Makes 4 poached pears; serves 4**

### Poached Pears
3 cups Merlot wine
¾ cup granulated sugar
2 cinnamon sticks
1 tablespoon whole cloves
1 vanilla bean
4 underripe Bartlett Pears, peeled and cored
2 cups apple juice
½ cup juniper berries (available in specialty food markets)
3 lemons, peeled, juice reserved from 1

### Chocolate Sauce
1½ cups granulated sugar
1½ cups water
1 cups unsweetened Dutch cocoa powder, sifted
1 cup heavy cream

Chef's Note

*Poached pears may be served alone, with a sauce, or baked in pastry. Martha Washington's recipe "TO STEW WARDENS" (firm New York pears) calls for poaching the fruit and then suggests either stewing or baking the pears to complete the preparation: "Boyle them first in faire water, then pare & stew them between 2 dishes with cinnamon, suger [sic], and rosewater; or with ye same seasoning you may put them in a pie & bake them" (Hess 99).*

1. Prepare the Poached Pears: In a large stainless steel or enameled saucepan, add the wine, sugar, cinnamon sticks, cloves, and vanilla bean; bring to a boil, stirring occasionally. Reduce the heat to a simmer.
2. Carefully stand the pears upright in the saucepan. To make sure that the pears are evenly submerged in the liquid, weight them down with a heat-safe dinner plate. Simmer, covered, until the thickest part of the pear can be easily pierced with a wooden skewer, 15 to 20 minutes. *Do not overcook.*
3. Meanwhile, fill a large bowl with ice water.
4. Remove the saucepan from the heat. With a slotted spoon, carefully transfer the pears to the ice water. Once cool, remove the pears from the ice water and let them sit to come to room temperature before serving.
5. Prepare the Chocolate Sauce: In a 2-quart saucepan, combine the sugar, water, and cocoa. Whisk to combine. Bring to a boil and immediately remove from the heat. Carefully whisk in the heavy cream.
6. Set a fine mesh sieve over a medium-size bowl. Strain the chocolate mixture through the sieve, and let cool to room temperature.
7. Final assembly: pour 2 tablespoons of the Chocolate Sauce on each dessert plate. Place a pear on each plate on top of the sauce. If desired, drizzle some of the remaining sauce over each pear, and garnish with biscotti, if desired.

# Poached Peaches

Makes 4 peaches; serves 4

4 peaches
1 lemon
2 tablespoons rose water
4 cups sweet dessert white wine (such as a Riesling)
1 Scotch bonnet chile (optional)
1 cup granulated sugar
2 cinnamon sticks
1 orange, peeled and juiced
1 teaspoon ground mace

1. Fill a large bowl with ice water.
2. Using a paring knife, cut an "X" into the bottom, just through the skin, of each peach.
3. In a large saucepan, bring 2 quarts of water to a boil. Carefully place the peaches in the boiling water. Cook the peaches for 10 seconds; then remove them with a slotted spoon and transfer to the bowl of ice water.
4. After the peaches have cooled, peel and discard the skins. Place the peaches in a mixing bowl, and squeeze the lemon juice over them so they will not discolor.
5. In a large stainless steel or enameled saucepan, add the rose water, wine, chile (if using), sugar, cinnamon sticks, orange juice, orange peel (the entire peel, not just the zest), and mace; bring to a boil, stirring occasionally. Reduce the heat to a simmer.
6. Add the peaches to the pan. To make sure the peaches are evenly submerged in the liquid, weight them down with a heat-safe dinner plate. Simmer, covered, until the peaches are fork tender, about 15 minutes.
7. With a slotted spoon, carefully remove the peaches from the pan and immediately transfer them to the ice water. Return the cooled fruit to the cooled poaching liquid, and store, covered and refrigerated, for up to 3 days.

# Applesauce

**Makes 6 cups**

¼ pound (1 stick) unsalted butter
16 apples (Gala, Granny Smith, or McIntosh), peeled, cored, and cut into ½-inch
  wedges
1 lemon, juiced
1 cinnamon stick
1¼ cups granulated sugar
½ cup maple syrup
⅛ teaspoon freshly grated nutmeg

1. In a large saucepan over medium heat, melt the butter.
2. Add the apples, lemon juice, and cinnamon stick; cook, stirring occasionally, until the apples are fork tender, about 10 minutes.
3. Add the sugar, maple syrup, and nutmeg, and stir to combine. Cook at a simmer, stirring occasionally, until the apples are soft and mashed, about 25 minutes.
4. Remove from the heat and cool to room temperature. If you prefer a smoother consistency, place the cooled applesauce in a blender or food processor and purée until it reaches the desired consistency.
5. Store refrigerated in an airtight container for up to 1 week.

# Preserves, Marmalades, Chutneys, and Compotes

Preserves, marmalades, chutneys, and compotes—all varieties of preserved fruit—were some of the most elegant sweetmeats served on eighteenth-century dessert tables. Whether prepared with imported fruits and spices or ingredients from local gardens, these dishes were always admired and celebrated. Sugar was costly in the eighteenth century, and, requiring copious amounts of it, so was preserved fruit. Certainly the expense of these dishes added to the panache associated with them, but other factors did so as well. Making preserves, marmalades, chutneys, and compotes was a long and often arduous process. Purchased in hard blocks or cones, sugar had to be refined (an involved process that included boiling, sieving, and recrystallizing), the fruit stemmed and washed, and the fire stoked; once the ingredients were combined, the sweetened fruit demanded a constant and watchful eye until it reached just the right consistency. The sweetmeats were then carefully placed into glass jars or ceramic pots and covered tightly with paper, leather, or layers of fat. Because this task required such skill, women often took pride in preparing these dishes themselves rather than delegating the work to domestics.

When a hostess presented a dessert table of preserved fruits, her guests would have implicitly understood and appreciated the high level of hospitality to which they were being treated. They understood that these were costly, labor-intensive dishes only available to those who could afford the money and time to prepare them. Just as importantly, however, a dessert table of sweetmeats must have appealed to the eighteenth-century sensibility that admired the luxurious sheen of silk damask, the glitter of candlelight, and the reflective surfaces of glass and silver. A candlelit table filled with glass and china dishes of preserved fruit shimmering with translucent color must have been a fanciful and inviting vision indeed.

# Stone Fruit Preserves

Makes 2 cups

8 apricots, or 4 peaches, or 6 plums
1½ cups granulated sugar
½ cup water
¼ cup honey
1 tablespoon freshly squeezed lemon juice
2 tablespoons rose water

1. Bring a medium-size saucepan of water to a boil. Fill a large bowl with ice water.
2. Wash the ripe fruit well. Slice the fruit in half and remove the pits. Cook the fruit in the boiling water until fork tender, about 3 minutes. Remove the fruit from the pot, and immediately submerge it in the ice water. Peel off the skin with a paring knife. Pat the fruit dry with a paper towel.
3. Transfer the fruit to a food processor and purée. You should have about 2 cups of fruit purée.
4. Choose a saucepan large enough to hold three times the amount of ingredients being used. Add the sugar, water, honey, and lemon juice; stir to combine. Wash down the sides of the pot with cool water and a pastry brush, making certain no sugar crystals remain. Bring the sugar syrup to a boil over high heat, washing down the sides of the pot often. Cook the syrup until it reaches a temperature of 285°F on a candy thermometer.
5. Remove from the heat. Carefully stir the fruit purée into the sugar syrup. The mixture will spatter, so add it slowly, close to the syrup, stirring constantly. Once all of the pulp has been added, return to the heat, and continue to stir the mixture until it returns to a boil. Reduce the heat to medium-high, and cook until the mixture is thickened.
6. Once the preserves have reached the desired thickness, stir in the rose water. Transfer the preserves to a stainless steel bowl, and place them in the ice bath to cool to room temperature.
7. Store the preserves in an airtight container in the refrigerator for up to 2 weeks.

# Berry Preserves

Makes 2 cups

> 2 pints berries, such as blackberries, raspberries, strawberries, gooseberries, or blueberries
>
> 2 cups granulated sugar
>
> ¾ cup water
>
> 1 tablespoon freshly squeezed lemon juice

1.  Fill a large bowl with ice water.
2.  Place the berries in a strainer and rinse well with cold water. Pat the berries dry with a paper towel.
3.  Choose a saucepan large enough to hold three times the amount of ingredients being used. Add the sugar, water, and lemon juice; stir to combine. Wash down the sides of the pot with cool water and a pastry brush, making certain no sugar crystals remain. Bring the sugar syrup to a boil over high heat, washing down the sides of the pot often. Cook the syrup until it reaches a temperature of 285°F on a candy thermometer.
4.  Remove from the heat. Carefully add a few berries at a time. The mixture will spatter, so add the berries slowly, close to the syrup, stirring constantly. Once all of the berries have been added, return to the heat, and continue to stir the mixture until it returns to a boil. Reduce the heat to medium, and cook until the mixture is thickened, 8 to 10 minutes.
5.  Once the preserves have reached the desired thickness, transfer them to a stainless steel bowl and set the bowl in the ice bath to cool to room temperature.
6.  Store the preserves in an airtight container in the refrigerator for up to 2 weeks.

In his letter from 1780, a visitor to Mount Vernon remarked little on most of the dishes served at dinner but expounded upon the elegant preserves the Washingtons offered:

> I paid no attention to them [all of the dishes] as I was restricted to a severe diet and they have escaped from my memory. I can only say that I saw there for the first time preserved strawberries whether that kind of sweetmeats was then not so common in France as in this country or whatever may be the cause, I had never seen any before. Those were very large and beautiful, and I indulged in eating a few of them. I have been very fond of them ever since ("Descriptions of Meals," Mount Vernon memo).

# Apple, Pear, or Quince–Wine Preserves

Makes 2 cups

> 5 apples (Gala or Granny Smith), or 5 pears, or 5 quinces
> 1¾ cups granulated sugar
> ½ cup honey
> ½ cup Madeira wine
> ½ cup water
> 2 teaspoons cider vinegar

1. Bring a medium-size saucepan of water to a boil. Fill a large bowl with ice water.
2. Wash the fruit well. Peel the fruit and slice it in half. Remove the core. Cook the fruit in the boiling water until fork tender, about 3 minutes. Remove the fruit from the pot and immediately submerge it in the ice water. Pat the fruit dry with a paper towel.
3. Transfer the fruit to a food processor and purée. You should have about 2 cups of fruit purée.
4. Choose a saucepan large enough to hold three times the amount of ingredients being used. Add the sugar, honey, wine, water, and vinegar; stir to combine. Wash down the sides of the pot with cool water and a pastry brush, making certain no sugar crystals remain. Bring the sugar syrup to a boil over high heat, washing down the sides of the pot often. Cook the syrup until it reaches a temperature of 285°F on a candy thermometer.
5. Remove from the heat. Carefully add the fruit pulp to the sugar syrup. The mixture will spatter, so add it slowly, close to the syrup, stirring constantly. Once all of the pulp has been added, return to the heat, and continue to stir the mixture until it returns to a boil. Reduce the heat to medium-high, and cook the mixture until it is thickened, 8 to 10 minutes.
6. Once the preserves have reached the desired thickness, transfer them to a stainless steel bowl and set the bowl in the ice bath to cool to room temperature.
7. Store the preserves in an airtight container in the refrigerator for up to 2 weeks.

# Cherry–Vanilla Preserves

Makes 2 cups

    3 cups cherries
    2 cups granulated sugar
    ½ cup plus 2 tablespoons water
    ¼ cup kirschwasser (cherry-flavored liqueur)
    2 teaspoons balsamic vinegar
    1 vanilla bean
    1 tablespoon vanilla extract

1.  Fill a large bowl with ice water.
2.  With a paring knife, slice the cherries in half and remove the pits.
3.  Choose a saucepan large enough to hold three times the amount of ingredients being used. Add the sugar, water, kirschwasser, vinegar, vanilla bean, and vanilla extract; stir to combine. Wash down the sides of the pot with cool water and a pastry brush, making certain no sugar crystals remain. Bring the sugar syrup to a boil over high heat, washing down the sides of the pot often. Cook the syrup until it reaches a temperature of 285°F on a candy thermometer.
4.  Remove from the heat. Carefully add a handful at a time of the cherries to the sugar syrup. The mixture will spatter, so add the cherries slowly, close to the syrup, stirring constantly. Once all of the cherries have been added, return to the heat, and continue to stir the mixture until it returns to a boil. Reduce the heat to medium, and cook, stirring with a wooden spoon, until the mixture thickens.
5.  Once the preserves have reached the desired thickness, transfer them to a stainless steel bowl and set the bowl in the ice bath to cool to room temperature.
6.  Store the preserves in an airtight container in the refrigerator for up to 2 weeks.

In The London Art of Cookery, John Farley devoted an entire chapter to "Preserving" and, as many authors of the period did, he offered his readers "Preliminary Hints and Observations" on the topic. He paid particular attention to the storing of these items; they demanded so much of a cook's time and money that these final details were of the utmost importance:

> Wet sweetmeats [preserves] must be kept in a dry and cool place; for a damp place will mould them, and a hot place will deprive them of their virtue. It is a good method to dip writing-paper into brandy, and lay it close to the sweetmeats. They should be tied well down with white paper, and two folds of cap-paper, to keep out the air, as nothing can be a greater fault than leaving the pots open, or tying them down carelessly (311).

# Orange Marmalade

Makes 2 cups

 2½ cups sugar
 2 teaspoons pectin powder (available in the jelly section of better supermarkets)
 4 oranges, cut in half widthwise
 1 lemon, cut in half widthwise
 1 cup water
 1 cup honey

1. In a small bowl, stir together the sugar and pectin.
2. Over a separate bowl, scoop out the flesh and pulp from the oranges and lemon fruits with a melon baller or tablespoon. Discard the seeds. Place the pulp, juice, and flesh in a medium-size pot. Slice the peel into ⅛-inch pieces, and reserve.
3. Add the water and honey to the pot, and stir to combine. Add the sugar-pectin mixture to the pot; stir to combine, and let stand for 2 minutes. Stir in the lemon and orange peel.
4. Wash down the sides of the pot with cool water and a pastry brush, making certain no sugar crystals remain. Bring the mixture to a boil, and cook, stirring occasionally, until thickened, 10 to 12 minutes.
5. Remove from the heat and let cool completely. Transfer to an airtight container, and store in the refrigerator for up to 1 week.


# Gooseberry Compote

Makes 4 cups

 1½ cups water
 1 cup granulated sugar
 ¼ cup orange juice
 ¼ cup orange liqueur (such as Triple Sec or Cointreau)
 1 vanilla bean
 1 tablespoon chopped fresh ginger
 3 pints gooseberries, husked
 ¼ cup thinly sliced Candied Ginger (see page 235)

1. Fill a large bowl with ice water.
2. In a large pot, add the water, sugar, orange juice, liqueur, vanilla bean, and fresh ginger; stir to combine, and bring to a boil.
3. Add the gooseberries and cook, stirring occasionally, until the berries begin to pop, 5 to 7 minutes. Add the Candied Ginger, and stir.
4. Transfer the compote to a stainless steel bowl, and set the bowl in the ice bath. Remove the vanilla bean, cool to room temperature, and store in an airtight container in the refrigerator for up to 1 week.

# Summer Fruit Compote

**Makes 2 cups**

> 6 stalks rhubarb
> 2 peaches
> ½ cup sweet dessert white wine (such as Riesling)
> ½ cup water
> 1 cup granulated sugar
> 1 vanilla bean
> 1 tablespoon rose water
> Pinch of mace

1. Fill a large bowl with ice water.
2. Peel the rhubarb with a vegetable peeler, and cut the stalks into ½-inch pieces. Slice the peaches in half, remove the pits, and cut the halves into ½-inch-thick cubes.
3. In a large pot, add the wine, water, sugar, vanilla bean, rose water, and mace; stir to combine. Bring the mixture to a boil.
4. Add the rhubarb to the pot and cook for 3 minutes. Add the peaches and cook until the fruit is tender, another 3 to 5 minutes.
5. Transfer the compote to a stainless steel bowl, and set it in the ice bath. Cool to room temperature, and store in an airtight container in the refrigerator for up to 3 days.

# Mixed Berry Compote

**Makes 4 cups**

> 1 cup water
> 1 cup granulated sugar
> 3 tablespoons freshly squeezed lemon juice
> ½ pint fresh strawberries, hulled and quartered
> ½ pint fresh blueberries
> ½ pint fresh raspberries
> ¼ cup thinly sliced Candied Lemon Peel (see page 234)
> 2 tablespoons chopped fresh mint

1. Fill a large bowl with ice water.
2. In a medium-size pot, add the water, sugar, and lemon juice; stir to combine, and bring to a boil. Remove from the heat. Add the berries, Candied Lemon Peel, and mint; stir to combine.
3. Transfer the compote to a stainless steel bowl, and set the bowl in the ice bath. Cool to room temperature, and store in an airtight container in the refrigerator for up to 3 days.

# Mango–Papaya Chutney

**Makes 2 cups**

3 mangoes
1 papaya
2 cups orange juice
½ cup granulated sugar
1 tablespoon honey
2 teaspoons finely minced fresh ginger
1 orange, zest grated
1 lime, zest grated and juiced
2 cinnamon sticks
2 teaspoons pectin powder (available in the jelly section of better supermarkets)
2 tablespoons sliced Candied Orange Peel (see page 234)

1. Fill a large bowl with ice water.
2. Peel the mangoes with a vegetable peeler. Trim the flesh from the center stone. Cut the mango into ½-inch pieces. Peel the papaya, slice it in half, and scoop out the seeds. Chop the papaya into ½-inch pieces. Set aside.
3. In a medium-size saucepan, stir together the orange juice, sugar, honey, ginger, orange zest, lime zest, lime juice, and cinnamon sticks. Sprinkle the pectin powder over the mixture, and let it stand for 2 minutes.
4. Slowly bring the mixture to a boil. Add the fruit, and cook the mixture until the fruit is tender and begins to break down, about 5 minutes. Add the Candied Orange Peel, and stir.
5. Transfer the chutney to a stainless steel bowl, and set it in the ice bath. Cool to room temperature, and store in an airtight container in the refrigerator for up to 1 week.

# Fall Fruit Compote

Makes 6 cups

4 Bartlett pears
1 lemon, zest grated
2 cups dried cherries
2 cups apple cider
1 cup granulated sugar
¼ cup light rum
2 tablespoons honey
1 cinnamon stick
3 whole cloves
1 vanilla bean
1 teaspoon whole black peppercorns
Pinch of mace

1. Fill a large bowl with ice water.
2. Peel, core, and cut the pears into ½-inch cubes. Squeeze the lemon juice over the pears and set aside.
3. In a medium-size pot, add the lemon zest, dried cherries, cider, sugar, rum, honey, cinnamon stick, cloves, vanilla bean, peppercorns, and mace; stir to combine, and bring to a boil.
4. Add the pears, and cook until the fruit is tender, 4 to 5 minutes.
5. Transfer the compote to a stainless steel bowl, and set the bowl in the ice bath. Remove the vanilla bean and cinnamon stick. Cool to room temperature, and store in an airtight container in the refrigerator for up to 1 week.

# Pineapple Compote

**Makes 6 cups**

> 1 pineapple
> ¼ cup Appleton gold rum
> 1 teaspoon cornstarch
> 2 cups pineapple juice
> 2 cups water
> ¼ cup granulated sugar
> 1 tablespoon whole allspice

1. Fill a large bowl with ice water.
2. Trim the skin from the pineapple, remove the core, and cut the pineapple into ½-inch cubes.
3. In a small bowl, stir together the rum and cornstarch.
4. In a medium-size pot, add the pineapple juice, water, and sugar; stir to combine, and bring the mixture to a boil. Add the allspice, and cook until the mixture reduces by half, about 5 minutes.
5. Add the rum-cornstarch mixture to the pot, stirring constantly. Add the pineapple, and cook for just 1 minute.
6. Transfer the compote to a stainless steel bowl, and set the bowl in the ice bath. Cool to room temperature, and store in an airtight container in the refrigerator for up to 1 week.

# Sources

**Albert Uster Imports**
For chocolate, pastry and baking equipment, and other pastry baking products
800-231-8154
www.auiswisscatalog.com

**Caviar Assouline**
For citronand plum purée
800-521-4491
www.caviarassouline.com

**King Arthur Flour**
For Sir Lancelot Hi-Gluten Flour, other premium flours, and pastry and baking equipment
800-827-6836
www.bakerscatalogue.com

**Pastry Chef Central**
For pastry and baking equipment (such as cookie spritzers)
888-750-2433
www.pastrychef.com

# Bibliography

Adams, Abigail. *New Letters of Abigail Adams, 1788-1801.* Edited by Stewart Mitchell. Boston: Houghton Mifflin Co., 1947.

Armes, Ethel, ed. and comp. *Nancy Shippen: Her Journal Book, the International Romance of a Young Lady of Fashion of Colonial Philadelphia.* Philadelphia: J. B. Lippincotte Co., 1935.

Belden, Louise Conway. *The Festive Tradition: Table Decoration and Desserts in America, 1650-1900.* New York: W.W. Norton & Co., 1983.

Bridenbaugh, Carl, ed. *Gentleman's Progress: The Itinerarium of Dr. Alexander Hamilton, 1744.* Pittsburgh: University of Pittsburgh Press, 1948.

Bushman, Richard L. *The Refinement of America.* New York: Alfred A. Knopf, 1992.

Carter, Susannah. *The Frugal Colonial Housewife: A Cook's Book wherein The Art of Dressing all Sorts of Viands with Cleanliness, Decency, and Elegance is explained. or Complete Woman Cook.* Edited by Jean McKibbin. Garden City, N.Y.: Doubleday & Co., 1976. Originally published as *The Frugal Housewife or Complete Woman Cook* (London: F. Newbery, 1772; Boston: Edes and Gill, 1772).

Carson, Barbara G. *Ambitious Appetites: Dining, Behavior, and Patterns of Consumption in Federal Washington.* Washington, D.C.: The American Institute of Architects Press, 1990.

Child, Lydia Maria. *The American Frugal Housewife.* Facsimile of the 12th ed., 1833. Bedford, Mass.: Applewood Books, n.d.

Drinker, Elizabeth Sandwith. *The Diary of Elizabeth Drinker.* Edited by Elaine Forman Crane. Vol. 1. Boston: Northeastern University Press, 1991.

Escoffier, A. *The Escoffier Cookbook: A Guide to the Fine Art of French Cuisine.* New York: Crown Publishers, Inc., 1969. Originally published as *Le Guide Culinaire* (Paris, 1903).

Faber, Eli. *The Jewish People in America. A Time for Planting: The First Migration, 1654-1820.* Baltimore: The Johns Hopkins University Press, 1992.

Farley, John. *The London Art of Cookery.* Edited by Ann Haly. Introduction by Stephen Medcalf. Lewes, East Sussex, England: Southover Press, 1988.

Glasse, Hannah. *The Art of Cooking Made Plain and Easy.* Facsimile of the 1805, Alexandria ed. Introduction by Karen Hess. Bedford, Mass.: Applewood Books, 1997.

Herbst, Sharon T. *Food Lover's Companion.* New York: Barron's Educational Series, 1990.

Hess, Karen, ed. and transcriber. *Martha Washington's Booke of Cookery.* New York: Columbia University Press, 1995.

Hooker, Richard J., ed. *A Colonial Plantation Cookbook: The Receipt Book of Harriott Pinckney Horry, 1770.* Columbia, S.C.: University of South Carolina Press, 1984.

Kimball, Marie. *Thomas Jefferson's Cook Book.* Richmond, Va.: Garrett & Massie, 1938.

Leslie, Eliza. *Directions for Cookery, in Its Various Branches.* Facsimile of the 1848, Philadelphia ed. Monterey, Ca: Creative Cookbooks, 2001.

_____. *Seventy-Five Receipts, for Pastry, Cakes, and Sweetmeats.* Facsimile of the 1st ed., 1828. Bedford, Mass.: Applewood Books.

Leighton, Ann. *American Gardens in the Eighteenth Century, "For Use or for Delight."* Boston: Houghton Mifflin Co., 1976. Reprint, Amherst: University of Massachusetts Press, 1986.

Lowenstein, Eleanor. *Bibliography of American Cookery Books, 1742-1860.* Worcester, Mass.: American Antiquarian Society, 1972.

Mariani, John. *The Encyclopedia of American Food and Drink.* New York: Lebhar-Friedman Books, 1999.

*Mount Vernon memos.* George Washington's Mount Vernon Estate and Gardens, Mount Vernon, Va.

Nutt, Frederick. *The complete confectioner, or, The whole art of confectionary made easy . . .* 1798. 4th ed. Reprint, New York: Richard Scott, 1807.

Ortiz, Elizabeth Lambert, ed. *The Encyclopedia of Herbs, Spices, and Flavorings: A Cook's Compendium.* New York: Dorling Kindersley, 1992.

Peckham, Howard H., ed. "Journal of Lord Adam Gordon." In *Narratives of Colonial America, 1704-1765.* Chicago: R.R. Donnelley & Sons Co., 1971.

*Pennsylvania Gazette,* 12 June 1766 to 4 July 1792.

Platt, John D.R. *Historic Resource Study: The City Tavern.* Denver: United States Department of the Interior, 1973.

Raffald, Elizabeth. *The Experienced English Housekeeper.* Facsimile of the 1st ed., 1769. Introduction by Roy Shipperbottom. Lewes, East Sussex, England: Southover Press, 1997.

Randolph, Mary. *The Virginia House-Wife.* Facsimile of the 1st ed., 1824. Historical notes and commentaries by Karen Hess. Columbia, S.C.: University of South Carolina Press, 1984.

Rice, Kym S. *Early American Taverns: For the Entertainment of Friends and Strangers.* Chicago: Regnery Gateway, 1983.

Roberts, Kenneth, and Anna Roberts, eds. *Moreau de St. Mery's American Journey, 1793-98.* Garden City, N.Y.: Doubleday and Co., 1947.

Rundell, Maria Eliza Ketelby. *A new system of domestic cookery: formed upon principles of economy, and adapted to the use of private families throughout the United States.* By a Lady. New York: R. M'Dermut and D.D. Arden, 1814.

Schweitzer, Mary McKinney. "The Economy of Philadelphia and Its Hinterland." In *Shaping a National Culture: The Philadelphia Experience, 1750-1800.* Edited by Catherine E. Hutchins. Winterthur, De.: Henry Francis du Pont Winterthur Museum, 1994.

Sherrill, Charles H. *French Memories of Eighteenth-Century America.* New York: Charles Scribner's Sons, 1915.

Simmons, Amelia. *American Cookery.* Facsimile of the 2nd ed., 1796. Introduction by Karen Hess. Bedford, Mass.: Applewood Books, 1996.

Smith, Eliza. *The Compleat Housewife.* Facsimile of the 1758, London ed. London: Studio Editions, 1994.

Thompson, Mary V. "'Look Into the Milk and Butter': Food Preservation at George Washington's Mount Vernon." Department of the Registrar, Mount Vernon Ladies' Association, Mount Vernon, Va., January 1996.

Verral, William. *The Cook's Paradise being William Verral's 'Complete System of Cookery' Published in 1759 with Thomas Gray's cookery notes in Holograph.* Introduction and appendices by R. L. Megroz, London: Sylvan Press, 1948.

Weaver, William W., Mary Anne Hines, and Gordon Marshall. *The Larder Invaded: reflections on three centuries of Philadelphia food and drink.* Philadelphia: Library Company of Philadelphia, Historical Society of Pennsylvania, 1987.

# Index

CITY TAVERN

DELAWARE